QUESTIONS & ANSWERS:
PAYMENT SYSTEMS

QUESTIONS & ANSWERS:
PAYMENT SYSTEMS

Multiple-Choice and Short-Answer Questions and Answers

Second Edition

By

Timothy R. Zinnecker
Professor of Law
Campbell University
Norman Adrian Wiggins School of Law

 LexisNexis

ISBN: 9781422493762
E-Book ISBN: 9780327174479

NOTE TO USERS

To ensure that you are using the latest materials available in this area, please be sure to periodically check the LexisNexis Law School web site for downloadable updates and supplements at www.lexisnexis.com/lawschool.

Editorial Offices
121 Chanlon Rd., New Providence, NJ 07974 (908) 464-6800
201 Mission St., San Francisco, CA 94105-1831 (415) 908-3200
www.lexisnexis.com

MATTHEW◆BENDER

DEDICATION

To Grace and Meredith, my most precious and priceless gifts of the Lord (Psalm 127:3).

ABOUT THE AUTHOR

Timothy R. Zinnecker is a professor at Campbell University's Norman Adrian Wiggins School of Law, where he teaches commercial law courses. Professor Zinnecker graduated with honors from the J. Reuben Clark Law School, Brigham Young University, in 1986, where he served on the law review and was a member of Order of the Coif. He then served as a judicial clerk for the Hon. Frank X. Gordon (Arizona Supreme Court), and the Hon. Edith H. Jones (United States Court of Appeals for the Fifth Circuit). He practiced commercial law in Dallas and Houston for five years before joining the faculty at South Texas College of Law in 1994. He joined Campbell University's law faculty in 2011. He has been a visitor at Samford University, Florida State University, the University of Richmond, and the University of Houston. He is the co-author of Q&A: SECURED TRANSACTIONS (2nd ed., LexisNexis 2010).

PREFACE

In general, a course in Payment Systems involves examining the law applicable to common forms of payment, such as checks, notes, credit cards, debit cards, wire transfers, and letters of credit. This study guide uses multiple-choice and short-answer questions to test your knowledge of the dominant bodies of law applicable to these forms of payment, including Articles 3, 4, 4A, and 5 of the Uniform Commercial Code, selected provisions of the Consumer Credit Protection Act (Truth in Lending Act), and a few federal regulations.

All statutory citations can be found in the softback statutory books used in most law schools; the materials do not reflect non-uniform amendments enacted by any particular state.

The short-answer questions can be answered in no more than 10 sentences and less than 15 minutes. You will better understand the materials if you prepare your own answer before peeking at the model answer.

This is the second edition of this study aid. My friend, Gregory E. Maggs, professor of law at The George Washington University Law School, was my co-author on the first edition. Other commitments have prevented Greg from participating in this second edition. Nevertheless, some of his original work, and his influence, remain herein.

Thank you for using this study guide to supplement your understanding of Payment Systems. Please contact me with your questions and comments.

Timothy R. Zinnecker
zinneckert@campbell.edu
Raleigh, North Carolina

TABLE OF CONTENTS

QUESTIONS

QUESTIONS

1. UCC Article 3 covers "negotiable instruments." Each of the following may be a negotiable instrument, except:

   (A) a teller's check for $1,000.

   (B) a $10 bill.

   (C) a promissory note for $1,000,000.

   (D) a personal check for less than $100.

Use the following facts to answer the next two questions.

Following a recent hurricane that devastated the Houston area, Julie wrote a personal check for $200, payable to the order of the American Red Cross. Julie maintains her checking account with First National Bank.

2. Under UCC Article 3, Julie is the:

   (A) borrower.

   (B) drawer.

   (C) drawee.

   (D) accommodation party.

3. Under UCC Article 3, First National Bank is the:

   (A) drawee.

   (B) remitter.

   (C) payee.

   (D) maker.

Use the following facts to answer the next two questions.

Last week, Tom Sullivan bought a new boat from Dealer for $18,000. He paid $3,000 in cash, and financed the $15,000 balance by executing a negotiable promissory note.

4. Under UCC Article 3, Tom's signature on the note makes him the:

(A) drawee.

(B) drawer.

(C) debtor.

(D) maker.

5. Which of the following provisions would render Tom's promise conditional, and remove the $15,000 note from the scope of UCC Article 3?

   (A) "In consideration of Dealer's agreement to sell a 2013 Polaris boat to me, I promise to pay $25,000 to the order of Dealer."

   (B) "Rights in any and all collateral that secures repayment of the indebtedness evidenced by this promissory note are stated in the Security Agreement executed contemporaneously herewith by and between the undersigned and Dealer."

   (C) "This promissory note is the 'Note' as defined in the Installment Sales Contract executed on this date by and between Maker (as 'Buyer') and Dealer (as 'Seller')."

   (D) "Maker's obligations hereunder are contingent on Dealer's delivery to Maker of a lien-free certificate of title on the Boat no later than ten calendar days after the date hereof."

6. To be a negotiable instrument, a promissory note must be payable to bearer or to order. Which of the following phrases will make a promissory note payable to bearer?

   (A) ". . . pay to the order of Jan, June, or John Smith . . ."

   (B) ". . . pay to the order of CASH . . ."

   (C) ". . . pay to Tom Wilson . . ."

   (D) ". . . pay to Mary Jones or her designee . . ."

7. In April of this year, Wendy executed a negotiable promissory note in which she promised to pay $10,000 on demand to Paul. At the same time, Wendy and Paul agreed in a separate writing that Paul would not demand payment before February 1 of the next year.

   Contrary to this separate writing (which is not referenced in the promissory note), Paul demanded payment from Wendy on November 1 of this year, relying on the terms of the promissory note. Wendy objected, relying on their separate agreement.

   Discuss which party the law favors. You may assume that a court will allow Wendy to introduce into evidence the separate agreement.

ANSWER:

8. A few months after they both arrived in Miami from Havana, Maria borrowed $350 from

her brother, Hector. To evidence repayment of the loan, Maria signed the following single-sentence writing on April 1: "The undersigned promises to pay 10,000 Cuban Pesos to the order of Hector one year from today."

When the note comes due in one year,

(A) Maria may tender Cuban Pesos or U.S. Dollars (converted as of the issue date).

(B) Maria may tender Cuban Pesos or U.S. Dollars (converted as of the payment date).

(C) Maria must tender Cuban Pesos.

(D) Maria must honor Hector's choice of Cuban Pesos or U.S. Dollars.

9. To evidence a $2,000 loan from her father, Melissa executed a promissory note that required her to repay the $2,000 "with interest at an annual rate equal to the 'Prime Rate' as defined in *The Financial Times Journal*, issue dated July 7, 2013." Subsequently, Melissa and her father become estranged, and Melissa refused to repay the loan. Only when litigation ensued did the parties discover that July 7, 2013, fell on a Sunday, and *The Financial Times Journal* only publishes an issue on weekdays.

The judge rules that the promissory note falls within the scope of UCC Article 3 and orders Melissa to repay the loan. He also should rule that the applicable interest rate is:

(A) 0%.

(B) the "Prime Rate" as defined in *The Financial Times Journal*, issue dated July 8, 2013.

(C) 6%.

(D) the appropriate judgment rate.

10. Three days ago, Tim wrote a check intending to pay his utility bill of $213.79. He inserted the correct amount in the numerical box on the check, but he wrote the amount as "two hundred seventy-nine and 13/100" dollars. No party catches the mistake until the check is presented to the payor bank for payment.

The payor bank should honor the check for:

(A) $279.13 because that number is the higher of the two numbers.

(B) $279.13 because words control over numbers.

(C) $246.46, the average of the two numbers.

(D) $213.79, because that number is the lower of the two numbers and the correct amount of the utility bill.

11. Ellen borrowed $2,500 from Frank. Frank has prepared a $2,500 promissory note for Ellen's signature. The parties are debating between themselves what might happen if

Ellen writes "VOID" or "NON-NEGOTIABLE" on the note.

What contribution might you make to the debate?

ANSWER:

12. A negotiable promissory note must be payable on demand or at a definite time. Which of the following provisions makes a note payable on demand?

    (A) ". . . payable on December 31, 2016."

    (B) ". . . payable on _____."

    (C) ". . . payable 45 days after the date hereof."

    (D) ". . . payable at the will of the undersigned."

13. Jill borrowed $25,000 from her parents a few years ago. To evidence the loan, Jill executed a promissory note. Jill's father, who drafted the promissory note, failed to include a place of payment. As a result,

    (A) the note will fall outside the scope of UCC Article 3.

    (B) the note is payable at Jill's address.

    (C) the note is payable at her parents' address.

    (D) the note is payable at any bank chartered under federal law.

14. Alex agrees to buy Karen's piano for $5,000. With Karen's permission Alex tenders his personal check for $5,000. Alex recalls from his business law class in college that he may not wish to release a negotiable instrument that could ultimately fall into the hands of a holder in due course, so he writes "NON-NEGOTIABLE" in the memo line in the lower left-hand corner of the check, and he also strikes through "to the order of" before writing Karen's name on the payee line.

Which statement is true?

    (A) Each of the two steps taken by Alex effectively removed his personal check from the scope of UCC Article 3.

    (B) Alex removed the check from the scope of UCC Article 3 by writing "NON-NEGOTIABLE" in the memo line.

    (C) Alex removed the check from the scope of UCC Article 3 by striking through "to the order of" on the payee line.

    (D) Nothing Alex has done is effective to remove the check from the scope of UCC Article 3.

15. Greg has a dental appointment tomorrow, and he has been told to bring a $150 check with him. This morning Greg wrote the check, filling in all spaces (including the signature line), except for the name of the payee. He left the check in his bedroom on a table.

This afternoon an electrician stole the check after installing a ceiling fan and light fixture in Greg's bedroom.

Which of the following statements is true?

(A) Without the name of the payee, the check is not a negotiable instrument.

(B) Because the electrician stole the check, he cannot be a person entitled to enforce the check.

(C) Because the electrician stole the check, no subsequent possessor can be a holder in due course.

(D) Greg is the issuer of the check, which itself has not been issued.

16. Lucas borrowed $2,500 from Stan for a business purpose. In return, Lucas executed and delivered to Stan a writing that stated: "I promise to pay $2,500 to Stan on demand."

Which statement is true?

(A) The writing falls outside the scope of UCC Article 3; therefore, the promise is unenforceable.

(B) The writing falls outside the scope of UCC Article 3, but the promise may be enforceable.

(C) The writing falls within the scope of UCC Article 3, provided that Stan demands payment within two years after taking delivery of the writing.

(D) The writing falls within the scope of UCC Article 3, provided that Stan demands payment within six years after taking delivery of the writing.

17. Shannon borrowed $5,000 from her sister, Lisa, earlier today. Both sisters agree that Shannon must repay the loan in a single payment due on the date of their mother's death. Their mother, Jennifer, just celebrated her 83rd birthday and is in good health.

Draft a promissory note that memorializes the agreed payment date and falls within the scope of UCC Article 3.

ANSWER:

18. Carmen wanted to a purchase a boat from a seller who insisted that she pay with a cashier's check. Carmen went to her bank, which issued a cashier's check for the requested amount (after withdrawing the same amount of funds, plus a $10 fee, from Carmen's account).

Which of the following statements is false?

(A) Carmen is the remitter if the check is payable to the seller.

(B) Carmen's bank is both the drawer and the drawee of the check.

(C) Carmen can place a stop-payment order on the check.

(D) Carmen can negotiate the check to the seller, regardless of whether the named payee is Carmen or the seller.

19.   What are teller's checks and cashier's checks, and how do they differ?

ANSWER:

20.   Jane executed and delivered to Patrick a negotiable promissory note for $12,000 two years ago. The note came due three months ago. Jane has yet to pay, so Patrick has commenced a lawsuit against her.

In order to prevail, and assuming that Jane raises no challenges to liability, Patrick must prove that:

(A) Jane's signature is authentic.

(B) Jane issued the note to him.

(C) he possesses the note.

(D) he timely presented the note to Jane.

21.   Romi and Nate Purewal are brothers. Shortly after moving to Florida from the country of India in 2012, Nate borrowed $500 from Romi. Romi wanted to be repaid in rupees (the official currency of India), rather than U.S. Dollars, so Nate executed the following note drafted by Romi:

PROMISSORY NOTE

I promise to pay 28,000 Indian Rupees to Romi Purewal on October 1, 2014.

Nate Purewal

Romi presented the note for payment on the maturity date, but Nate refused to pay. After his repeated demands for payment went unanswered, Romi initiated a lawsuit against Nate sometime thereafter.

Romi's lawsuit is timely only if the note is a negotiable instrument governed by UCC Article 3. Nate contends that the note is not a negotiable instrument because Nate promised to pay in a foreign currency rather than in U.S. Dollars. Therefore, Nate argues that the lawsuit is time-barred.

Is Nate correct?

ANSWER:

22. John intends to give his parents (Wallace and Helen) a $200 check as a wedding anniversary gift. If John makes the check payable to the order of "Helen and/or Wallace Smith," then:

    (A) both parents must indorse the check, and Helen must indorse before Wallace indorses.

    (B) both parents must indorse the check, but the order of indorsements is not important.

    (C) Helen must indorse the check, but Wallace's indorsement is optional.

    (D) either parent may indorse the check.

23. A few days ago, Wendy won an Internet auction for some children's books. The seller, Rosaria Giacona, allowed Wendy to pay with her personal check. Wendy did so, but incorrectly made the check payable to "Rosie Giacconi." Rosaria received the check and intends to deposit it into her bank account tomorrow. If Rosaria wants to follow established commercial practices, how should she indorse the check?

ANSWER:

24. Section 3-104 requires that a negotiable instrument state an "unconditional" promise or order. Section 3-106 expands on the meaning of "unconditional." Subsection (b)(ii) expressly permits language that limits payment "to a particular fund or source" (e.g., ". . . provided that Maker's payment hereunder shall not exceed the balance in his XYZ Investment Account on the maturity date of this note . . .").

    What policy argument underlies Section 3-106(b)(ii), which is a departure from earlier versions of UCC Article 3?

ANSWER:

NEGOTIABLE INSTRUMENTS: PERSONS ENTITLED TO ENFORCE; DEFENSES TO PAYMENT; HOLDER IN DUE COURSE DOCTRINE

25. ABC Company executed and delivered a negotiable promissory note to (and payable to the order of) ZinnCorp. Later, ZinnCorp sold the note to FinCo.

    FinCo will not be a person entitled to enforce the note if:

    (A) FinCo has not yet obtained possession of the note from ZinnCorp.

    (B) FinCo has possession of the note, which is unindorsed by any party.

    (C) ABC Company has yet to receive goods and services from ZinnCorp, for which the note was executed.

    (D) ABC Company has yet to receive, from either ZinnCorp or FinCo, notice of the sale of the note from ZinnCorp to FinCo.

26. John fills out all parts of a check, except the name of the payee, and then signs the check. John then loses the check. Ginny finds the check. She is:

    (A) not a person entitled to enforce the check because she gave no value for it.

    (B) not a person entitled to enforce the check because John did not place her name on the payee line.

    (C) a person entitled to enforce the check because she is the owner of the check.

    (D) a person entitled to enforce the check because she is the holder of the check.

27. Helen encloses a $50 check in a wedding card for her friends, Robert and Elaine. She makes the check payable "to the order of Elaine and Robert Jackson." Robert and Elaine get married, open Helen's card, and find her check.

    Which statement is true?

    (A) Elaine is a person entitled to enforce the check while it is in her possession.

    (B) Elaine or Robert, acting separately, can each be a person entitled to enforce the check.

    (C) Elaine and Robert, acting together as a unit, can be persons entitled to enforce the check.

(D) Robert, acting alone, can be a person entitled to enforce the check because the last name of "Jackson" appears on the payee line immediately after "Robert."

28. Which of the following statements is true?

(A) Only a person in possession of an instrument can be a person entitled to enforce the instrument.

(B) A thief can be a person entitled to enforce the instrument.

(C) A party cannot be a person entitled to enforce an instrument unless that party's name appears on the instrument, either as the original payee or in an indorsement.

(D) An owner of an instrument is a person entitled to enforce the instrument.

29. Gwen Clark is the president of MegaCorp. She has corporate authority to sign checks for amounts that do not exceed $5,000.

Two months ago, Gwen signed and issued a corporate check for $4,300 for a legitimate corporate purpose. The drawee timely dishonored the check. The depositary bank then sued Gwen for personal liability on the check.

The check has been introduced into evidence. MegaCorp's name and address appear in the upper left corner of the check. Gwen's signature appears in the lower right corner as "Gwen Clark" and is not accompanied by any other words.

The court should rule that:

(A) Gwen is personally liable for signing the check.

(B) Gwen may be personally liable for signing the check, but only if the depositary bank is a holder in due course.

(C) Gwen may be personally liable for signing the check, but only if she received notice of dishonor within 30 days from the date on which she signed the check.

(D) Gwen is not personally liable for signing the check.

30. Grace received a $25 birthday check in recent days. Her name appeared on the payee line. Upon receipt, she indorsed the check and placed it in her purse. A few hours later, Thief stole her purse (and the check inside the purse).

Thief will be a person entitled to enforce the check if:

(A) Grace indorsed as follows: For Deposit Only - Account 54321987 / Grace Smith.

(B) Grace indorsed as follows: Pay to Alan Johnson / Grace Smith.

(C) Grace indorsed as follows: Without Recourse Or Warranty / Grace Smith.

(D) Thief demands payment from the drawer within 30 days after the issue date.

31. Because § 3-301(iii) permits eligible non-possessors to enforce a lost or stolen instrument,

it is conceivable that an issuer (maker or drawer) may be confronted with demands for payment from both a possessor (asserting enforcement rights under § 3-301(i) or (ii)) and a non-possessor (asserting enforcement rights under § 3-301(iii)). From which of those two parties would the issuer prefer to receive the *initial* demand for payment?

ANSWER:

Use the following facts to answer the next two questions.

On March 1, the law firm of Smith & Jones issued and delivered a $50,000 promissory note to CompuTech as payment for a computer system to be delivered and installed by March 31. The note was due and payable on August 31.

On May 4, CompuTech negotiated the note to FinCorp for $40,000. As agreed, FinCorp paid $30,000 to CompuTech and $10,000 to one of CompuTech's designated creditors.

On September 3, FinCorp presented the note to Smith & Jones for payment. The law firm refused to pay, citing CompuTech's failure to deliver and install the computer system (a fact previously unknown to FinCorp).

32. FinCorp is a holder in due course to the extent of, and the law firm must pay,

    (A) $50,000.

    (B) $40,000.

    (C) $37,500.

    (D) $30,000.

33. Would your answer change if FinCorp had yet to pay the $10,000 to CompuTech's designated creditor on September 3?

ANSWER:

Use the following facts to answer the next two questions.

First Church bought a new grand piano from Dealer on credit for $25,000, executing a negotiable promissory note for the purchase price. Dealer negotiated the note to Bank as collateral for a $20,000 secured loan. After paying $8,000 to Bank, Dealer defaulted on the secured loan. Bank then presented the $25,000 note to First Church on the maturity date. First Church refused to pay, citing a legitimate contract defense enforceable against Dealer (previously unknown to Bank).

34. With respect to the $25,000 note, Bank can assert rights as a holder in due course against First Church for:

    (A) $25,000.

    (B) $20,000.

    (C) $17,000.

(D) $12,000.

35. Assume the same facts, except Dealer sold the note to Providence Finance, a holder in due course. Providence Finance then negotiated the note to Bank as collateral for a $22,000 secured loan. After paying $14,000 to Bank, Providence Finance defaulted on the secured loan. Bank then presented the $25,000 note to First Church on the maturity date. First Church refused to pay, citing a legitimate contract defense enforceable against Dealer (previously unknown to Bank).

With respect to the $25,000 note, Bank can assert rights as a holder in due course against First Church for:

(A) $25,000.

(B) $22,000.

(C) $11,000.

(D) $8,000.

36. Gwen's son recently passed his driver's test and needed a car of his own. Gwen's elderly neighbor, Frank, agreed to sell one of his cars to Gwen in return for $6,500 cash and a negotiable promissory note for $6,000. So Gwen executed a negotiable $6,000 note and delivered it to Frank. The note was payable to the order of Frank.

Three months later, Frank, in need of cash, sold the $6,000 note to his nephew, Jack, for a fair price. Not until Jack presented the note to Gwen for payment did the parties discover that Frank had failed to indorse the note when he sold it to Jack. And Frank died unexpectedly before the note matured, so the parties can no longer obtain his indorsement.

Is Jack a person entitled to enforce the note?

ANSWER:

37. Amy bought a used car from Barton on July 1, paying with a $4,000 negotiable promissory note that was due and payable in three months. At the time of sale, Barton represented that the odometer reading was correct. In fact, Barton had tampered with the odometer, rolling it back from a reading of 85,437 miles to a reading of 55,437 miles.

On September 14, Barton sold the note to Claire, a holder in due course. On October 5, Claire gave the note to her father, David, as a birthday present.

On October 15, David demanded payment of the note from Amy. Amy refused, arguing that Barton misrepresented the genuineness of the odometer reading.

Does David have the rights of a holder in due course?

ANSWER:

38. Tim and Lisa are makers on a $15,000 negotiable promissory note, originally payable to the order of Jennifer. Jennifer has sold the note to Marcus. Marcus may be a holder in due course, even if he had notice on the date that he took possession of the note that:

(A) Tim and Lisa had dishonored the note.

(B) Jennifer had fraudulently raised the amount of the note to $18,000.

(C) Jennifer had voluntarily discharged Tim's liability.

(D) Jennifer had stolen the note, while in bearer form, from Tim and Lisa.

39. Tony and Vincent had a $500 wager on the outcome of a political election. Tony lost the bet and was unable to immediately pay the wager. Vincent agreed to accept a $500 negotiable promissory note payable in 60 days. Tony then executed and delivered to Vincent a negotiable promissory note with those terms. Ten days later, Vincent sold the note to George for $380, telling George that the note represented a short-term loan by Vincent to enable Tony to pay some unexpected medical expenses.

Assume that governing law makes gambling on political events illegal. Tony discovers the law shortly before the note becomes due and asserts this defense against George when George demands payment on the due date.

Which of the following statements is true?

(A) George cannot be a holder in due course because his purchase price reflected more than a 20 percent discount.

(B) George cannot be a holder in due course because the underlying gambling transaction was illegal.

(C) George may be a holder in due course, but he will be subject to George's defense based on the illegality of the underlying transaction.

(D) If George is a holder in due course, he may (or may not) be subject to George's defense based on the illegality of the underlying transaction.

Use the following facts to answer the next two questions.

Celeste bought a car from Dealer. She made a $2,000 cash payment and financed the $18,000 balance. At Dealer's insistence, Gerard (Celeste's father) co-signed the $18,000 negotiable promissory note.

Celeste defaulted on the note when the unpaid balance was $12,000. Without the knowledge or consent of Gerard, Dealer and Celeste agreed that Celeste would pay $2,000 and be released from any further liability on the note. Celeste made the $2,000 payment. The written release did not address Gerard's remaining liability (if any).

Dealer then sued Gerard for the unpaid balance of $10,000. Gerard refused to pay, contending that Dealer's discharge of Celeste's liability also discharged his liability.

40. Which of the following statements is true?

(A) Gerard's liability has been discharged, but only if the settlement agreement between Celeste and Dealer was in writing.

(B) Gerard's liability has been discharged, whether or not the settlement agreement between Celeste and Dealer was in writing.

(C) Gerard's liability has not been discharged, but he continues to have rights of reimbursement against Celeste.

(D) Gerard's liability has not been discharged, and he no longer has any rights of reimbursement against Celeste.

41. Assume that Dealer sold the note to FinCo after Dealer and Celeste reached their settlement agreement. Dealer disclosed the terms of the settlement agreement to FinCo when FinCo took possession of the note.

   Which of the following statements is true?

   (A) Notice of the settlement agreement prevents FinCo from being a holder in due course.

   (B) FinCo may be a holder in due course and, if so, the settlement agreement has no effect on FinCo's enforcement rights on the note.

   (C) FinCo may be a holder in due course; even so, however, the terms of the settlement agreement are binding on FinCo.

   (D) FinCo may be a holder in due course, but only against Gerard.

42. Jack and Jill bought a home on credit, paying $25,000 in cash and signing a $175,000 negotiable promissory note for the balance, payable to the order of Lender. The terms of the note called for Jack and Jill to make monthly payments of $1,200.

   About six months ago, Lender sold the note to Wabash Finance. Neither party notified Jack and Jill of the sale, so they continued to send monthly payments to Lender. Lender did not forward the payments to Wabash Finance, who now demands these same (and now past due) payments from Jack and Jill. They agree to make future payments to Wabash Finance but refuse to pay, for a second time, payments previously remitted to Lender after the sale of the note.

   Which of the following statements is true?

   (A) Wabash Finance is not a holder in due course.

   (B) Wabash Finance may be a holder in due course and, if so, may enforce the note against Jack and Jill free of their payment defense.

   (C) Wabash Finance may be a holder in due course; even so, it is subject to Jack and Jill's payment defense.

    (D) Wabash Finance may be a holder in due course, but only to the extent of payments due and payable by Jack and Jill after they learn that Wabash Finance holds the note.

43.   Maker bought furniture on credit from Dealer on February 1, paying with a negotiable promissory note due and payable in six months.

    Dealer sold and delivered the note to Friendly Finance, acting in good faith, on June 15.

    Friendly Finance sold and delivered the note to ZinnCorp, acting in good faith, on August 20.

    When ZinnCorp asserts enforcement rights against Maker, Maker refuses to pay, citing Dealer's failure to deliver the furniture (a problem not previously known by Friendly Finance or ZinnCorp).

    Which of the following statements is true?

    (A) Whether ZinnCorp is (or is not) a holder in due course is irrelevant, because Maker's defense is effective even against a holder in due course.

    (B) ZinnCorp should assert that it qualified as an independent holder in due course when it acquired the note.

    (C) ZinnCorp should assert that Friendly Finance was a holder in due course, and ZinnCorp was sheltered to that status when ZinnCorp acquired the note.

    (D) ZinnCorp cannot enjoy the status of a holder in due course, either independently on its own or derivatively through Friendly Finance.

Use the following facts to answer the next two questions.

Dealer and Supplier frequently buy and sell products from and to each other. On April 1, Dealer bought goods from Supplier by delivering to Supplier a $5,000 negotiable promissory note. On April 10, Supplier bought goods from Dealer by delivering to Dealer a $1,600 negotiable promissory note.

On April 20, Supplier negotiated Dealer's $5,000 promissory note to Finance Company for a cash payment of $4,300.

When Finance Company demanded payment of $5,000 from Dealer on the maturity date of the promissory note, Dealer argued that its liability should be reduced by both (x) the $1,600 owed by Supplier to Dealer under the unpaid promissory note from April 10 and (y) a $700 claim for damages arising from a defect in the goods bought by Dealer from Supplier on April 1.

44.   How much is Finance Company entitled to recover on the $5,000 note if it is a holder in due course?

ANSWER:

45.   How much is Finance Company entitled to recover on the $5,000 note if it is *not* a holder in due course?

ANSWER:

46. For the past three years, Tim has understated his earnings and overstated his charitable contributions on his federal income tax return. He recently bragged about his conduct to a circle of friends after having a bit too much to drink.

Evan (one of these "friends") threatened to disclose Tim's wrongdoing to the IRS unless Tim delivered a $15,000 check to Evan within 10 days. Tim, fearing a much larger monetary penalty, and perhaps jail time, believed he had no choice but to comply with Evan's demand.

Tim's check bounced because he did not have adequate funds in the account. The drawee timely returned the check to Fidelity Savings (Evan's bank). Evan's account no longer had a $15,000 balance, so Fidelity Savings attempted to recover the funds from Tim, arguing that it was a holder in due course on the dishonored check. Tim refused to pay, arguing that he was blackmailed into writing the check.

Which of the following statements is true?

(A) Fidelity Savings cannot be a holder in due course of a dishonored check.

(B) Tim's defense is a real defense, making Fidelity Savings' status as a possible holder in due course irrelevant.

(C) Tim's defense is a personal defense, making Fidelity Savings' status as a possible holder in due course relevant.

(D) Tim's defense may be a real defense.

Use the following facts to answer the next three questions.

Jill borrowed $45,000 from First Bank in 2013. In connection with this loan, Jill executed and delivered to First Bank a $45,000 negotiable promissory note payable to the order of First Bank.

A few months later, First Bank became insolvent and the Federal Deposit Insurance Corporation (FDIC), acting as a receiver, took over the bank and acquired all of the bank's assets (including Jill's note).

A few days later, the FDIC sold Jill's note to MegaBank in an isolated transaction. Jill was timely informed that MegaBank had become the owner of her note.

When MegaBank demanded payment on the note under its terms, Jill asserted that she was entitled to a $25,000 offset, or credit, arising from an unpaid $25,000 certificate of deposit that she had purchased from First Bank in 2011.

47. If MegaBank wishes to assert that it owns Jill's note as a holder in due course, it will need to prove that the note has been indorsed by:

(A) First Bank and the FDIC.

(B) First Bank.

(C) the FDIC.

(D) neither First Bank nor the FDIC.

48. MegaBank:

(A) will not take subject to Jill's offset claim, whether or not MegaBank is a holder in due course of Jill's note.

(B) will not take subject to Jill's offset claim, but only if MegaBank is a holder in due course of Jill's note.

(C) will take subject to Jill's offset claim, whether or not MegaBank is a holder in due course of Jill's note.

(D) will take subject to Jill's offset claim, but only if MegaBank is not a holder in due course of Jill's note.

49. Assume that First Bank had sold 200 notes (including Jill's note) as part of a bulk transfer to MegaBank before the FDIC placed First Bank into receivership.

MegaBank:

(A) cannot be a holder in due course of Jill's note.

(B) cannot be a holder in due course of Jill's note in its own capacity, but MegaBank could acquire First Bank's status as a holder in due course through the shelter doctrine.

(C) can be a holder in due course of Jill's note, but only if it gave value for Jill's note equal to at least 80% of Jill's unpaid debt at the time of purchase.

(D) can be a holder in due course of Jill's note.

50. Ronald Clark, a legendary real estate magnate, wants to buy a large parcel of real estate that is currently for sale in downtown Boston. Mindful that negotiations may be more difficult, and competing bids might arise, if his interest becomes known, he prefers to remain anonymous if possible.

To accomplish his purpose, Clark authorizes his obscure lawyer, Timmy Zee, to negotiate the transaction on two conditions: (i) the purchase price cannot exceed $25 million and (ii) Zee cannot disclose (or otherwise mention) Clark's name. Zee honors both conditions, agreeing with the seller to purchase the property for $23.5 million. Zee delivers a $3.5 million cashier's check at the closing and executes a negotiable promissory note, for the $20 million balance, as "Timmy Zee, Agent." Per Clark's instructions, his name never came up in the negotiations, and his name does not appear in the note or any of the related real estate documents. The seller is aware, however, that Timmy Zee has been acting merely as an agent for an undisclosed principal.

Within two months, the seller has negotiated the $20 million note to Fargo Finance Company (FFC). When the note comes due, FFC demands payment from both Clark (whose involvement is now known) and Zee.

Which of the following statements is true?

(A) Neither Clark nor Zee has signature liability on the note.

(B) Clark has signature liability on the note, and Zee may have signature liability on the note.

    (C)   Clark does not have signature liability on the note, but Zee may have signature liability on the note.

    (D)   Both Clark and Zee have signature liability on the note.

51.   A holder in due course takes an instrument subject to a defense, asserted by a corporate maker, that:

    (A)   executing the note was an *ultra vires* act that renders its liability void.

    (B)   the note arose from an illegal transaction.

    (C)   the goods purchased in the underlying transaction were knowingly, and materially, misdescribed by the seller/payee.

    (D)   the note was executed under duress, brought about by settlement negotiations with the federal government concerning alleged violations of environmental laws.

Use the following facts to answer the next two questions.

Last month, Elaine wrote a $10,000 check for deposit into the college fund of her granddaughter (Meredith) that Elaine's son (Tim) had recently opened for Meredith. She mailed the check to Tim. The check was payable "to the order of Tim Smith, in trust for Meredith Smith, a minor." The accompanying letter directed Tim to add the proceeds to Meredith's college fund.

Tim took the check and deposited it into his personal account at Metro Bank after adding the following two-line indorsement: "for deposit only / Tim Smith". ZeeBank, the drawee, paid the check.

Soon thereafter, Tim withdrew the funds to pay off some uninsured medical expenses and overdue credit card bills. Greatly annoyed at this, Elaine and Meredith initiated a lawsuit against both Metro Bank and ZeeBank, seeking to recover $10,000, on the theory that Tim had violated his fiduciary duties, a fact that each bank knew or should have known.

52.   Tim's two-line indorsement is:

    (A)   a blank and restrictive indorsement.

    (B)   a special and restrictive indorsement.

    (C)   an anomalous and restrictive indorsement.

    (D)   a restrictive indorsement only.

53.   The lawsuit will succeed against:

    (A)   both banks.

    (B)   Metro Bank but not ZeeBank.

    (C)   ZeeBank but not Metro Bank.

    (D)   neither bank.

54. In early July, Jennifer agreed to purchase a painting from Helen for $2,500. Jennifer paid with her personal check, made payable to the order of Helen. Jennifer delivered the check to Helen on July 7. Helen deposited the check into her account at Jamestown Bank on July 11.

Jamestown Bank presented the check to Cromwell Savings on July 13. Unknown to Helen, Jennifer had placed a timely stop-payment order on the check, genuinely believing that Helen had misrepresented certain material details of the painting. Therefore, Cromwell Savings dishonored the check and timely returned it to Jamestown Bank on July 14.

Jamestown Bank had permitted Helen to withdraw funds credited against the check, so reversing the credit and creating a sizeable overdraft balance was not an attractive option. Therefore, Jamestown Bank has sued Jennifer, as drawer, for payment of the check.

Will Jamestown Bank's lawsuit against Jennifer be successful if evidence reveals that: (i) Helen never indorsed the check and (ii) Jennifer's reasons for placing the stop-payment order have merit?

ANSWER:

55. ZinnCorp executed a $1 million negotiable promissory note, payable to the order of Elliot Finance. Elliott Finance negotiated the note to Farmington Credit, which became a holder. Somehow, Farmington Credit lost the note. Nevertheless, after Farmington Credit executed a "lost note affidavit" and agreed to indemnify Weatherford Company, Farmington Credit assigned all of its right, title, and interest in the note to Weatherford Company. Farmington Credit provided Weatherford Company with a photocopy of the lost note.

Weatherford Company demanded payment from ZinnCorp a few days after the note came due. ZinnCorp refused to pay, contending that Weatherford Company could not enforce a note that it never possessed. Weatherford Company responded with a timely lawsuit against ZinnCorp, seeking payment of the indebtedness evidenced by the lost note.

How should the court decide the case?

ANSWER:

NEGOTIABLE INSTRUMENTS: FORMS OF LIABILITY ON NOTES, ORDINARY CHECKS, AND BANK CHECKS

Use the following facts to answer the next two questions.

Beth Davenport borrowed $12,000 from her mother, Grace, on July 1, 2013. At Grace's request, Beth executed the following negotiable promissory note on that date:

> The undersigned promises to pay $12,000 (twelve thousand U.S. Dollars) to the order of Grace Davenport on June 30, 2017.

> *Beth Davenport*

56.   The applicable statute of limitations on an action to enforce Beth's obligation is:

   (A)   four years after June 30, 2017.

   (B)   six years after June 30, 2017.

   (C)   four years after July 1, 2013.

   (D)   eight years after July 1, 2013.

57.   Assume that the language "on June 30, 2017" is replaced with a new sentence that states: *"This note is payable on demand."* Also assume that Grace negotiated the note to Marci in January 2015.

   Marci demanded payment from Beth on August 15, 2015, but Beth refused to make payment.

   To be timely, any action by Marci against Beth to enforce Beth's signature liability on the note must be commenced within:

   (A)   four years after August 15, 2015.

   (B)   six years after August 15, 2015.

   (C)   eight years after August 15, 2015.

   (D)   a reasonable period of time, not to exceed six years after August 15, 2015.

58.   Helen's father passed away in January 2014. While taking an inventory of her father's belongings, Helen found a $1,000 check in a desk. The check, payable to the order of her father, was an automobile rebate check issued by Motor Company of America (MCA) and drawn on MegaBank. The check had an issue date of October 1, 2008.

   On March 1, 2014, Helen presented the check to MegaBank for payment, offering proof that her father had recently died and that Helen was the executor of his estate. MegaBank refused to pay the check because MCA had closed its account several years ago.

Helen has come to you for advice on whether to sue MCA for drawer liability on the check. She is concerned that her lawsuit may be time-barred by the applicable statute of limitations.

How do you respond to her concern?

ANSWER:

Use the following facts to answer the next two questions.

Ima Bilder is a well-known real estate developer. Audra MacLaine is Ima's agent, authorized to execute promissory notes, real estate mortgages, and other related contracts on Ima's behalf.

Ima wants to buy real estate in downtown Memphis from TRZ Partners, the seller. Given her reputation, Ima believes that TRZ Partners will attempt to negotiate a higher price if Ima's involvement in the sale is known. Therefore, Ima authorizes Audra to negotiate the transaction as her agent. So Audra negotiates the deal and signs a negotiable promissory note simply as "Audra MacLaine, Agent." The promissory note and other loan documents never mention Ima or her involvement in the transaction.

The note is never repaid. TRZ Partners initially sues Audra as maker. Then TRZ Partners timely sues Ima as maker after discovering her role in the transaction.

59. Who is liable as a maker?

    (A) Ima and Audra are both liable as a maker.

    (B) Ima is liable as a maker; Audra may be liable as a maker.

    (C) Ima is not liable as a maker; Audra may be liable as a maker.

    (D) Ima is not liable as a maker; Audra is liable as a maker.

60. Who will be liable as a maker if evidence reveals that ABC Equity Group is the holder of the note (and ABC Equity Group purchased the note from TRZ Partners six months before the note's maturity date)?

ANSWER:

Use the following facts to answer the next two questions.

In November 2014, Molly issued and delivered a $5,000 negotiable promissory note to Eric. The note was payable to the order of Eric. A few months later, Eric negotiated the note to Harry.

The note is completely silent on the matter of presentment and notice of dishonor.

61. Molly's liability as maker:

    (A) turns on timely presentment.

(B)   turns on timely presentment, but only if the note is payable on demand.

(C)   turns on timely presentment, but only if the note is not payable on demand.

(D)   does not turn on timely presentment.

62.   Eric's indorser liability:

(A)   turns on timely notice of dishonor.

(B)   turns on timely notice of dishonor, but only if his indorsement was a special indorsement.

(C)   turns on timely notice of dishonor, but only if the note is a time instrument (and not a demand instrument).

(D)   does not turn on timely notice of dishonor.

Use the following facts to answer the next three questions.

Maker executed and delivered to Archie a negotiable promissory note payable to the order of Archie. Archie negotiated the note by blank indorsement to Barry, who negotiated the note by special indorsement to Charlie, who negotiated the note by special indorsement to David, a holder.

David demanded payment from Maker on the due date, but Maker refused to pay. Three weeks later, David informed Barry of the dishonor by telephone. David never gave notice of dishonor to Archie or Charlie because David did not know how to contact them.

Two months have passed since the note was dishonored.

63.   Barry is:

(A)   not liable to David on his indorsement because David's notice of dishonor was not in writing.

(B)   not liable to David on his indorsement because David's notice was not timely.

(C)   liable on his indorsement, but only to Charlie (the person to whom Barry negotiated the note).

(D)   liable to David on his indorsement.

64.   Assume that Barry and Charlie are business acquaintances, and Barry gave written notice of dishonor to Charlie two days after David telephoned Barry.
      Charlie is:

(A)   liable to David on his indorsement.

(B)   not liable to David on his indorsement because Charlie received notice of dishonor from Barry, not David.

(C)   liable to Barry on his indorsement if David collects payment from Barry.

    (D) not liable on his indorsement if it was accompanied by the phrase "without warranty."

65.   The facts indicate that Charlie negotiated the note by special indorsement to David. Describe Charlie's special indorsement, and contrast it with what his blank indorsement would look like.

ANSWER:

Use the following facts to answer the next two questions.

66.   Ashley agreed to purchase a painting from Gwen for $10,000. As agreed, Ashley executed and delivered to Gwen a short-term negotiable promissory note for the purchase price. The note was payable to the order of Gwen.

    Later, Gwen agreed to sell the note to Monica. Gwen asks Monica whether she prefers Gwen's special, or blank, indorsement.

    How should Monica respond?

ANSWER:

67.   Assume that Gwen placed her blank indorsement on the back of the note before delivering it to Monica. Monica noticed this, a few days after taking delivery of the note. She then wrote "Pay to Monica Johnson" in the space above Gwen's blank indorsement, making no attempt to match Gwen's handwriting or color of ink.

    Has Monica taken inappropriate action?

ANSWER:

68.   Two years ago, Hal bought a car on credit from Dealer. At Dealer's insistence, Hal's father (Keith) executed the negotiable promissory note as a co-maker. Dealer took all steps necessary to obtain a perfected security interest in the car.

    Hal recently dishonored the note. Dealer has sued Keith for co-maker liability.

    Which of the following responses by Keith should cause Dealer the most concern?

    (A) "I don't owe you a penny because you tampered with the odometer on the car."

    (B) "Forget about collecting from me, since Hal had this debt discharged in his recent bankruptcy proceeding."

    (C) "Since I didn't receive any consideration for my signature on the note, I therefore have no personal liability on the note."

    (D) "Sell the car first and apply the proceeds to the unpaid debt. Then we'll talk."

69.   In August 2013, Meredith purchased a used car from Dealer. She made a $5,000 cash down

payment and executed a negotiable $20,000 promissory note for the balance. Dealer expressly warranted that the odometer reading of 18,561 miles was true and correct. In fact, but unknown to Dealer, the previous owner had adjusted the odometer reading by 7,000 miles (meaning that the true and correct mileage at the time of Meredith's purchase was 25,561 miles).

After holding the note for two years, Dealer discounted and negotiated Meredith's note to Finance Company. Dealer delivered the note to Finance Company after adding the following two-line indorsement to the note: "Without Recourse / Dealer."

Three weeks ago, Meredith defaulted on the note.

Finance Company may be able to recover the unpaid balance of the note from Dealer on which statutory legal theory (or theories)?

(A) indorser liability and transfer warranty liability

(B) indorser liability, but not transfer warranty liability

(C) transfer warranty liability, but not indorser liability

(D) neither transfer warranty liability, nor indorser liability

70. As payment for taking care of her dog for two weeks, Holly issued her $200 personal check to Andrew on July 1.

Andrew owed $1,000 to his father, Luke. Andrew took Holly's check, indorsed it in blank, and delivered it to his father on July 15 as partial payment of his debt.

Luke deposited the $200 check into his account at Metropolitan Bank on August 30.

Metropolitan Bank timely presented the check to AmeriBank on September 2, which dishonored the check on September 3 because Holly's account had insufficient funds to cover the check. AmeriBank gave timely notice of the dishonor to Metropolitan Bank, which immediately reversed the $200 credit that it had previously given to Luke.

Luke now seeks recovery of $200 from Holly (drawer liability) and Andrew (indorser liability).

Which of the following statements is true?

(A) Luke should be able to recover the $200 from either party for signature liability.

(B) Holly no longer has any signature liability because more than 60 days have passed from the date of issuance to the date of AmeriBank's dishonor.

(C) Andrew no longer has any signature liability because more than 30 days have passed from the date of his indorsement to the date of Luke's deposit.

(D) Luke cannot recover the $200 from either Holly or Andrew until he exhausts any possible recovery he may have against Metropolitan Bank or AmeriBank.

Use the following facts to answer the next four questions.

Melissa and Hannah are business partners. They want to buy a small office building for $200,000, and they intend to borrow the funds. At Lender's insistence, their respective parents (Mark and Ruth, John and Abigail) also execute the negotiable promissory note. Melissa and Hannah sign their names at the end of the text of the note, and Mark, Ruth, John, and Abigail sign their respective names on the back of the last page of the note.

71.   Which of the following statements is true?

   (A) Melissa and Hannah are accommodated parties, and Mark, Ruth, John, and Abigail are accommodation parties.

   (B) Each of the six individuals is a co-maker.

   (C) Mark, Ruth, John, and Abigail are anomalous indorsers, but they are not sureties.

   (D) Mark, Ruth, John, and Abigail are not entitled to notice of dishonor as a condition to any signature liability.

72.   Which of the following statements is true?

   (A) If Melissa pays the note, she has a right of reimbursement from Hannah and a right of contribution from Abigail.

   (B) If Mark pays the note, he has a right of reimbursement from Melissa and a right of contribution from John.

   (C) If Hannah pays the note, she has a right of contribution from Melissa and a right of reimbursement from Ruth.

   (D) If Ruth pays the note, she has a right of reimbursement from John and a right of contribution from Hannah.

73.   Assume that Ruth pays $60,000 when the note comes due. The $140,000 balance remains unpaid, and Lender does not intend to forgive that piece of the debt.

   Which of the following statements is true?

   (A) Ruth has a reimbursement claim against Melissa for $60,000, and a contribution claim against Abigail for $15,000.

   (B) Ruth has a contribution claim against Hannah for $30,000.

   (C) Ruth has a reimbursement claim against Hannah for $60,000, and a contribution claim against John for $10,000.

   (D) Ruth has a reimbursement claim against Abigail for $60,000, and a contribution claim against Hannah for $50,000.

74.   Assume that Melissa pays $100,000 and John pays $40,000. The $60,000 balance remains

unpaid, and Lender does not intend to forgive that piece of the debt.

Which of the following statements is true?

(A) Lender does not have a claim against John for the $60,000 balance.

(B) Melissa has a contribution claim against Hannah for $50,000.

(C) John has a contribution claim against Mark for $15,000.

(D) John has a reimbursement claim against Hannah for $40,000, and a contribution claim against Ruth for $10,000.

Use the following facts to answer the next two questions.

The Jazz Club purchased a new grand piano, on credit, for its business. At Dealer's insistence, one of the club's wealthy investors, Ziggy Malone, executed the $25,000 promissory note as a co-maker. Repayment of the negotiable promissory note was secured by an enforceable security interest in the piano. Through oversight, Dealer never filed a financing statement, leaving its security interest in the piano unperfected.

During the term of the loan, and without Malone's knowledge or permission, the Club granted an enforceable security interest in the piano to Creditor to secure repayment of a $10,000 debt. Creditor timely perfected its security interest. As a result, under applicable commercial law (UCC Article 9), Creditor's perfected security interest in the piano enjoys priority over Dealer's earlier, but unperfected, security interest in the piano.

The Club defaulted on the $25,000 note. Dealer has sued Malone for the unpaid $17,000 balance and has made no attempt to sell the piano and apply any proceeds to the unpaid debt.

75. If the fair market value of the piano is $20,000, and the Club still owes $4,000 to Creditor, then Malone, after asserting a defense of collateral impairment, remains liable to Dealer for

(A) $20,000.

(B) $17,000.

(C) $16,000.

(D) $13,000.

76. If the fair market value of the piano is $15,000, and the Club still owes $4,000 to Creditor, then Malone, after asserting a defense of collateral impairment, remains liable to Dealer for

(A) $17,000.

(B) $15,000.

(C) $13,000.

(D) $11,000.

77. Two years ago, John bought some business equipment on credit for $24,000. The debt is evidenced by a negotiable promissory note (and neither the note, nor any other agreement, provide for a waiver of any suretyship defense). John had poor credit, so at Dealer's insistence John's mother, Alice, also signed the note.

In recent months John has incurred large uninsured medical costs and has informed Dealer that he is unable to make any additional payments on the note. The unpaid balance is $15,000. Three weeks ago, Dealer executed a one-sentence release in favor of John: "Dealer hereby releases John from all liability remaining on the Note (photocopy attached)."

As a result of this release,

    (A)   Alice's remaining liability on the note has been discharged.

    (B)   Alice continues to remain liable for $15,000 to Dealer, but she also retains her rights of recourse against John.

    (C)   Alice continues to remain liable for $15,000 to Dealer, but she no longer has any rights of recourse against John.

    (D)   The release is unenforceable if Alice, an original party to the note, did not know of, or consent to, the release.

Use these facts to answer the next two questions.

Two months ago, Sharon received a brochure from Getaway Vacations that invited her to purchase a holiday vacation package for $395. She responded by mailing her personal check to the address on the brochure. The next day she read a newspaper article in which several people complained about being "ripped off" by Getaway Vacations. So that day, Sharon drove to her bank, accurately completed the necessary paperwork, and placed a stop-payment order on the check that she had mailed to Getaway Vacations.

When Sharon received her next monthly bank statement, she was surprised to discover that the bank had paid her check to Getaway Vacations. Payment of the check left Sharon with an account balance insufficient to pay six subsequent checks. Her bank dishonored those six checks, resulting in an aggregate fee of $150 payable to the bank, and fees aggregating $120 payable to the payees of the dishonored checks. She contacted her bank and asked for an explanation. The bank officer explained that although the check written to Getaway Vacations was not presented for payment until four days after Sharon had placed the stop-payment order, the bank paid the check because its employee had accidentally transposed a digit when inputting the check number into its computer, preventing the bank's computer from flagging the check for nonpayment. When Sharon responded by demanding a $665 credit to her account ($395 for the check, plus $270 in fees), the bank officer reminded her that her deposit account agreement and the stop-payment order form both stated: "*Our liability for paying your check that is subject to a proper and timely stop-payment order is limited to your actual loss, which will not exceed the amount of the check unless our payment of your check resulted from our gross negligence or willful and intentional disregard of your stop-payment order.*" The bank officer agreed that Sharon was entitled to a credit, but only for $395 (the amount of the check). Sharon replied with some not-so-polite words and slammed down her phone.

78. Sharon has come to you for advice. What do you tell her?

ANSWER:

79. Assume the same facts, except Sharon erroneously completed the stop-payment order form by listing the amount of the check at $400 (instead of $395). The bank employee accurately input the information provided by Sharon (all of which was correct, except for the amount). The bank's technology flags a check subject to a stop-payment order by the amount of the check. Because the bank's computer was told to look for a $400 check, the Getaway Vacations check was paid, rather than flagged for nonpayment. Neither the deposit account agreement nor the stop-payment order form stated that the customer must provide the exact amount of the check in order for the stop-payment order to be effective. The deposit account agreement does require Sharon to describe the check with "reasonable certainty" when placing a stop payment order (although the agreement does not elaborate on the intended meaning of the phrase).

   Will Sharon's error prevent her from recovering any damages resulting from the bank's payment of the check?

ANSWER:

Use the following facts to answer the next two questions.

Two months ago, Tim (operating under the name of his sole proprietorship, "Tim's Lawncare") agreed to perform major landscaping work for Lisa at the rate of $60 per hour, plus the cost of materials. When the project was finished, Tim submitted an invoice for $2,500 (25 hours of work, plus $1,000 for materials). Lisa, who had been carefully watching Tim during the landscaping project, calculated an amount due of $2,200 (20 hours of work, plus $1,000 for materials). Based on her calculations, Lisa mailed a $2,200 check to Tim, conspicuously marked "payment in full for landscape work," accompanied by a letter explaining the $300 discrepancy from Tim's invoice amount.

Soon after receipt, Tim deposited Lisa's check. He then mailed a second invoice to Lisa, demanding payment of the additional $300.

80. Which of the following statements is true?

   (A) Lisa must pay the $300, unless she can prove material fraud by Tim.

   (B) Lisa must pay the $300 because the underlying contract was for services rendered (rather than for goods sold).

   (C) Lisa need not pay the $300 if she has acted in good faith.

   (D) Lisa need not pay the $300 because the UCC favors the maker of a check if the amount in dispute represents less than 15% of the amount originally demanded by the payee.

81. Discuss the merits of the following statement: *Tim can preserve a claim of $2,500 against Lisa if he timely returns $2,200 to her.*

ANSWER:

82. Robert agreed to purchase Helen's car for $12,500. Helen agreed to take a $12,500 check from Robert. Helen comes to you for advice on whether to take Robert's personal check, or a cashier's check issued by Robert's bank, and whether the difference will affect Helen's ability to sue Robert on the underlying contract.

Offer a brief response.

ANSWER:

83.   Jim owed Robert $1,000. He placed his personal $1,000 check (payable to the order of Robert) in a stamped envelope, which he put in his mailbox at the end of his driveway. Frank noticed the mailbox flag in the "up" position, opened the mailbox, and took the envelope addressed to Robert. Frank then forged Robert's special indorsement ("Pay to Frank / Robert"), drove to First Bank, and deposited the check into his account. First Bank timely presented the check to Second Bank, which timely honored the check.

Which statement is true?

(A)   First Bank breached the transfer warranty regarding its status as a person entitled to enforce the check.

(B)   Robert has a claim against Second Bank for statutory conversion.

(C)   Second Bank is liable for statutory conversion.

(D)   Frank breached the presentment warranty regarding his status as a person entitled to enforce the check.

Use the following facts to answer the next three questions.

Two weeks ago, Lisa mailed a $4,000 check to her twin daughters, who were college sophomores. The check was payable to the order of "Grace and Meredith," and Lisa's cover letter indicated that the $4,000 was to be shared in equal parts by both daughters.

Grace received and opened the letter. She took the check to a local branch of the payor bank, which cashed the check for Grace after she indorsed the check in blank. The payor bank debited Lisa's account for $4,000.

Soon thereafter, Grace went on an online shopping spree, spending nearly all of the $4,000.

Lisa discovered Grace's mischief three days ago. Meredith never saw the letter, had no knowledge that her mother had mailed the check, and was unaware of Grace's actions until two days ago. Both Lisa and Meredith are quite unhappy and disappointed with Grace.

84.   The payor bank:

(A)   properly debited Lisa's account for $4,000.

(B)   should have debited Lisa's account for only $2,000.

(C)   should not have debited Lisa's account at all.

    (D) breached its duty of ordinary care by cashing a check for more than $1,000.

85. The payor bank has a claim against Grace for:

    (A) breach of transfer warranty.

    (B) breach of presentment warranty.

    (C) indorser liability.

    (D) statutory conversion.

86. Meredith has a claim against:

    (A) Grace for breaching a presentment warranty.

    (B) Grace for breaching a transfer warranty.

    (C) the payor bank for statutory conversion.

    (D) the payor bank for violating the "properly payable rule."

87. Ima Saint is a member of MegaChurch. She is one of several members who serve as ushers who take up the weekly church offering. During the last eight months, Ima has clandestinely stolen several tithing checks payable to MegaChurch and then deposited them into her personal account at Cardinal Bank. Sometimes she forged MegaChurch's indorsement. Sometimes she added her own blank indorsement. Sometimes a stolen check bore both indorsements. In total, the thefts aggregated nearly $43,000.

MegaChurch discovered Ima's financial sins last week. It seeks to recover the stolen funds from Cardinal Bank. MegaChurch is not quite sure of what legal theory it should pursue, but one church member (a lawyer who vaguely recalls bits and pieces of his UCC coursework) suggests that Cardinal Bank failed to exercise ordinary care by allowing a customer to deposit into a personal account numerous checks payable to a well-known business.

Briefly discuss the merits of this suggestion.

ANSWER:

Use the following facts to answer the next three questions.

John Johnson, the bookkeeper for Smith & Jones, L.L.C., prepares payroll checks for signature by Smith. For six months, John has included checks payable to (and in the name of) a former employee, Alex Johnson. Smith has signed all of the checks submitted by John, and returned them to John for distribution to the employees. John has then taken the checks that list Alex as the payee (individually in amounts ranging from $1,800 to $2,300, and in the aggregate amount of $25,700), forged Alex's blank indorsement, and deposited the checks into his account at Fidelity Bank. Fidelity Bank has presented the checks for payment to Commerce Bank, the drawee, which has timely paid each check.

Smith discovered John's mischief during a recent internal audit. John can no longer be found. Smith & Jones seeks recovery of the $25,700 from Commerce Bank.

88. As between Smith & Jones and Commerce Bank,

    (A) Commerce Bank should take the loss under Section 4-401(a).

    (B) Smith & Jones should take the loss under Section 4-406.

    (C) Smith & Jones should take the loss under Section 3-405.

    (D) Smith & Jones should take the loss under Section 3-404(b).

89. Regardless of your previous answer, assume that Smith & Jones, rather than Commerce Bank, takes the entire $25,700 loss.

    Discuss whether Smith & Jones can recover some or all of its loss from Fidelity Bank under Sections 3-416(a)(2) or 4-207(a)(2) (breach of transfer warranty re authentic and authorized signatures), Sections 3-417(a) or 4-208(a) (breach of presentment warranty), or Section 3-405(b) (comparative negligence).

ANSWER:

90. Regardless of your previous answers, assume that Smith & Jones is able to deflect part of the loss (e.g., $12,850) to Fidelity Bank. Assume that Fidelity Bank acted in good faith, but failed to exercise ordinary care, in taking the checks from John.

    Discuss whether Fidelity Bank has a cause of action against John for breaching a transfer warranty.

ANSWER:

91. To which situation does the "imposter rule" of Section 3-404(a) *not* apply?

    (A) Sarah issues a check, payable to the order of Gary Thompson, to Barry after Barry tells Sarah that he is Gary Thompson. Barry forges Gary's indorsement and obtains payment of the check.

    (B) Sarah issues a check, payable to the order of Gary Thompson, to Barry after Barry tells Sarah, "I'm Barry, Gary's authorized agent for delivery." Barry forges Gary's indorsement and obtains payment of the check.

    (C) Sarah prepares a check, payable to the order of Gary Thompson. Gary has informed Sarah that his agent, Bill, will stop by and pick up the check. Sarah later delivers the check to Barry after Barry tells Sarah, "I'm Bill, and Gary asked me to stop by and pick up the check." Barry forges Gary's indorsement and obtains payment of the check.

(D) Sarah issues a check, payable to the order of Gary Thompson, to Barry after Barry tells Sarah that he is Gary Thompson. Barry never indorses the check, but he does deposit the check into an account that he opened in the name of "Gary Thompson."

Use the following facts to answer the next six questions.

ZinnCorp ("ZC") has its checking account with Fidelity Bank. All checks written on the account for more than $2,000 require the signature of two ZC officers (and this dual signature requirement is preprinted on each check). Fidelity provides ZC with a monthly bank statement (but not the checks themselves), which lists for each check paid during that reporting period the check number, the date paid, and the amount of the check.

Over the course of three months, ZC's chief financial officer engaged in improper check-related behavior. He improperly wrote three checks payable to himself, signing only his name on two of the checks (#2 and #4 below), and signing his name and forging another corporate officer's name on one check (#6 below). On two outgoing checks (#1 and #5 below) signed by other authorized corporate officers, the CFO used chemicals to alter in an expert manner the amount (both numbers and words) from $2,477 and $3,985 to $5,900 and $8,300, respectively (splitting the excess with the named payees after they deposited the checks). Also, the CFO intercepted two outgoing checks (#3 and #7 below) signed by other authorized corporate officers and payable to legitimate suppliers, forged the indorsement of each payee, added his own blank indorsement, and then cashed the checks at his bank.

Fidelity paid and returned the checks (ranging in amount from $3,800 to $8,750) on the following dates:

check #1 (alteration of amount) paid on June 5 and returned on June 12;

check #2 (missing signature) paid on June 13 and returned on July 12;

check #3 (forged indorsement) paid on June 17 and returned on July 12;

check #4 (missing signature) paid on July 8 and returned on July 12;

check #5 (alteration of amount) paid on July 16 and returned on August 12;

check #6 (one forged signature) paid on July 31 and returned on August 12; and

check #7 (forged indorsement) paid on August 4 and returned on August 12.

ZC did not discover the CFO's wrongdoing until November. Its general counsel then immediately informed Fidelity of the corporate mischief. Fidelity has expressed reluctance to recredit ZC's account for the amount of the seven checks.

92. Section 4-406 has no application to the loss allocation of:

   (A) check #2.

   (B) check #3.

   (C) check #5.

   (D) check #6.

93. As between ZC and Fidelity, Section 4-406 probably will place the loss on ZC for:

(A) check #1.

(B) check #2.

(C) check #6.

(D) check #7.

94. As between ZC and Fidelity, Section 4-406 probably will place the loss on Fidelity for:

(A) check #1.

(B) check #4.

(C) check #5.

(D) check #6.

95. Among Sections 3-404, 3-405, and 3-406, which statutes may be relevant to the loss allocation of check #5?

(A) all three statutes

(B) Sections 3-404 and 3-406 only

(C) Sections 3-405 and 3-406 only

(D) Section 3-406 only

96. Among Sections 3-404, 3-405, and 3-406, which statutes may be relevant to the loss allocation of check #6?

(A) all three statutes

(B) Sections 3-404 and 3-405 only

(C) Section 3-405 only

(D) Section 3-406 only

97. Among Section 3-404, 3-405, and 3-406, which statutes may be relevant to the loss allocation of check #7?

(A) all three statutes

(B) Sections 3-404 and 3-406 only

(C) Sections 3-405 and 3-406 only

(D) Section 3-406 only

Use the following facts to answer the next two questions.

Monica has a checking account with Oxford Savings. Monica and Oxford Savings have agreed that Oxford Savings will mail a bank statement to Monica every month. However, Monica and Oxford Savings also have agreed that Oxford Savings will not return the physical checks to Monica.

98.   If Oxford Savings wishes to impose on Monica the "examine and notify" duties of Section 4-406(c), Oxford Savings must include on the monthly bank statement information that describes each check by check number and:

   (A) date paid and payee.

   (B) payee and amount paid.

   (C) date paid and amount paid.

   (D) date paid, amount paid, and payee.

99.   If Oxford Savings provides Monica with sufficient information to allow Monica to reasonably identify checks paid, Monica has a duty under Section 4-406(c) to examine her statement for checks bearing:

   (A) alterations, forged indorsements, and her unauthorized drawer signature.

   (B) alterations and forged indorsements.

   (C) forged indorsements, and her unauthorized drawer signature.

   (D) alterations and her unauthorized drawer signature.

Use the following facts to answer the next five questions.

Nancy contractually agreed to buy Mark's grand piano for $20,000. Mark insisted on payment in the form of a cashier's check, so Nancy purchased a $20,000 cashier's check from her bank, Heritage Bank. Heritage debited Nancy's account for $20,000, plus $25 as a service fee.

Heritage Bank issued the cashier's check to Nancy on July 1. The check was payable to the order of Mark.

100.   While Nancy possessed the check (before she delivered it to Mark), she was:

   (A) a remitter, a holder, and a PETE.

   (B) a nonholder in possession with rights of a holder, and a PETE.

   (C) a remitter, and a PETE under the shelter doctrine.

   (D) a remitter, but not a PETE.

101.   Thief stole the check from Nancy on July 3 before she delivered the check to Mark.

   Which of the following statements is true?

(A) Mark can bring a cause of action against Nancy on the underlying obligation to pay for the piano even though the parties contemplated payment of that obligation with a cashier's check.

(B) Thief cannot be a holder in due course, but one or more of Thief's direct or indirect transferees may become a holder in due course.

(C) Mark has standing to assert an enforceable claim under Section 3-312 even though he never possessed the check.

(D) Nancy is not a person entitled to enforce the check after its theft.

102. Nancy discovered the theft on July 4. She visited Heritage Bank on July 5, informed the bank officer of the theft, and completed a "declaration of loss" and other paperwork requested by the officer.

Nancy's claim to the stolen check became enforceable:

(A) on July 5, when she completed all of the paperwork.

(B) 30 days after July 1.

(C) 90 days after July 1.

(D) the later of the presentment date, and 30 days after July 1.

103. Thief forged Mark's blank indorsement and deposited the check into his account at Pemberton Bank on July 7. Pemberton Bank presented the check for payment to Heritage Bank on July 8, which timely paid the check.

When Nancy's claim becomes enforceable, Heritage Bank:

(A) must pay her claim.

(B) is excused from paying her claim because Heritage Bank already paid the check on presentment.

(C) is excused from paying her claim because Heritage Bank previously made payment to a person entitled to enforce the check.

(D) is excused from paying her claim because Nancy's underlying contract obligation to pay for the piano has been discharged.

104. Assume that Heritage Bank had issued the check payable to Nancy (instead of Mark) and Nancy had written her blank indorsement on the check prior to its theft. How does this affect Nancy's claim when it becomes enforceable?

ANSWER:

Use the following facts to answer the next three questions.

Tim, a Dallas resident, mails a $250 check to his mother, Helen, who lives in Phoenix. Helen deposits the check into her account at Arizona Bank. Arizona Bank forwards the check to the local Federal Reserve bank ("FRB-Phoenix"), which forwards the check to the Federal Reserve bank in Dallas ("FRB-Dallas"), which forwards the check to Dallas National Bank for payment.

105. Using Article 4 terminology, Arizona Bank is the depositary bank and:

    (A) a collecting bank.

    (B) an intermediary bank.

    (C) a collecting bank and an intermediary bank.

    (D) a collecting bank and a presenting bank.

106. Using Article 4 terminology, FRB-Dallas is:

    (A) an intermediary bank.

    (B) a collecting bank.

    (C) an intermediary bank and a collecting bank.

    (D) an intermediary bank, a collecting bank, and a presenting bank.

107. Assume that Dallas National Bank receives the check at 4:30 p.m. on Tuesday, when Tim's account balance is less than $200.

    Which of the following statements is true?

    (A) The check is not properly payable if payment will create an overdraft of more than $100.

    (B) The check is not properly payable if payment will create an overdraft of any amount.

    (C) Dallas National Bank may be liable for the amount of the check if it holds the check beyond Tuesday midnight without settling for it.

    (D) Dallas National Bank has until Thursday midnight to make its "pay or dishonor" decision without becoming liable for the amount of the check.

108. Hal and Shirley have a joint checking account with Paradise Savings. The deposit account

agreement permits either party to write checks without the signature of the other spouse. The agreement also states: *"If you have a joint account, then you are responsible for repayment of any overdraft created by any check drawn on the account, whether written by you or any other joint owner."*

Without Shirley's knowledge or consent, Hal purchased a golf membership for himself (Shirley hates golf!) on April 12, paying the annual $2,000 fee with a check drawn on the joint account. Knowing that the account had a balance of only $1,300, but expecting an electronic deposit of $1,500 in three days, Hal postdated the check with a date of April 17. Hal asked the membership manager to wait until April 18 to deposit the check. The manager agreed. But the manager's assistant deposited Hal's check (along with several other checks) the next day. Paradise Savings honored the check on April 15, creating a $700 overdraft, which remained for several weeks because the electronic deposit never occurred.

Which of the following statements is true?

(A) Paradise Savings can collect the overdraft from Shirley, even though she neither signed the check nor received any benefit from it.

(B) Paradise Savings cannot collect the overdraft from Shirley because a check that creates an overdraft is not properly payable, leaving Paradise Savings responsible for any overdraft balance.

(C) Paradise Savings cannot collect the overdraft from either Shirley or Hal because it honored the postdated check before it became properly payable on April 17.

(D) Article 4 of the UCC prevents Paradise Savings from collecting the overdraft from Shirley.

109. Connie issued a $300 check to Marvin on April 2. Marvin gave the check to his daughter, Alice, on April 29, as a birthday gift. Marvin placed his blank indorsement on the check immediately prior to delivery. Alice misplaced the check and did not find it until November 10. On November 12, Alice presented the check to Broadway Bank, the payor bank, for payment. Connie's account balance is approximately $750.

At the time of presentment,

(A) the check is not overdue.

(B) the check is no longer properly payable.

(C) Marvin no longer has any indorser liability.

(D) Broadway Bank risks liability for wrongful dishonor if it refuses to pay the check.

110. Francine owes $2,000 to Mark. They have agreed that Francine will make monthly payments of $200.

Last week Francine mailed a $200 check to Mark for the first payment. Mark deposited the check in his account at Integrity Bank and received a $200 credit to his account. Integrity Bank erroneously encoded the check for $2,000. Integrity Bank forwarded the check to the local branch of the Federal Reserve Bank ("FRB-Local"), which forwarded the check to Francine's bank, Fidelity Bank, for payment. Fidelity Bank honored the check and debited Francine's account for the encoded amount of $2,000.

Which of the following statements best states the path of recovery of the $1,800 problem?

(A) Francine takes the loss and cannot recover the $1,800 from any party because she owed $2,000 to Mark.

(B) Francine recovers from Fidelity Bank, which recovers from FRB-Local, which recovers from Integrity Bank.

(C) Francine recovers from Fidelity Bank, which recovers from Integrity Bank.

(D) Francine recovers from Integrity Bank.

Use the following facts to answer the next two questions.

Alice has been interested in buying a used piano for some time. In recent days she noticed an advertisement in the paper that caught her eye. She called the seller, Karen, and made an appointment to look at the piano. During the inspection Alice noticed what she thought might be a hairline crack in the metal soundboard. Karen assured Alice that this was no more than a cosmetic defect. Alice gave Karen a $3,500 check (the amount Karen was asking) to "hold" the piano. Alice asked Karen not to deposit the check until Alice could return in two or three days with a piano technician who could confirm whether the soundboard was cracked. Karen agreed.

But Karen did not honor her agreement. Instead, she immediately deposited the check in her account at Dollar Bank, which took the check in good faith and without notice of any problems. Dollar Bank credited Karen's account immediately, and Karen withdrew and spent all the credit. Two days later, Alice returned with the piano technician, who confirmed Alice's fears that the soundboard was indeed cracked. Alice demanded the return of her $3,500 check. Karen said that she had deposited the check, annoying Alice greatly. But in a show of good faith, Karen offered to give Alice her (Karen's) personal check for $3,550 (knowing the check would bounce). Alice took the $3,550 check and left with the technician.

Alice still feels uneasy about the situation and has decided to place a stop payment order on her $3,500 check.

111. Which of the following statements is true?

(A) Alice cannot place a stop payment order on the check after Karen has deposited the check.

(B) Alice cannot place a stop payment order on the check after Karen has withdrawn the credit she received from Dollar Bank for the check.

(C) Alice cannot place a stop payment order on the check after Dollar Bank has forwarded the check to the next financial institution in the collection process.

(D) Alice can place an oral stop payment order on the check.

112. Assume the same facts, except that Alice did not offer her personal check for $3,500. Instead, she offered a cashier's check for $3,500, which had been issued by her bank in bearer form. All other facts remain the same.

Which of the following statements is true?

(A) A stop payment order cannot be placed on a cashier's check, if the cashier's check was issued by a financial institution chartered under federal law.

(B) A stop payment order cannot be placed on a cashier's check issued in bearer form.

(C) A stop payment can be placed on a cashier's check, but Alice may not place the order.

(D) A stop payment cannot be placed on a cashier's check once a special indorsement is placed on the check.

113. Richard and Celia, husband and wife, have a joint checking account. A few days ago, Celia received an expense reimbursement check from her employer. This morning, she gave the check to Richard to deposit into their joint checking account. When Richard arrived at the bank, he discovered that Celia had not indorsed the check.

Discuss what may happen when he offers the deposit slip, and the check, to the bank teller.

ANSWER:

114. Meredith maintains her checking account with ABC Bank. This morning, ABC Bank received seven checks drawn on Meredith's account. The checks range from a low of $700 to a high of $2,100. The total amount of the seven checks equals $8,300. Meredith's account balance is $5,700. In such a situation, the UCC mandates that ABC Bank:

(A) dishonor all seven checks.

(B) honor as many checks as it can, starting with the smallest check.

(C) honor as many checks as it can, starting with the check bearing the smallest check number.

(D) honor as many checks as it can, in any order it desires.

115. What is the difference between a cashier's check and a teller's check?

ANSWER:

116. What is a remitter? Give an example.

ANSWER:

117. On Friday morning, July 14, ZeeCorp deposited into its account with First Bank a cashier's

check drawn on Prosperity Bank in the amount of $55,000. First Bank placed a hold on ZeeCorp's account, pending payment of the check. On Monday morning, July 17, the first business day after deposit, First Bank presented the check to Prosperity Bank and received provisional credit.

Hearing nothing further from Prosperity Bank, First Bank informed ZeeCorp on July 20 that the hold on its account had been lifted.

On July 21, Prosperity Bank notified First Bank that it was returning the $55,000 check because it was counterfeit. First Bank promptly notified ZeeCorp of the problem and then debited ZeeCorp's account for $55,000, plus a $25 chargeback fee.

Which of the following statements is true?

(A) First Bank cannot charge back the $55,000 check because there has been final settlement for the check.

(B) First Bank cannot charge back the $55,000 check because more than five days have passed since the check was deposited.

(C) First Bank cannot charge back the $55,000 check because it had already lifted the hold on ZeeCorp's account.

(D) First Bank can charge back the $55,000 check because it acted within a reasonable time after being informed by Prosperity Bank that the check was counterfeit.

118. On July 2, Dru mailed to American Motors a $300 check. American Motors received the check on July 7 and deposited the check with Wembley Savings on July 8. Wembley Savings presented the check to University Bank on July 10. University Bank timely paid the check on July 11.

Dru had a sudden heart attack and died on July 4. His obituary was prominently featured in *The Scranton Daily News* (July 8 edition). University Bank is located in Scranton. Numerous employees and officers of University Bank read the obituary. Several bank officers attended Dru's funeral on July 6.

University Bank's authority to pay the $300 check:

(A) terminated at Dru's death on July 4.

(B) terminated when bank officers attended Dru's funeral on July 6.

(C) terminated on July 8, the publication date of Dru's obituary.

(D) was not terminated prior to payment on July 11.

119. On August 1, Nancy had some minor contracting work done by Grant at her home at a cost of $450. Grant asked for a check before he left. Nancy had only $395 in her account, but her salary was scheduled to be wired into her account on August 7. She gave a $450 check dated August 8 to Grant, asking him to wait until that date to deposit the check. She explained that her account was low on funds, but that adequate funds would be available on August

8 and thereafter. Grant said he could, and would, wait.

Not quite convinced that Grant would postpone his deposit, Nancy telephoned her bank officer on August 2, explained that she had given a payee a postdated check, accurately described all of the relevant details of the check, and asked the officer to flag the check in such a manner that her bank would not pay the check until August 8. The officer agreed.

Grant deposited the check on August 3. His bank presented the check to the drawee on August 4. The drawee honored and paid the check on August 5, creating an overdraft balance in Nancy's account.

Four checks drawn on Nancy's account were presented for payment on August 6. The drawee dishonored each of the four checks because the account had a negative balance. As a result of the multiple dishonors, Nancy incurred fees and charges from various parties in the total amount of $140. And one of the payees of a dishonored check, Jim's Gym, terminated Nancy's athletic membership.

As she had expected, Nancy received an electronic deposit of $1,200 on August 7.

Evidence reveals that the $450 check slipped through the system because the bank officer became distracted after talking with Nancy and never forwarded the necessary information to the appropriate bank department.

Nancy has demanded that her bank pay various damages in the amount of $2,000.

Nancy's bank has pointed her attention to the following provision in the bank account agreement: *"Bank's liability for wrongful payment of a postdated check shall never exceed the amount of that check."*

Discuss how this dispute will play out, under the UCC.

ANSWER:

120. Last week, Lisa issued a $400 check, drawn on her account at Omega Bank, to Edith as payment for consulting services. Edith deposited the check into her account at Alpha Bank. Alpha Bank timely presented the check to Omega Bank for payment. Omega Bank timely, but wrongfully, dishonored the check. Omega Bank gave timely notice of the dishonor to Alpha Bank, which immediately made a $400 debit to Edith's account.

Edith has a cause of action:

   (A) against Alpha Bank for a wrongful debit to her account, and against Lisa on the check.

   (B) against Omega Bank for wrongful dishonor, and against Alpha Bank for a wrongful debit to her account, and against Lisa on the check.

   (C) against Lisa on the check.

   (D) against Omega Bank for wrongful dishonor, and against Lisa on the check.

121. In a successful action for wrongful dishonor, the injured party is entitled:

(A) to be put in as good a position as if the other party had fully performed, but neither consequential or special damages nor penal damages may be had except as specifically provided in the UCC or by other rule of law.

(B) to the amount of the item, reduced by an amount that could not have been realized by the exercise of ordinary care.

(C) to actual damages proved (which may include consequential damages).

(D) to actual damages proved, plus a statutory penalty (to be determined by the trier of fact) in the minimum amount of $100 and the maximum amount of $5,000.

122. UCC Article 4 provides a cause of action for wrongful dishonor. Give three examples of *rightful* dishonor.

ANSWER:

Use the following facts to answer the next two questions.

Buyer agreed to make an online purchase of a rare set of baseball cards at a cost of $2,000. Because Buyer had such a great online record for timely payments, Seller agreed to take Buyer's personal check. Buyer then mailed a $2,000 personal check to Seller.

The next day, Buyer found the same rare set of baseball cards being offered online by a different merchant at a price of $1,600. Concluding that he had overpaid for his purchase, Buyer immediately and timely placed a written stop-payment order on his $2,000 check, accurately describing all of the pieces of information on the check.

Through its own negligence, the drawee overlooked Buyer's stop-payment order and paid the check.

123. Discuss the two different approaches that courts have taken in addressing what Buyer must prove in order to recover the amount of the check from the drawee.

ANSWER:

124. Assume that the drawee complies with Buyer's written stop-payment order and dishonors the check. The check is timely returned to Seller. If Seller has the patience and the inclination, it may wish to hold the check and resubmit it for deposit and ultimate payment in approximately:

(A) 30 days.

(B) 60 days.

(C) 90 days.

(D) 180 days.

125. The Electronic Fund Transfer Act (the "EFTA") applies, as one would assume, to "electronic fund transfers" as that term is defined by the EFTA. To be an "electronic fund transfer," the funds being transferred must result in:

   (A) a debit, but not a credit, to a consumer's account.

   (B) a debit or a credit to a consumer's account of at least $100.

   (C) a debit or a credit to a consumer's account in any amount.

   (D) a debit or a credit to any bank account (whether or not the account is established primarily for personal, family, or household purposes).

126. Which of the following transactions will *not* be an "electronic fund transfer" as defined by the EFTA?

   (A) Melissa authorizes her mortgage company to electronically withdraw her monthly mortgage payment from her personal checking account. The monthly withdrawal will exceed $1,000.

   (B) Melissa and her bank agree that if Melissa writes a personal check that creates an overdraft in her family's checking account, the bank may electronically transfer funds from the family's savings account in an amount sufficient to cover the overdraft.

   (C) At the request of the checkout clerk, Melissa tenders a blank check to the clerk. The clerk swipes the check through a machine that reads the MICR line information on the check. The clerk manually enters the amount of the transaction and returns the check to Melissa. Melissa's checking account (used primarily for a family purpose) is electronically debited for the amount of the transaction.

   (D) Melissa's personal checking account is credited twice a month with an electronic deposit of her wages. The initiator of the transfer is Melissa's corporate employer.

127. Congress has delegated to "the Board" the authority to prescribe rules to carry out the purposes of the EFTA.

   The "Board" means:

   (A) the Board of Governors of the Federal Reserve System.

   (B) the Federal Financial Services Board.

    (C) the Federal Trade Commission.

    (D) the Consumer Credit Protection Board.

128. Congress also has delegated to "the Bureau" the authority to prescribe rules to carry out the purposes of the EFTA. The "Bureau" means the:

    (A) Federal Bureau of Investigation.

    (B) Bureau of Consumer Financial Protection.

    (C) Federal Bureau of Financial Management.

    (D) Bureau of Electronic Fund Transfers.

129. Which regulation enacted by the Board is most closely associated with the Electronic Fund Transfer Act?

    (A) Regulation CC

    (B) Regulation M

    (C) Regulation E

    (D) Regulation Z

Use the following facts to answer the next five questions.

Meredith keeps her MegaBank debit card in her purse. Evidence reveals the following activity:

Monday 8:45 p.m.	Thief steals Meredith's purse. Thief withdraws $200 from ATM using the stolen card.
Tuesday 9:00 a.m.	Meredith discovers the theft of her purse and card.
Tuesday 9:35 a.m.	Thief withdraws $250 from ATM using the stolen card.
Tuesday 2:15 p.m.	Thief withdraws $200 from ATM using the stolen card.
Tuesday 4:20 p.m.	Meredith visits MegaBank and discloses the theft of her purse and ATM card. MegaBank immediately cancels Meredith's card.

130. Assuming that MegaBank can satisfy its burden of proof, Meredith's maximum liability for the unauthorized withdrawals should be:

    (A) $500.

    (B) $100.

    (C) $50.

    (D) $0.

131. Would your answer change if Meredith admitted that she kept her personal identification

number taped to the card?

ANSWER:

132. Assume that Meredith's contract with MegaBank included the following provision: *"Cardholder agrees that he or she is liable for any and all unauthorized electronic fund transfers, excluding any such transfer that results in whole or in part from the Bank's negligence, gross negligence, or failure to exercise ordinary care."* Would this contract provision affect your liability allocation under the original facts?

ANSWER:

133. Assume that applicable state law provides that Meredith incurs no liability for unauthorized electronic fund transfers resulting from a stolen access device. Would this state law provision affect your liability allocation under the original facts?

ANSWER:

134. Assume that Meredith did not visit MegaBank on Tuesday at 4:20 p.m. Instead, Meredith telephoned her MegaBank account representative on Tuesday at 4:20 p.m. The representative was away from the office for a few days (although the voicemail response did not indicate the absence). As a result, the account representative did not listen to Meredith's voicemail until Friday and did not cancel the card until Friday at 10:30 a.m. Between Tuesday at 4:20 p.m. and Friday at 10:30 a.m., Thief used Meredith's ATM card to make several unauthorized withdrawals that aggregated $1,100.

Discuss how these revised facts affect the loss allocation between Meredith and MegaBank.

ANSWER:

Use the following facts to answer the next two questions.

Tommy has a personal account at AmeriBank. He receives an activity statement each month that reflects checks paid, deposits made, and any electronic fund transfers (such as ATM transactions).

Yesterday, while reconciling his bank statement to his personal records, Tommy noticed a $250 ATM withdrawal for which he did not have a receipt. He assumed that his wife made this withdrawal and simply forgot to record the transaction in the checkbook register. He discussed this matter with his wife last night, reminding her to timely document her ATM transactions. She replied that she had been doing so, to the best of her knowledge. They then both looked at the statement and noticed that the $250 withdrawal in question had occurred at a cross-town terminal which neither of them had visited. They then reviewed previous statements and noticed that a similar $250 ATM withdrawal had taken place once a month, at the same terminal location, for eight months. As with the most recent withdrawal, Tommy had been assuming in past months that these transactions were legitimate, but that he or his wife had failed to record the withdrawals in the check register.

Tommy visited his AmeriBank account representative this morning and explained that, unknown to him and his wife, someone had been making a monthly unauthorized withdrawal from his family's personal bank account. He demanded that AmeriBank credit the account for $2,000 ($250 each month, for eight months).

Evidence confirms that someone was using an unauthorized access device to make the monthly $250 withdrawals.

135. If AmeriBank can satisfy its burden of proof, Tommy and his wife will incur a loss of:

    (A) $50.

    (B) $550.

    (C) $1,550.

    (D) $2,000.

136. Just before AmeriBank is prepared to credit Tommy's account for the appropriate amount, its lawyer informs Tommy that the bank has decided against any credit. When Tommy asks for an explanation, the bank lawyer responds as follows. "An 'error' under the EFTA includes an unauthorized electronic fund transfer, as we acknowledge happened on numerous occasions to your account. But the error resolution process (as stated in EFTA § 908) requires you to give us *timely* notice of the error. Timely notice is loosely defined as sixty days. We delivered to you the statement on which appeared the initial unauthorized ATM withdrawal more than seven months before you informed us of the problem. You waited too long to assert the problem, so under the EFTA you have to take the entire loss."

How should Tommy (or his lawyer) respond?

ANSWER:

Use the following facts to answer the next seven questions.

On June 10, Holly visited a local department store and purchased some new dinnerware, priced at $173.46. She paid for the purchase by swiping her debit card, issued by FirstBank. FirstBank transmitted to Holly her monthly bank statement on July 1. Holly received the statement on July 5. After reviewing her statement, Holly concluded that the dinnerware purchase was incorrectly reflected twice, not once.

137. To trigger the error resolution process under applicable federal law, Holly must timely notify FirstBank:

    (A) in writing.

    (B) orally or in writing.

    (C) orally, electronically, or in writing.

    (D) "by any reasonable means, including, without limitation, orally, electronically, or in writing."

138. Assume that Holly contacts FirstBank in writing. Holly's notice need not include:

    (A) her account number.

    (B) the amount of the alleged error.

    (C) the reason(s) for her belief that the statement contains an alleged error.

    (D) a copy of the department store receipt.

139. To be timely, FirstBank must receive Holly's letter within:

    (A) 30 days after July 1.

    (B) 60 days after July 1.

    (C) 45 days after July 1.

    (D) 45 days after July 5.

140. Assume that Holly mailed proper notice of the alleged error to FirstBank on August 10. FirstBank received Holly's letter on August 16.

    Unless FirstBank provisionally credits Holly's account for the amount of the alleged error, FirstBank must investigate and determine the merits of Holly's allegation within:

    (A) seven business days.

    (B) 10 business days.

    (C) 20 business days.

    (D) 30 business days.

141. FirstBank opts to credit Holly's account for the amount of the alleged error on August 19, three days after it receives Holly's letter. FirstBank must conclude its investigation not later than

    (A) 20 days after August 19.

    (B) 30 days after August 16.

    (C) 30 days after August 19.

    (D) 45 days after August 16.

142. Assume that FirstBank conducts a timely investigation and correctly determines that no error occurred. In fact, the allegedly duplicate charge reflected Holly's purchase of matching glassware.

    FirstBank must transmit its explanation to Holly:

(A) in writing and within three business days after concluding its investigation.

(B) in writing and "within a reasonable period of time, not to exceed five business days" after concluding its investigation.

(C) orally or in writing within seven days after concluding its investigation.

(D) orally or in writing within three business days after concluding its investigation.

143. Assume that FirstBank breaches one of the technical requirements of applicable federal law. Holly suffers no damages, but she is a litigious person and sues FirstBank under the EFTA. She is entitled to recover:

(A) nothing.

(B) costs of her action, plus a reasonable attorney's fee not to exceed $500.

(C) at least $100.

(D) at least $1,000.

144. A "funds transfer" under UCC Article 4A always involves:

   (A) at least one bank.

   (B) a payment of at least $1 million.

   (C) a physical exchange of money.

   (D) at least two payment orders.

Use the following facts to answer the next nine questions.

BigCo owes $1 million to MegaFirm. BigCo contacts its investment advisor, ABC Securities, and instructs ABC to sell some of BigCo's investments and remit $1 million to MegaFirm's account at Integrity Bank. ABC complies with BigCo's instructions by selling certain investments and then sending a message to its bank, Fidelity Bank, to credit MegaFirm's account at Integrity Bank for $1 million. Integrity Bank receives the message and timely credits MegaFirm's account for $1 million.

145. BigCo's instruction to ABC Securities:

   (A) will not be governed by UCC Article 4A.

   (B) is a "payment order" under UCC Article 4A if the instruction is in writing.

   (C) is a "payment order" under UCC Article 4A if the instruction is oral or written.

   (D) is a "payment order" under UCC Article 4A if the instruction is oral, written, or electronic.

146. ABC's message to Fidelity Bank will *not* be governed by UCC Article 4A if:

   (A) it is oral.

   (B) it is conditional on MegaFirm's delivery to Fidelity Bank of a notarized billing statement, documenting services rendered to BigCo for $1 million.

   (C) it informs Fidelity Bank to postpone sending the message to Integrity Bank for seven business days.

   (D) it is transmitted on a Sunday.

147. Assume that ABC transmits its message to Fidelity Bank in a manner that triggers application of UCC Article 4A. Fidelity Bank then transmits a message to Integrity Bank, directing Integrity Bank to credit the account of its customer, MegaFirm.

    Under UCC Article 4A,

    (A) Fidelity Bank is an originator.

    (B) Integrity Bank is a sender and a receiving bank.

    (C) Integrity Bank is a receiving bank and the beneficiary's bank.

    (D) Fidelity Bank is an intermediary bank and a sender.

148. This transaction will involve:

    (A) three payment orders and one funds transfer.

    (B) two payment orders and one funds transfer.

    (C) three payment orders and two funds transfers.

    (D) two payment orders and two funds transfers.

149. ABC incurs liability to pay $1 million under UCC Article 4A when:

    (A) ABC transmits its message to Fidelity Bank.

    (B) Fidelity Bank receives ABC's message.

    (C) Fidelity Bank transmits its message to Integrity Bank.

    (D) Integrity Bank credits MegaFirm's account for $1 million.

150. When does Fidelity Bank incur liability to pay $1 million under UCC Article 4A?

ANSWER:

151. BigCo's contractual liability of $1 million to MegaFirm is deemed paid under UCC Article 4A when:

    (A) ABC transmits its message to Fidelity Bank.

    (B) ABC pays $1 million.

    (C) Fidelity Bank executes ABC's instruction.

    (D) Integrity Bank accepts Fidelity Bank's instruction.

152. Assume that ABC's message to Fidelity Bank directed payment of $1 million. In response to ABC's message, Fidelity Bank transmitted a message to Integrity Bank, directing Integrity Bank to credit MegaFirm's account for $10 million (instead of $1 million).

As a result of Fidelity Bank's error,

(A) Fidelity Bank has not executed ABC's message.

(B) ABC must pay $10 million to Fidelity Bank and attempt to recover the $9 million overpayment from MegaFirm under the law governing mistake and restitution.

(C) ABC must pay only $1 million to Fidelity Bank, and Fidelity Bank must attempt to recover the $9 million overpayment from Integrity Bank under the law governing mistake and restitution.

(D) ABC must pay only $1 million to Fidelity Bank, and Fidelity Bank must attempt to recover the $9 million overpayment from MegaFirm under the law governing mistake and restitution.

153. Assume that ABC's message to Fidelity Bank accidentally directed payment of $1.5 million, rather than $1 million. ABC discovers its mistake about five hours after transmitting the message to Fidelity Bank.

Discuss ABC's ability to cancel or amend its message.

ANSWER:

154. A "payment order" under UCC Article 4A means "an instruction of a sender to a receiving bank . . . if . . . *the receiving bank is to be reimbursed by debiting an account of, or otherwise receiving payment from, the sender . . .*" What is meant by the italicized language?

ANSWER:

Use the following facts to answer the next five questions.

First Bank has agreed that it will honor a payment order placed by its customer, BizCorp, if the payment order passes certain "security procedures" as that term is defined by UCC Article 4A.

155. A security procedure:

(A) may be as simple as First Bank's comparison of a signature on BizCorp's payment order with an authorized specimen signature previously provided by BizCorp.

(B) can be unilaterally dictated by First Bank.

(C) need not be commercially reasonable.

(D) must involve at least one of the following: a callback procedure, the use of an algorithm, or encryption.

156. On March 1, First Bank accepted a $2 million payment order allegedly submitted by its customer, BizCorp. The parties had agreed to specific security procedures. First Bank accepted the order and debited BizCorp's account for $2 million. Evidence later revealed that a criminal wrongdoer submitted the payment order. BizCorp insists that First Bank promptly credit its account for the unauthorized transaction.

In determining loss allocation,

   (A) First Bank must prove that it accepted the payment order in good faith, and BizCorp must prove that First Bank failed to comply with the security procedures.

   (B) the court will treat the commercial reasonableness of the security procedures as a question of law, but it will address First Bank's compliance (or noncompliance) with the security procedures as a question of fact.

   (C) the commercial reasonableness of the security procedures is not relevant because the amount in question is less than $5 million.

   (D) First Bank need not prove that it accepted the payment order in good faith if the security procedures are commercially reasonable.

157. Assume that evidence favors First Bank on matters of good faith, compliance, and commercial reasonableness.

As a result,

   (A) the parties will share the loss in an equitable fashion.

   (B) First Bank will take the entire loss.

   (C) BizCorp will take the entire loss.

   (D) the court may conclude that the payment order is effective against BizCorp, whether or not authorized by BizCorp.

158. Again, assume that evidence favors First Bank on matters of good faith, compliance, and commercial reasonableness.

Evidence also reveals that the wrongdoer initiated the payment order by hacking into First Bank's computer system.

The unauthorized wire transfer is reflected on BizCorp's bank statement, which it receives from First Bank on March 25.

BizCorp forfeits its ability to recover any amount from First Bank if BizCorp fails to notify First Bank of the unauthorized transfer:

   (A) within 90 days from the date of the unauthorized transfer.

   (B) within one year from the date on which BizCorp received notice of the unauthorized transfer.

   (C) within 180 days from March 25.

(D) within a "reasonable period of time," not to exceed one year from the date of the unauthorized transfer.

159. Given the dollars at stake, BizCorp also may seek interest on any recovery. UCC Article 4A permits BizCorp to recover interest if it timely notifies First Bank of the unauthorized transfer. BizCorp gives timely notice if it contacts First Bank within:

(A) a reasonable period of time, not to exceed 90 days from the date on which BizCorp received notice of the transaction.

(B) 60 days from the date of the transaction.

(C) 180 days from the date on which BizCorp received notice of the transaction.

(D) one year from the date of the transaction.

160. Megan operates a cake shop as a sole proprietorship. At the suggestion of her insurance agent, she recently purchased a policy covering her shop. She agreed to pay the annual premium of $3,000 by authorizing her agent to make an electronic withdrawal of $250 every month from her business account at Midtown Bank.

Which body of law governs these electronic fund transfers: the federal Electronic Fund Transfer Act, or the state UCC Article 4A?

ANSWER:

Use the following facts to answer the next two questions.

Last year, Mockingbird Bank issued a credit card to Daphne (and, in the process, complied with all statutory duties and disclosures). Daphne contractually agreed to all terms of the credit card agreement. One of the provisions stated: *"Cardholder shall be liable for all charges made by Cardholder or anyone else to the Credit Card, whether authorized or unauthorized."*

A week ago, an unknown person broke into Daphne's car, stole her purse, and used her Mockingbird Bank credit card to go on a shopping spree. By the time Daphne had discovered and timely reported the theft, the thief had charged $13,567.83 to the card.

161. Daphne's maximum liability for the unauthorized charges is:

    (A) $50.

    (B) $500.

    (C) $1,000

    (D) $13,567.83.

162. Would your answer change if the applicable state law stated: *"A cardholder's liability for unauthorized use of that cardholder's credit card shall not exceed $25."*

ANSWER:

163. Several years ago, Francine's Fashions issued a credit card to Linda Johnson (and, in the process, complied with all statutory duties and disclosures).

    Linda has a teenage daughter, also named Linda, who goes by the nickname of "Penny."

    Last week, over Linda's express objections, Penny took her mother's credit card and bought clothing at Francine's Fashions valued at $873.64.

    When Linda received her bill, she was shocked to see these charges. She told Francine's Fashions that she would not be paying the charges, which Linda asserted were "unauthorized." An official from Francine's Fashions reviewed its internal documentation, confirmed that its clerk had asked for (and received) a driver's license identification that matched the name on the credit card, and viewed the charges as "authorized."

    Which statement is true?

    (A) Linda has no liability because Penny did not have permission to use her mother's card.

(B)   The charges were unauthorized, but Linda is liable for $50.

(C)   Under federal law, household dependents are deemed to have apparent authority to use a parent's credit card.

(D)   A court is likely to impose liability on both Linda and Francine's Fashions in an equitable fashion, given that Linda forbade Penny from using the card, and Francine's Fashions asked for and received identification that matched the name on the credit card.

164.   Jill, a Denver resident, received a brochure in the mail in November from Rocky Mountain Sports Club, advertising a calendar-year gym membership at a nearby facility for $500. Jill called the number on the brochure and charged the $500 membership to her credit card. When Jill asked what would happen if she changed her mind before January 1, the representative called Jill's attention to the "money back guarantee" stated in the brochure if Jill contacted the Club no later than December 15.

The $500 charge first appeared on the credit card statement that Jill received in late November. Jill paid $100 of the charge in early December.

A few days later, Jill started reading some news articles that suggested the Club was having financial problems. She then decided to cancel her calendar-year membership. But by the time she placed her first cancellation call on December 11, the Club had already ceased its operations and closed its doors. The Club's recorded telephone message offered no guidance on how to proceed, and Jill was unable to reach an actual representative or employee of the Club.

When Jill received her credit card statement in late December, she informed her card issuer, in writing, that she was asserting her rights under TILA § 170, 15 U.S.C. § 1666i, and was refusing to pay the $400 balance of the charge for the gym membership because the Club had promised a "money back guarantee." Jill also demanded a $100 credit, reflecting the portion of her previous monthly payment that had been applied against the original $500 charge.

Which of the following statements is true?

(A)   Jill cannot assert any rights under TILA § 170, 15 U.S.C. § 1666i, because that statute exempts from its coverage "any disagreement arising out of a credit card transaction involving a services contract lasting more than six months."

(B)   Jill cannot assert any rights under TILA § 170, 15 U.S.C. § 1666i, because she partially paid the original $500 charge before contacting her card issuer.

(C)   Jill can assert her rights under TILA § 170, 15 U.S.C. § 1666i, and avoid paying the $400 balance, but she will not receive a $100 credit for the payment already applied against the original $500 charge.

(D)   Jill can assert her rights under TILA § 170, 15 U.S.C. § 1666i, which permits her to avoid paying the $400 balance and to receive a credit for the $100 payment already applied against the original $500 charge.

Use the following facts to answer the next eight questions.

In February, Lauren bought a light fixture and charged the purchase price of $183.67 to her credit card issued by MegaBank.

This charge first appeared on a statement mailed by MegaBank on February 20, which Lauren received on February 25. After reviewing her statement, Lauren concluded that she had been double-billed for the purchase price of the light fixture (the $183.67 purchase price appeared twice, as if she had bought two of the fixtures).

165. To comply with the dispute resolution process under applicable federal law, Lauren must timely notify MegaBank:

   (A) in writing.

   (B) orally or in writing.

   (C) electronically or in writing.

   (D) orally, electronically, or in writing.

166. To be timely, Lauren's notice must be:

   (A) sent within 30 days of February 20.

   (B) sent within 60 days of February 25.

   (C) received by MegaBank within 60 days of February 20.

   (D) received by MegaBank within 60 days of February 25.

167. Assume that Lauren notifies MegaBank by letter. She mails her letter on March 17. MegaBank receives her letter on March 22.

   Unless it has already resolved Lauren's alleged billing error, MegaBank must acknowledge, in writing, Lauren's letter. To be timely under applicable federal law,

   (A) MegaBank must send its acknowledgment within 20 days after March 17.

   (B) MegaBank must send its acknowledgment within 30 days after March 22.

   (C) Lauren must receive the acknowledgment within 20 days after March 17.

   (D) Lauren must receive the acknowledgment within 30 days after March 22.

168. MegaBank must resolve Lauren's alleged billing error within:

   (A) 45 calendar days from the date on which MegaBank received Lauren's letter.

   (B) a "reasonable period of time," not to exceed 60 calendar days from the date on which MegaBank received Lauren's letter.

(C) two complete billing cycles (in no event later than 90 days) from the date on which MegaBank received Lauren's letter.

(D) a "reasonable period of time," not to exceed one complete billing cycle after MegaBank received Lauren's letter.

169. During the dispute resolution process, MegaBank:

(A) may not reflect the disputed amount on billing statements mailed during the dispute resolution process.

(B) may reflect the disputed amount (but not any related finance charges) on billing statements mailed during the dispute resolution process.

(C) may reflect the disputed amount, together with any related finance charges, on billing statements mailed during the dispute resolution process.

(D) may reflect the disputed amount, together with any related finance charges, on billing statements mailed during the dispute resolution process, accompanied by a statement informing Lauren that such amounts are not due and payable until MegaBank has concluded its investigation of the alleged billing error.

170. During the dispute resolution process, MegaBank:

(A) may not apply the disputed charge against Lauren's credit limit.

(B) may apply the first $50 of the disputed charge against Lauren's credit limit.

(C) may apply the first $100 of the disputed charge against Lauren's credit limit.

(D) may apply the entire disputed charge against Lauren's credit limit.

171. Briefly state the rules that govern MegaBank's ability to report (or threaten to report) Lauren to a third-party credit bureau.

ANSWER:

172. Assume MegaBank breaches one or more of its duties while investigating Lauren's alleged billing error, prompting Lauren to file a lawsuit against MegaBank. Citing TILA § 161(e), 15 U.S.C. § 1666(e), MegaBank prepares a $50 check and offers it to Lauren's attorney as final payment of the matter.

Is that the best Lauren can hope for?

ANSWER:

Use the following facts to answer the next three questions.

Emma lives in Kansas City, Missouri. While visiting a friend in St. Louis (more than 100 miles from Emma's billing address), Emma bought a $45 purse and a $375 dress from different merchants, charging both purchases on her credit card issued by Midtown Bank. After returning home to Kansas City, she discovered both items were materially defective. Emma has written several letters and made numerous telephone calls to both merchants but has been unable to obtain any relief. She also has given timely written notice to Midtown Bank of her intent not to pay for these two charges.

173. Emma can assert against Midtown Bank her merchant disputes as a defense against paying the charges for:

    (A) neither the purse nor the dress.

    (B) the purse, but not the dress.

    (C) the dress, but not the purse.

    (D) both the purse and the dress.

174. Would your analysis change if Emma had bought the purse and the dress from different merchants located in Kansas City, Kansas?

ANSWER:

175. Assume under the original facts that Emma, while shopping in St. Louis, bought the purse at Tilly's (and charged the price to her Tilly's credit card) and bought the dress at Francine's Fashions (and charged the price to her Francine's Fashions credit card). Would these revised facts affect your analysis?

ANSWER:

176. A letter of credit:

    (A)   must be issued by a financial institution that has received its charter from the Office of the Comptroller of the Currency.

    (B)   must be issued by a financial institution that has received its charter from the Office of the Comptroller of the Currency or a similar state regulatory agency.

    (C)   may be issued by any entity, but not an individual.

    (D)   may be issued by an individual who is not doing so for personal, family, or household purposes.

177. A letter of credit must be:

    (A)   signed by the issuer, and acknowledged by the beneficiary.

    (B)   signed by the issuer, and acknowledged by the applicant and the beneficiary.

    (C)   authenticated by the issuer.

    (D)   in writing.

178. Which of the following statements, concerning consideration for the issuance of a letter of credit, is correct?

    (A)   Consideration is irrelevant, and lack thereof is no defense to enforceability of the letter of credit.

    (B)   Consideration is irrelevant, and lack thereof is no defense to enforceability of the letter of credit, if the beneficiary is a U.S. citizen or an organization created under state or federal law.

    (C)   The issuer can assert the defense of lack of consideration, but only if the issuer's potential liability under the letter of credit exceeds $1 million.

    (D)   A beneficiary is not entitled to request payment under the letter of credit unless it timely proves that the issuer received consideration, from the applicant, for issuing the letter of credit.

179. A letter of credit that is silent on whether it is revocable or irrevocable is:

    (A)　unenforceable.

    (B)　enforceable, and revocable.

    (C)　enforceable, and irrevocable.

    (D)　enforceable, and revocable, unless the beneficiary timely exercises its statutory option to declare the letter of credit to be irrevocable.

180. A letter of credit that fails to state an expiration date is:

    (A)　unenforceable.

    (B)　unenforceable, but only if the issuer timely exercises its statutory option to declare the letter of credit unenforceable.

    (C)　enforceable, with a statutory duration of 90 days.

    (D)　enforceable, with a statutory duration of one year.

181. Briefly explain the difference between a documentary (or commercial) letter of credit, and a standby letter of credit.

ANSWER:

182. Briefly explain the primary difference between a confirmer and an adviser.

ANSWER:

183. Briefly explain the independence principle.

ANSWER:

184. Briefly explain the strict compliance doctrine.

ANSWER:

Use the following facts to answer the next three questions.

Sunshine Flowers agreed to buy 4,000 tulip bulbs from Holland Nurseries, a European company. At the insistence of Holland Nurseries, Sunshine Flowers requested its financing institution, Morgantown Bank, to issue a letter of credit in favor of Holland Nurseries. Morgantown Bank complied with the request and issued a letter of credit that included terms acceptable to all parties.

185. Which of the following statements is true?

    (A)　Sunshine Flowers is a beneficiary, and Holland Nurseries is an accommodated party.

(B) Sunshine Flowers is an account party, and Holland Nurseries is a beneficiary.

(C) Sunshine Flowers is an applicant, and Holland Nurseries is a beneficiary.

(D) Sunshine Flowers is an account party, and Holland Nurseries is a nominated person.

186. If Holland Nurseries timely tenders all required documents to Morgantown Bank, then Morgantown Bank must review the documents and elect to honor or dishonor the presentment by Holland Nurseries within a reasonable time, not to exceed:

(A) three business days.

(B) five calendar days.

(C) seven business days.

(D) ten calendar days.

187. Holland Nurseries makes a timely presentment that strictly complies with the terms of the letter of credit. Nevertheless, Morgantown Bank wrongfully dishonors its obligation to pay the requested amount, $25,000. Holland Nurseries could mitigate its damages by selling the bulbs to another party for $10,000, but Holland Nurseries decides not to do so, allowing the bulbs to rot.

In an action by Holland Nurseries against Morgantown Bank for wrongful dishonor, Holland Nurseries is entitled to recover:

(A) $25,000, plus interest from the date of dishonor, plus its reasonable attorney's fees and litigation expenses.

(B) $25,000, plus interest from the date of dishonor, plus consequential damages not to exceed the face amount of the letter of credit.

(C) $15,000, plus interest from the date of dishonor, plus its reasonable attorney's fees and litigation expenses.

(D) $15,000, plus interest from the date of dishonor, plus consequential damages.

Use the following facts to answer the next four questions.

On June 10, 2012, Giacona Chocolates Corp. contracted to buy five tons of sugar from Bradford Sugar Company for $5 million. Giacona Chocolates agreed to arrange for payment through a letter of credit issued by Warren Falls Bank.

All three parties realize that the letter of credit may shift the risk of nonpayment or nonperformance by one of the parties, but the letter of credit will not completely eliminate potential lawsuits between and among the parties.

188. Which of the following lawsuits is least likely to arise under UCC Article 5?

(A) Bradford Sugar v. Warren Falls Bank, for wrongful dishonor.

(B) Warren Falls Bank v. Giacona Chocolates, for reimbursement following the Bank's proper honor of Bradford Sugar's presentation.

(C) Warren Falls Bank v. Bradford Sugar, for restitution after the Bank mistakenly honors Bradford Sugar's presentation.

(D) Warren Falls Bank v. Bradford Sugar, for breach of warranty.

189. On July 1, 2013, Warren Falls Bank issued the following letter of credit, which was reviewed and approved by all parties:

LETTER OF CREDIT
July 1, 2013

TO: Bradford Sugar Company

RE: Giacona Chocolates Corp.

Warren Falls Bank hereby establishes its irrevocable Letter of Credit No. 070113 for five million and no/100 U.S. dollars (U.S. $5,000,000.00) on your behalf. Your draft must be marked "DRAWN UNDER WFB LETTER OF CREDIT NO. 070113" and must be accompanied by a bill of lading dated no later than October 15, 2013, referencing your shipment of five tons of white refined granulated sugar to Giacona Chocolates Corp. This Letter of Credit expires October 31, 2013.

This letter of credit incorporates by reference, and is subject to, the terms and provisions of the Uniform Customs and Practice for Documentary Credits (2007 Revision), fixed by the International Chamber of Commerce (I.C.C. Pub. No. 600).

WARREN FALLS BANK
by: Baxter Honeycutt III, Vice President

On October 25, 2013, Bradford Sugar submitted to the Bank a draft for $5 million and additional paperwork that strictly complied with the terms of the letter of credit. However, while the bill of lading reflected a shipping date of October 15, the actual shipping date was October 17 (the shipper had backdated the bill of lading at the request of Bradford Sugar). The intentional misstatement of the shipping date on the bill of lading did not affect compliance with the underlying sales contract and would not be deemed material to either Bradford Sugar or Giacona Chocolates.

Before paying the $5 million to Bradford Sugar, the Bank discovered the misstatement of the shipping date on the bill of lading.

The Bank should:

(A) dishonor Bradford Sugar's presentation because Bradford Sugar has knowingly submitted a bill of lading with an incorrect shipping date.

(B) dishonor Bradford Sugar's presentation because it does not strictly comply with the terms of the letter of credit.

(C) honor Bradford Sugar's presentation because the misstatement is immaterial to Giacona Chocolates and Bradford Sugar.

(D) honor Bradford Sugar's presentation because the misstatement falls within the "harmless error" exception to the strict compliance doctrine.

190. Assume that Bradford Sugar's draft is marked "DRAWN UNDER WARREN FALLS BANK LETTER OF CREDIT NUMBER 070113" and accompanied by a bill of lading correctly dated October 15, 2013, evidencing its shipment of "five metric tons of white granulated sugar" to Giacona Chocolates.

Which of the following statements is true?

(A) Giacona Chocolates is not obligated to reimburse the Bank if the Bank honors the draft.

(B) The Bank will be liable for wrongful dishonor if it refuses to pay the draft.

(C) Prior to honoring Bradford Sugar's presentation, the Bank should seek confirmation from Giacona Chocolates that Bradford Sugar has not violated any material terms of the underlying contract.

(D) The letter of credit is a standby letter of credit.

191. Briefly describe what is intended by the last paragraph of the letter of credit.

ANSWER:

Use the following facts to answer the next two questions.

At the request of its customer, Dumbarton Industries, OmniBank issued a $500,000 letter of credit for the benefit of Justin Resources. The standby letter of credit required Justin Resources to tender a draft for the requested amount, accompanied by this written statement, signed by its chief executive officer or general counsel: *Dumbarton Industries has committed a "default" under the terms of the Sales Agreement dated July 20, 2013, executed by and between Dumbarton Industries and Justin Resources; as a result, the amount of the draft is due and owing by Dumbarton Industries to Justin Resources.*

Six calendar days before the letter of credit was scheduled to expire, Justin Resources tendered a draft for the correct amount, together with a certificate of default, signed by its chief financial officer, stating: *Dumbarton Industries has defaulted under the Sales Agreement executed by and between itself and Justin Resources. Therefore, the amount of the requested draft is now due and payable by Dumbarton Industries to Justin Resources.*

Within two calendar days, OmniBank informed Justin Resources that it was dishonoring the presentation because the language of the certificate of default did not track the language required by the letter of credit. OmniBank did not mention a second problem: the wrong corporate officer signed the certificate of default.

192. Which of the following statements is true?

(A) Under the "one shot" rule of letter of credit law, Justin Resources has no ability to attempt to cure the defects of its initial presentation and timely make a second presentation.

(B) Justin Resources has no ability to cure the defects of its initial presentation and timely make a second presentation because its initial presentation occurred within ten business days of the expiration date of the letter of credit.

(C) OmniBank must honor a second presentation timely made by Justin Resources if the revised certificate of default tracks the language required by the letter of credit, even if the revised certificate of default is executed again by Justin Resources' chief financial officer.

(D) OmniBank should dishonor a second presentation timely made by Justin Resources that is executed by Justin Resources' chief financial officer, even if the revised certificate tracks the language required by the letter of credit.

193. Assume that the Sales Agreement required Dumbarton Industries to make ten $50,000 payments to Justin Resources (one payment per month, for ten months). The Sales Agreement defined "default" to include, among other events, failure to make any scheduled payment on time. The Sales Agreement permitted Justin Resources, on default, to accelerate future payments. The acceleration clause was optional, triggered only if Justin Resources declared, in writing, that it was electing to accelerate future payments.

When Dumbarton Industries missed its payment due in the fourth month, Justin Resources tendered a draft for $350,000, accompanied by a written statement that conformed to the terms of the letter of credit and signed by the appropriate corporate officer. Justin Resources had yet to trigger the acceleration clause. OmniBank honored the presentment and paid $350,000 to Justin Resources.

Shortly thereafter, OmniBank decided to sue Justin Resources for breach of warranty, alleging that Justin Resources was not entitled to $350,000 because it had not yet triggered the acceleration clause in a manner required by the Sales Agreement. (OmniBank will not assert material fraud, however.)

Which of the following statements is true?

(A) Once OmniBank honored the presentment, it lost its ability to bring a warranty action against Justin Resources.

(B) Because OmniBank's cause of action is predicated on the terms of the underlying Sales Agreement, OmniBank cannot sue Justin Resources without violating the independence principle.

(C) OmniBank can bring a warranty action against Justin Resources and recover damages as provided by UCC Article 5.

(D) OmniBank should seek reimbursement from Dumbarton Industries, who should sue Justin Resources for breach of warranty.

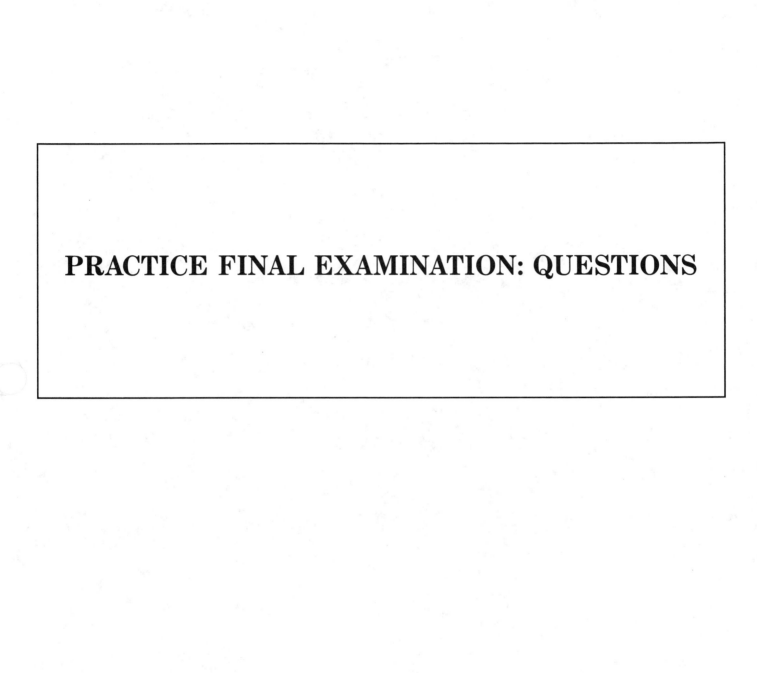

PRACTICE FINAL EXAMINATION: QUESTIONS

PRACTICE FINAL EXAMINATION

Instructions: This exam consists of 28 multiple choice questions and 11 short-answer questions. Try to answer all 39 questions in no more than three hours.

194. A provision in a promissory note that refers the reader to another transaction-related agreement may render the promise conditional and effectively remove the note from the scope of UCC Article 3. Which of the following provisions is most likely to do that?

    (A) "Notwithstanding the foregoing, Maker enjoys prepayment rights as stated in the Credit Agreement."

    (B) "Unpaid principal shall accrue interest at an annual rate equal to the 'Prime Rate' as defined in the Loan Agreement."

    (C) "Rights and obligations of Maker and Holder with respect to the Note are stated in the Trust Indenture."

    (D) "Maker's payment and performance obligations are secured by the 'Collateral' as defined in the Security Agreement."

195. To be a negotiable instrument, a promissory note must be payable to bearer or to order. Which of the following phrases will make a promissory note payable to order?

    (A) ". . . pay to Fran Martin . . ."

    (B) ". . . pay to the order of Gwen Turner or bearer . . ."

    (C) ". . . pay to Jesse Buckman or order . . ."

    (D) ". . . pay to the order of _____ . . ."

196. A negotiable promissory note must be payable on demand or at a definite time. Which of the following provisions makes a note payable at a definite time?

    (A) ". . . payable upon presentment."

    (B) ". . . payable in installments, due on the first Monday of each calendar month, beginning with July 2013 and ending with June 2020."

    (C) ". . . payable at the complete discretion of the holder hereof."

    (D) ". . . payable on the enshrinement date of Albert Pujols into baseball's Hall of Fame in Cooperstown, New York."

197. On July 1 of this year, Amos borrowed $2,500 from his brother, Dan. At the time of the loan, Amos executed a promissory note in favor of Dan, promising repayment, with interest, on June 30 in five years. The note is undated, and it fails to state a place of payment.

Which of the following statements is true?

   (A) The omission of the date is irrelevant, and UCC Article 3 provides for a place of payment if one is not otherwise stated.

   (B) The omission of the date is irrelevant, but the failure to state a place of payment effectively removes the note from the scope of UCC Article 3.

   (C) The omission of the date has legal significance if Amos's signature was not notarized.

   (D) The failure to state a place of payment means that Amos may tender payment on the maturity date anywhere within the United States.

198. Derek wrote a check for the purpose of making a $450.00 payment on his car. The checks in his checkbook contained spaces for indicating the amount of the check in both words and numbers. Derek correctly wrote the words "four hundred fifty dollars and no cents." But when he attempted to write the amount of the check in numbers, he mistakenly wrote "$540.00."

Which of the following statements is true?

   (A) The amount of the check is $450.00.

   (B) The amount of the check is $540.00.

   (C) The amount of the check will be determined by parol evidence.

   (D) The check is voidable because it contains contradictory terms.

199. Jessica Alexander bought a used grand piano from her neighbor, Helen Floyd, on credit. To evidence the purchase price of $20,000, Jessica executed and delivered to Helen the following promissory note:

Promissory Note

   The undersigned promises to pay $20,000 to _____.

   Jessica Alexander

Later, Helen filed a bankruptcy petition. One of her creditors, BigBank, is claiming a perfected security interest in the $20,000 note (still held by Helen). The bankruptcy trustee is challenging that claim. A review of BigBank's security agreement and financing statement reveals that BigBank has a perfected security interest in the note only if it is a "negotiable instrument" under UCC Article 3. The trustee argues that the note is not a "negotiable instrument" governed by Article 3 because the note is not dated and does not state a payee, an interest rate, a payment date, or a place of payment.

Is the trustee right?

ANSWER:

200. Give an example of a thief who qualifies as a person entitled to enforce an instrument.

ANSWER:

201. Give an example of an owner of an instrument who is not a person entitled to enforce the instrument.

ANSWER:

202. In January 2014, Molly bought a used car from her neighbor, Earl, for $6,500. Molly paid $1,500 in cash and signed a negotiable promissory note for the $5,000 balance. When Molly executed and delivered the note to Earl, she failed to complete the blank in the following sentence: "The indebtedness evidenced by this promissory note shall be due and payable on December 31, ___." Molly and Earl had agreed that the note would be due and payable on December 31, 2016. Contrary to that agreement, however, Earl filled in the blank by writing "2015."

In June 2015, Earl sold and negotiated the note to Baxter, a holder in due course.

In November 2015, Baxter sold the note to Jennifer, a holder in due course. Baxter negotiated the note by writing his blank indorsement, accompanied by the phrase "without recourse," on the back of the note.

In early January 2016, Jennifer contacted Molly and demanded payment. Molly refused to pay, relying on her agreement with Earl that payment was not due until December 31, 2016.

Jennifer is aware that, as a holder in due course, she can enforce the note against Molly according to its completed terms. But can she also enforce the note against, or recover any damages from, Baxter, her transferor, who was a holder in due course?

ANSWER:

203. MS Enterprises agreed to pay $2,300 to a contractor for installing a new water heater at its place of business on March 1, 2014. The contractor, William Hammond, agreed to accept a promissory note as payment. So MS Enterprises executed the following note:

PROMISSORY NOTE

In consideration for installation of a new water heater at the undersigned's place of business, the undersigned promises to pay $2,300 to _____ on July 1, 2014.

MS ENTERPRISES

By: *Margie Smith*
Title: President

Hammond negotiated the note to Ronald Garcia on May 10, 2014, for $1,800. At Ronald's insistence, Hammond inserted Ronald's name ("Ronald Garcia") on the blank line in the note.

On the due date, Ronald presented the note to MS Enterprises for payment. MS Enterprises refused to pay because Hammond had improperly installed the water heater, resulting in damages to its place of business. Ronald is sympathetic but contends that he is a holder in due course because he bought the note for value, in good faith, and without notice of the improper installation. MS Enterprises responds by suggesting that when Ronald bought the note after Hammond inserted "Ronald Garcia" on the blank line, the note was not payable to bearer or order. Therefore, the promissory note is not a "negotiable instrument," so UCC Article 3 does not apply and Ronald cannot be a holder in due course.

Is MS Enterprises right?

ANSWER:

204.   Lisa bought a car from Dealer on credit, signing a promissory note that contained the following statutory provision as mandated by applicable law:

> *ANY HOLDER OF THIS PROMISSORY NOTE IS SUBJECT TO ALL CLAIMS AND DEFENSES WHICH THE MAKER MAY ASSERT AGAINST DEALER ARISING FROM THE TRANSACTION OUT OF WHICH THIS PROMISSORY NOTE AROSE.*

Two days after Lisa bought the car, Dealer negotiated her note to Finance Company for a fair price.

The quoted provision:

(A)   does not prevent the note from being a negotiable instrument under UCC Article 3 and Finance Company from being a holder in due course.

(B)   does not prevent the note from being a negotiable instrument under UCC Article 3; it does, however, prevent Finance Company from being a holder in due course if Finance Company had notice of the provision when it acquired the note.

(C)   does not prevent the note from being a negotiable instrument under UCC Article 3; it does, however, prevent Finance Company from being a holder in due course whether or not Finance Company had notice of the provision when it acquired the note.

(D)   prevents the note from being a negotiable instrument because Lisa's promise to pay is conditional on the absence of any claims and defenses that she can assert against Dealer.

205. Adam issued a negotiable promissory note to Elliott on February 13. The note called for quarterly interest payments and a single principal payment of $3,000 on the maturity date in five years. At Elliott's insistence, Marvin placed his anomalous indorsement on the back of the note.

On October 3, Elliott negotiated the note to Wanda as payment for a previous debt that Elliott owed to Wanda.

Wanda:

(A) cannot be a holder in due course because taking the note as payment for a previous debt is not "value."

(B) can be a holder in due course even if, at the time she took the note, she had notice that Elliott had discharged Marvin from his indorser liability.

(C) cannot be a holder in due course if, at the time she took the note, she had notice that Adam had failed to pay the last interest payment.

(D) cannot be a holder in due course if, two weeks after she took the note, she learns that Adam has a legitimate defense to payment of the note.

206. Two years ago, Matt (the original payee and holder) negotiated a promissory note to Sarah, via Matt's special indorsement. Yesterday the maker dishonored the note, which is silent on the matter of notice of dishonor.

Matt will not be liable on his indorsement unless he receives notice of the dishonor within:

(A) 10 days from yesterday.

(B) 14 days from yesterday.

(C) 30 days from yesterday.

(D) 60 days from yesterday.

207. Wallace Corporation borrows $400,000 from Bank. Wallace executes a negotiable promissory note to evidence the loan. Bank insists that two corporate officers also be personally liable on the debt. So Alex signs his name on the back of the note, and Charlene executes a separate unconditional guaranty. Loan proceeds are used solely for corporate purposes, which enhance the value of Wallace's capital stock. Alex and Charlene each own approximately 10% of the authorized, issued, and outstanding shares of Wallace's capital stock.

Discuss whether Alex and Charlene are accommodation parties.

ANSWER:

208. Harry Hinton is authorized by Danny Davis to execute agreements, documents, and

instruments on behalf of Danny that do not create liability in excess of $10,000.

With Danny's permission and authority, Harry borrows $5,000 for Danny's benefit from Sally Sloan. Harry executes the following one-sentence note:

> The undersigned promises to pay $5,000 to the order of Sally Sloan on December 1, 2016.

> [Signature]

Which of the following statements is true?

(A) Harry will not be personally liable if he signs the note "Danny Davis."

(B) Danny will not be personally liable if his name does not appear anywhere in the note.

(C) Both Harry and Danny will be personally liable if Harry signs the note "Harry Hinton, as agent for Danny Davis."

(D) Harry will be personally liable if he signs the note "Harry Hinton, Agent."

209. Grant performed some yard work for Meredith last week. Meredith paid the bill with her $350 personal check (which she completed by exercising ordinary care). Grant then raised the amount to $3,350 by using chemicals that eliminated any trace of his mischief. Grant deposited the $3,350 check into his account at Everett Bank, which presented the check for payment to the drawee, Pasco Savings, which timely paid the check in good faith by debiting Meredith's account for $3,350.

In allocating the $3,350 loss among the various parties other than Grant (who cannot be located, and who has closed his account at Everett Bank), the most likely scenario is that:

(A) Pasco Savings will incur a $3,350 loss.

(B) Everett Bank will incur a $3,350 loss.

(C) Pasco Savings may debit Alice's account for $350 and will absorb a $3,000 loss.

(D) Pasco Savings may debit Alice's account for $350 and may recover $3,000 from Everett Bank.

Use the following facts to answer the next two questions.

Kate stole several blank checks from her employer, Arco Products. Kate forged the signature of Arco's chief financial officer on the checks, which Kate made payable to the order of Arco's legitimate suppliers. Kate then forged the indorsement of the suppliers and, with the assistance of a co-conspirator who was a teller at Allied Bank, deposited the checks into her account at Allied Bank. Allied Bank presented the checks to Tuttle Savings, which timely honored the checks.

Arco Products has discovered Kate's mischief (and Kate has conveniently disappeared after emptying her account at Allied Bank), which resulted in a loss to Arco of more than $83,000.

210. In an attempt to recover its loss, Arco Products should bring a lawsuit against Allied Bank:

(A) under the "imposter rule."

    (B) for breach of its duty of ordinary care.

    (C) under the "properly payable rule."

    (D) for breach of transfer warranty.

211. In an attempt to recover its loss, Arco Products should bring a lawsuit against Tuttle Savings:

    (A) under the "properly payable rule."

    (B) for breach of transfer warranty.

    (C) for breach of presentment warranty.

    (D) for conversion.

Use the following facts to answer the next two questions.

Gwen placed her monthly $1,500 mortgage payment in her mailbox for delivery to Friendly Finance on May 28. Noticing that Gwen's mailbox flag was up, Milton Garvis opened the mailbox and took the envelope containing the check. Using chemicals, Milton then expertly changed the name of the payee from "Friendly Finance" to "Milton Garvis." The revision could not be detected by the average person. Milton then deposited the check into his account at Bayview Bank on May 29 after adding his blank indorsement to the check. Bayview Bank presented the check for payment to Wellford Savings, which timely paid the check on June 1. By June 12, Milton had closed his account at Bayview Bank, withdrawing all funds (including funds credited for the stolen check).

When Gwen's mortgage company inquired as to the status of her alleged nonpayment, Gwen began investigating the problem. By July 1, she and the other financial institutions involved had discovered Milton's theft. Gwen immediately insisted that Wellford Savings re-credit her account for $1,500. Wellford Savings complied with Gwen's request (after which Gwen issued a replacement check to her mortgage company).

212. Wellford Savings should attempt to recover the $1,500 from Bayview Bank:

    (A) on a mistake theory.

    (B) for breaching a presentment warranty.

    (C) for indorser liability.

    (D) for breaching the "properly payable rule."

213. Wellford Savings should attempt to recover the $1,500 from Milton:

    (A) on a mistake theory, for breaching a transfer warranty, and for breaching a presentment warranty.

    (B) on a mistake theory and for breaching a presentment warranty only.

    (C) for breaching a transfer warranty only.

     (D) on a mistake theory only.

Use the following facts to answer the next two questions.

Marty forged Len's signature, as maker, on a $5,000 promissory note payable to Marty's order. Marty then negotiated and discounted the note to Grant for $4,400 after indorsing it in blank and "without recourse." Later, Grant negotiated and discounted the note to Norm for $4,100.

Norm demanded payment of the note from Len on the due date. Len refused, informing Norm that his signature had been forged (a fact unknown to all parties except Marty).

214. Briefly discuss the merits of this statement: *In an action by Norm against Grant under Section 3-416 ("Transfer Warranties"), Grant is liable for breaching the warranty that the note was not subject to any defense that could be asserted against him.*

ANSWER:

215. Briefly discuss the merits of this statement: *In an action by Norm against Marty under Section 3-416 ("Transfer Warranties"), Marty is not liable for breaching the warranty that he was a person entitled to enforce the note.*

ANSWER:

Use the following facts to answer the next two questions.

Ellen, a Texas resident, mailed a $300 check to Fran, a New York resident. Fran deposited the check into her account maintained with Prosperity Bank. Prosperity Bank sent the check to the Buffalo branch of the Federal Reserve Bank ("FRB-Buffalo"), which sent the check to the Dallas branch of the Federal Reserve Bank ("FRB-Dallas"), which sent the check to Ellen's bank, Commerce Bank, for payment.

216. Using UCC terminology,

     (A) Ellen is the maker and Commerce Bank is the drawee.

     (B) Ellen is the drawee and Commerce Bank is the drawer.

     (C) Prosperity Bank is a depositary bank and an intermediary bank.

     (D) FRB-Buffalo is an intermediary bank and a collecting bank.

217. Assume that Prosperity Bank erroneously encoded the check for the amount of $3,000 (rather than $300). Ellen discovers the $2,700 discrepancy when she receives her monthly bank statement, and she promptly reports the error to Commerce Bank, which credits her account for $2,700.

    Commerce Bank can recover the $2,700, on a theory of encoding warranty breach, from:

     (A) Fran, Prosperity Bank, FRB-Buffalo, and FRB-Dallas.

     (B) only Prosperity Bank, FRB-Buffalo, and FRB-Dallas.

(C) only Prosperity Bank and FRB-Buffalo.

(D) only Prosperity Bank.

218. Arnie paid his monthly utility bill by mailing a $265 check to American Utility Company. Meredith, a mailroom clerk at American Utility Company, stole the check, forged the payee's blank indorsement, and deposited the check into her account at Graham Bank. Drawce Western Savings received the check for presentment on the morning of Monday, August 1. Western Savings dishonored the check because Arnie's account had a balance of only $47.39. Western Savings mailed the dishonored check, along with a notice of dishonor, to Graham Bank on Thursday, August 4. Graham Bank received the check and the notice on Saturday, August 6, one day after Meredith had closed her account and withdrawn the entire balance (including funds from the dishonored check).

Graham Bank contacted Western Savings on Wednesday, August 10, arguing that Western Savings was obligated to pay $265 to Graham Bank because Western Savings waited too long before mailing the check and its notice of dishonor to Graham Bank.

As between Graham Bank and Western Savings, which financial institution will take the loss if both financial institutions stipulate the inapplicability of UCC Sections 3-404, 3-405, and 3-406?

ANSWER:

219. What is the "midnight deadline"?

ANSWER:

220. In response to a telephone solicitation, Kerry mailed a $200 check to The Paradise Vacation Club on August 1. Within days, Kerry began feeling the symptoms of "buyer's remorse." On August 6, she telephoned her bank and orally placed a stop-payment order on the check, providing the bank employee with all relevant information about the check. The payee received the check on August 4. The check was presented for payment on August 9.

The stop-payment order:

(A) is not effective because it was placed on August 6, more than three days after the issue date of August 1.

(B) is not effective because it was placed on August 6, after the payee received the check on August 4.

(C) is not effective because it was oral, rather than written.

(D) should be effective.

221. In February, Avery received a check from her parents as a birthday gift. Avery misplaced the check and did not find it until November. She now intends to deposit the check into her account maintained with First Fidelity Bank.

Which statement is true?

(A) The check is no longer properly payable.

(B) The check is properly payable, but the payor bank may rightfully dishonor the check upon presentment.

(C) The check is not overdue, and First Fidelity Bank may qualify as a holder in due course.

(D) Whether or not the check is overdue is irrelevant because a depositary bank, such as First Fidelity Bank, cannot be a holder in due course.

222. Which of the following ATM transactions is *not* covered by the EFTA?

(A) a cash deposit in excess of $500

(B) a balance inquiry

(C) a deposit of a check for an amount greater than $5,000

(D) a cash withdrawal less than $250

223. Grace keeps her MegaBank debit card in her purse. Evidence reveals the following activity:

Monday 8:45 p.m.	Thief steals Grace's purse. Thief withdraws $250 from ATM using the stolen card.
Tuesday 9:00 a.m.	Grace discovers the theft of her purse and card.
Tuesday 9:35 a.m.	Thief withdraws $250 from ATM using the stolen card.
Wednesday 4:25 p.m.	Thief withdraws $250 from ATM using the stolen card.
Thursday 11:50 a.m.	Thief withdraws $250 from ATM using the stolen card.
Friday 9:15 a.m.	Thief withdraws $250 from ATM using the stolen card.
Friday 2:20 p.m.	Grace telephones MegaBank and discloses the theft of her purse and ATM card. MegaBank immediately cancels Grace's card.

Assuming that MegaBank can satisfy its burden of proof, Grace's maximum liability for the unauthorized withdrawals should be:

(A) $1,250.

(B) $800.

(C) $750.

(D) $300.

224. On June 10, Gordon visited a sporting goods store and purchased some new running shoes for $128.56. He paid for the purchase by swiping his debit card, issued by FirstBank.

FirstBank transmitted to Gordon his monthly bank statement on July 1. Gordon received the statement on July 5. Gordon noticed that the statement reflected a purchase price for the shoes at $228.56, not $128.56.

To trigger the error resolution process under applicable federal law, Gordon must notify FirstBank

(A) orally or in writing, and FirstBank must receive Gordon's notice within 30 days after July 1.

(B) in writing, and FirstBank must receive Gordon's notice within 45 days after July 1.

(C) orally or in writing, and FirstBank must receive Gordon's notice within 60 days after July 1.

(D) in writing, and FirstBank must receive Gordon's notice within 60 days after July 5.

Use the following facts to answer the next two questions.

ZinnCo Industries owes $2.5 million to MegaCorp. ZinnCo instructs its bank, Fidelity Bank, to credit MegaCorp's account at Integrity Bank for $2.5 million. Fidelity Bank timely sends the message to Integrity Bank. Integrity Bank receives the message and timely credits MegaCorp's account for $2.5 million.

225. In this funds transfer,

(A) there are three payment orders.

(B) Integrity Bank is a receiving bank and the beneficiary's bank.

(C) Fidelity Bank is the originator.

(D) Integrity Bank is an intermediary bank.

226. ZinnCo incurs liability to pay $2.5 million under UCC Article 4A when:

(A) ZinnCo transmits its message to Fidelity Bank.

(B) Fidelity Bank receives ZinnCo's message.

(C) Fidelity Bank accepts ZinnCo's message.

(D) Integrity Bank credits MegaCorp's account for $2.5 million.

227. Three years ago, Diamond Bank issued a credit card to Adam (and, in the process, complied with all statutory duties and disclosures).

Last week, Robert stole Adam's credit card issued by Diamond Bank and used it to purchase goods priced at $8,375.88 at Barrington Jewelers.

If Robert cannot be found, then liability, under federal law, for the unauthorized charges falls on:

(A)   Diamond Bank for the full amount.

(B)   Adam for $50, Barrington Jewelers for $5,000, and Diamond Bank for $3,325.88.

(C)   Adam for $50, and Diamond Bank for $8,325.88.

(D)   Adam for $50, and Barrington Jewelers for $8,325.88.

228.   In July 2013, Grace bought a dress and charged the purchase price of $250 to her credit card issued by MegaBank. The original purchase price was $300, but Grace used a valid promotional coupon that entitled her to a $50 discount.

The charge for the dress first appeared on a statement mailed by MegaBank on July 28 and which Grace received on August 2. After reviewing her statement, Grace concluded that she had been improperly billed for $300, rather than $250 (as if the merchant had failed to apply the promotional coupon at the register).

To trigger the dispute resolution process under federal law, Grace must contact Mega-Bank:

(A)   orally or in writing, and MegaBank must receive the notice within 30 days of July 28.

(B)   in writing, and MegaBank must receive the notice within 30 days of August 2.

(C)   in writing, and MegaBank must receive the notice within 60 days of July 28.

(D)   orally or in writing, and MegaBank must receive the notice within 60 days of August 2.

229.   Three weeks ago, Jeff used a bank-issued credit card to purchase several items at a department store. In recent days, Jeff has discovered some product defects on the items.

What must Jeff prove, under federal law, before he can successfully assert *against the bank* these product defects as a reason not to pay the charges?

ANSWER:

Use the following facts to answer the next three questions.

ABC Shrimp Company agreed to lease a boat from Outboard Industries for one year, agreeing to pay $10,000 each month, for twelve months. The lease agreement required ABC to provide a letter of credit in the amount of $60,000 to secure the last six monthly payments.

Marine Bank agreed to issue the letter of credit, which permitted Outboard Industries to draw under the letter of credit in $10,000 increments upon providing a written statement that ABC had missed the appropriate number of monthly payments.

After ABC made eight payments, a hurricane destroyed the boat. Under the lease, this damage excused ABC from making the remaining four monthly payments. Even so, Outboard Industries requested payment of $40,000 under the letter of credit by submitting paperwork to Marine Bank that strictly complied with the terms of the letter of credit. Marine Bank honored the request and paid $40,000 to Outboard Industries.

230. Marine Bank:

   (A) cannot recover the $40,000 from ABC because ABC was excused under the terms of the lease from paying Outboard Industries.

   (B) has a right to reimbursement from ABC for $40,000.

   (C) has a right to reimbursement from ABC for $40,000, but only if Marine Bank obtained timely permission from ABC to pay the $40,000 to Outboard Industries.

   (D) has no reimbursement claim under UCC Article 5 and must look elsewhere for a remedy.

231. ABC:

   (A) has no rights against Outboard Industries because Outboard Industries complied with the terms of the letter of credit.

   (B) may have a statutory claim against Outboard Industries for breach of warranty.

   (C) may have a contract claim against Outboard Industries, based on the underlying lease agreement.

   (D) may have a statutory claim against Outboard Industries for breach of warranty, and a contract claim based on the underlying lease agreement.

232. Assume that Marine Bank dishonored Outboard Industries' presentment (which strictly complied with the terms of the letter of credit) because Marine Bank knew that the terms of the lease excused ABC's post-hurricane obligations.

   Outboard Industries:

   (A) can recover from Marine Bank for wrongful dishonor.

   (B) can recover from either Marine Bank or ABC for wrongful dishonor.

   (C) has no rights against either Marine Bank or ABC because Outboard Motors was not entitled to the $40,000 payment.

   (D) should file a claim against Marine Bank, seeking recovery of the $40,000 as an insured deposit under the FDIC insurance program.

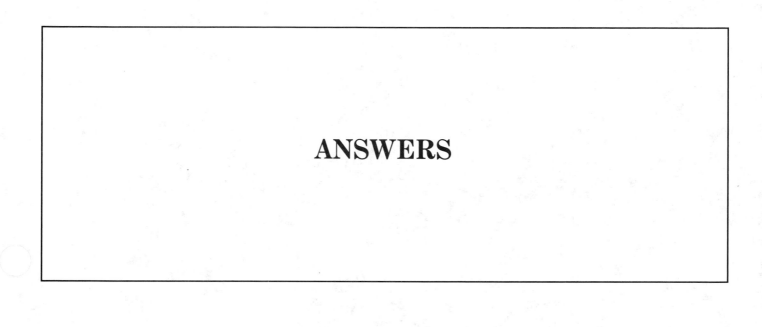

ANSWERS

<table>
<tr><td>TOPIC 1:</td><td>ANSWERS</td></tr>
<tr><td colspan="2">NEGOTIABLE INSTRUMENTS: DEFINITIONS; BASIC PRINCIPLES</td></tr>
</table>

1. **Answer (B) is the correct answer.** A $10 bill is "money," as that term is defined in Section 1-201. Article 3 expressly excludes "money" from its scope. *See* § 3-102(a). Therefore, **Answer (B) is the correct answer.**

   Section 3-104 contemplates that checks (e.g., personal checks, teller's checks, and cashier's checks) may be negotiable instruments. *See* § 3-104(f), (g), and (h). Therefore, **Answer (A) and Answer (D) are incorrect answers**.

   Section 3-104 also contemplates that a promissory note may be a negotiable instrument. *See* § 3-104(e). Therefore, **Answer (C) is an incorrect answer.**

2. **Answer (B) is the correct answer.** Section 3-103(a)(5) defines "drawer" as the person who signs, and orders payment of, a draft (e.g., a check). Julie wrote, or issued, the check, so she is the drawer of the check, **making Answer (B) the correct answer.**

   Her order ("pay") is directed at First National Bank, the bank that maintains Julie's checking account. Therefore, First National Bank is the "drawee," as defined in Section 3-103(a)(4), **making Answer (C) an incorrect answer**.

   Article 3 never defines "borrower," so **Answer (A) is incorrect**.

   Article 3 does define "accommodation party" in Section 3-419(a), but the few facts found in the problem fail to trigger the term, **making Answer (D) an incorrect answer.**

3. **Answer (A) is the correct answer.** As noted in the previous answer, Julie is writing a check, a writing in which she is ordering her bank, First National Bank, to make payment. Therefore, First National Bank falls within the definition of "drawee" at Section 3-103(a)(4), **making Answer (A) the correct answer.**

   Article 3 defines "remitter" in Section 3-103(a)(15). The typical example is a person who buys a cashier's check from a bank that names a third person as payee (typically a person who has sold goods or provided services to the buyer). First National Bank is not a remitter, so **Answer (B) is incorrect.**

   The term "payee" is not defined in Article 3, but the common understanding is that the payee is the party to be paid. In this case, the payee is the American Red Cross, not First National Bank. Therefore, **Answer (C) is an incorrect answer**.

   Article 3 defines "maker" in Section 3-103(a)(7) as the person who executes a promissory note in which that person promises payment. The facts involve a check, not a promissory note, so we have no "maker" in the problem and **Answer (D) is incorrect.**

4. **Answer (D) is the correct answer.** Section 3-103(a)(7) defines a "maker" as "a person who signs or is identified in a note as a person undertaking to pay." Tom signed a note (as contrasted with a check, or some other writing). As the note contains no other signatures, it

is safe to assume that Tom signed the note as evidence of his obligation, or promise, to pay $15,000 to Dealer. Therefore, his signature makes him the "maker," and **Answer (D) is the correct answer**.

Section 3-103 defines "drawer" and "drawee," terms that are associated with checks, not notes. Tom signed a note, not a check, so those terms are inapplicable and **Answers (A) and (B) are incorrect answers**. (Tom may later pay some or all of his $15,000 debt with one or more personal checks, at which time he will be a "drawer" on each such check.)

As used in everyday conversation, Tom may be the "debtor" or the "borrower," two terms that are not defined in Article 3. Therefore, **Answer (C) is an incorrect answer**.

5. **Answer (D) is the correct answer.** Section 3-104(a) states that a "negotiable instrument" must state "an *unconditional* promise or order" (emphasis added). Section 3-106 offers guidance on the meaning of this phrase.

    Section 3-106(a)(i) prohibits language that creates an "express" condition to payment. Answer (A) offers an example of an implied, rather than an express, condition to payment (a point illustrated in the first paragraph of Official Comment 1), so that provision does not create a conditional promise or order. Therefore, **Answer (A) is an incorrect answer**.

    Sections 3-106(a)(ii) and (iii) warn that cross-referencing other agreements *may* create a "conditional" promise or order. However, Section 3-106(b)(i) permits cross-references to other agreements "for a statement of rights with respect to collateral . . . ." Answer (B) does exactly that, so the provision is permissible, **making Answer (B) an incorrect answer**.

    The last sentence of Section 3-106(b) reminds the reader that the mere act of referencing another agreement "does not of itself make the promise or order conditional." Answer (C) offers a definition explanation, and nothing more. The cross-reference is acceptable, **making Answer (C) an incorrect answer**.

    As noted above, express conditions to payment render a promise or order conditional and remove the writing from the scope of Article 3. Answer (D) states that the maker's obligations are "contingent," or conditional, on Dealer's delivery of a particular piece of paper. This is an example of an express condition, which makes Tom's promise conditional. While Tom's obligation may remain enforceable, the provision has effectively removed the writing from the scope of Article 3. **Therefore, Answer (D) is the correct answer.**

6. **Answer (B) is the correct answer.** Section 3-104(a)(1) states that a negotiable instrument must be "payable to bearer or to order at the time it is issued or first comes into possession of a holder." The "payable to bearer or to order" language is explained in Section 3-109. Subsection (a) addresses "payable to bearer" and subsection (b) explains "payable to order."

    Section 3-109(a)(3) states that a promise or order is "payable to bearer" if it is "payable to or to the order of cash." Answer (B) offers such language, making it "payable to bearer." **Therefore, Answer B is the correct answer.**

    Other examples of "payable to bearer" language include "pay to bearer" or "pay to the order of bearer," as well as the omission of any named payee. Answers (A), (C), and (D) each name a particular payee and do not use terms such as "bearer" or "cash." These three examples do not create an obligation "payable to bearer," **making Answers (A), (C), and (D) incorrect answers**.

7.   The law favors Wendy over Paul, allowing the terms of the separate agreement to trump the contrary language in the promissory note. Section 3-117 states in relevant part: ". . . the obligation of a party to an instrument to pay the instrument may be modified . . . by a separate agreement of the obligor [Wendy] and a person entitled to enforce the instrument [Paul], if the instrument is issued or the obligation is incurred in reliance on the agreement . . ." This statutory provision allows Wendy to successfully argue that the separate agreement controls. Accordingly, any demand by Paul prior to February 1 of the next year is premature.

Under slightly different facts, Wendy may lose, however. First, the facts stipulate that Wendy can introduce into evidence the separate agreement. Section 3-117 acknowledges in its opening language ("Subject to applicable law regarding exclusion of proof of contemporaneous or previous agreements . . .") that the introduction of such evidence may pose a problem. Second, if the person demanding payment is not Paul, but a subsequent holder, the subsequent holder may not be bound by the separate agreement if that person took the note as a holder in due course. *See* § 3-117, cmt. 1.

8.   **Answer (B) is the correct answer.** Section 3-104(a) states that a negotiable instrument must include a promise or order to pay "money," a term defined in Section 1-201 in a manner that includes foreign currency. As of the publication date of this book, the peso is a form of currency used in Cuba (unlike some former currencies in Europe that have been replaced by the Euro).

Foreign currencies, when measured against the U.S. Dollar, can fluctuate in value over time, making the use of foreign currency in a negotiable instrument a somewhat risky venture for both parties (usually one party will benefit from market fluctuations, while the other will suffer a detriment). To address this fluctuation risk, the parties should consider including language in the instrument that specifies a currency conversion rate as of a particular date. If the instrument is silent, then Section 3-107 provides the rule: the obligation is payable in foreign currency, or an equivalent amount in U.S. dollars, "calculated by using the current bank-offered spot rate at the place of payment for the purchase of dollars on the day on which the instrument is paid."

Because the statute offers an option (pesos or dollars), **Answer (C) and Answer (D) are incorrect answers**.

The statutory conversion date is the date of payment, rather than the date of issue. For that reason, **Answer (B) is the correct answer** and **Answer (A) is an incorrect answer.**

9.   **Answer (D) is the correct answer.** Section 3-112 addresses the topic of interest. Subsection (b) states in part: "If an instrument provides for interest, but the amount of interest payable cannot be ascertained from the description, interest is payable at the judgment rate in effect at the place of payment of the instrument and at the time interest first accrues." Melissa executed a promissory note that assessed interest at a rate tied to a non-existent external source. The interest rate in the note "cannot be ascertained from the description," so the interest is payable at the appropriate judgment rate. **This makes Answer (D) the correct answer** and **Answer (A), Answer (B), and Answer (C) each an incorrect answer.**

10.   **Answer (B) is the correct answer.** Section 3-114 states the rule that "words prevail over numbers" when resolving contradictory terms. Therefore, the textual amount (two hundred seventy-nine and 13/100 dollars) prevails over the numerical amount ($213.79). For that

reason, **Answer (B) is the correct answer,** and **Answer (A), Answer (C), and Answer (D) are incorrect answers.**

The conflict is not resolved by comparing the amounts of the two numbers and picking the higher or the lower. Therefore, **Answers (A) and (D) are incorrect answers.**

The conflict is not resolved by calculating an average of the two numbers, so **Answer (C) is an incorrect answer.**

The conflict cannot be resolved by examining the underlying contractual obligation (e.g., the utility bill) because any such paperwork does not accompany the check through the check-clearing process. Therefore, **Answer (D) is incorrect for that additional reason.** Nevertheless, appreciate that Tim's mistake will trigger an overpayment, presumably resulting in a $65.34 credit against next month's charges.

11.   A note marked "VOID" may be treated as if Ellen's obligation has been discharged, a result that will not please Frank. *See* § 3-604(a) (cancellation possible by "the addition of words to the instrument indicating discharge"). In contrast, writing "NON-NEGOTIABLE" (in a conspicuous manner) leaves Ellen's obligation enforceable, but removes the note from the definition of "instrument" and the scope of UCC Article 3. *See* § 3-104(d). And if the note is not governed by UCC Article 3, no party will be a holder in due course. This is a result that would favor Ellen if she wished to preserve her liability defenses and assert them against Frank's direct or indirect transferees. If Frank contemplates the possibility of selling the note, he may wish to preserve the possibility that the buyer of the note may be a holder in due course. Because a holder in due course takes the instrument free and clear of almost all claims and defenses, the sale of the note to a potential holder in due course may command a higher price. For that reason, Frank may object to a "NON-NEGOTIABLE" legend on the note as it could adversely affect the note's marketability.

12.   **Answer (B) is the correct answer.** Section 3-104(a)(2) requires a negotiable instrument to be "payable on demand or at a definite time." The quoted language is addressed in Section 3-108. Subsection (a) indicates that an instrument is payable on demand if it states that it is payable on demand, states that it is payable on sight, states that it is payable at the will of the holder, or fails to state a time of payment. Answer (B) offers language that fails to state a time of payment, making it the correct answer.

Answer (A) and Answer (C) are incorrect because they state payment dates.

Answer (D) is incorrect because it is payable at the will of the undersigned (presumably the maker), not the holder.

13.   **Answer (B) is the correct answer.** Section 3-111 addresses the place of payment. But before looking there, observe that Section 3-104 (which defines "negotiable instrument") nowhere requires that a promissory note mention a place of payment. Therefore, **Answer (A) can be eliminated as an incorrect answer.** Because Jill has executed a note, rather than a check, she is the maker (and not the drawer). *See* § 3-103(a)(7). Under Section 3-111, a note that fails to state a place of payment is payable at the maker's address if stated in the note. If the maker's address is not stated in the note, then the note is payable at the maker's place of business; if the maker has no place of business, then the note is payable at the maker's residence. Without mentioning which of her possible addresses (business or residence), Answer (B) does state Jill's "address," **making Answer (B) the best, and**

therefore the correct, answer.

Nothing in Section 3-111 suggests that, absent contrary language in the note itself, the note is payable either at Jill's parents' address or any bank chartered under federal law. Therefore, **Answer (C) and Answer (D) are incorrect answers**.

14. **Answer (D) is the correct answer**.

As a general rule, parties can remove a writing from the scope of UCC Article 3 by including conspicuous language, "however expressed, to the effect that the promise or order is not negotiable or is not an instrument governed by [UCC Article 3]." *See* § 3-104(d). Writing "NON-NEGOTIABLE" in the memo line of the check would seem to accomplish the intended result. However, parties cannot exercise this opt-out option with respect to checks. *See* § 3-104(d) (". . . other than a check . . ."). Possible reasons for this exclusion include: banks rely on the possibility of holder-in-due-course status in the check-collection process; extraneous language on checks may not be viewed by all parties in the check-collection process (which utilizes electronic or machine processing); and most of us view checks as cash or cash equivalents. Therefore, a check cannot be removed from the scope of UCC Article 3 by writing "NON-NEGOTIABLE" on it, so **Answer (A) and Answer (B) are incorrect answers**.

As a general rule, a negotiable instrument requires language that makes the promise "payable to bearer or to order." *See* § 3-104(a)(1). Striking through, or otherwise removing, "to the order of" language on the payee line would seem to frustrate that requirement and effectively remove the check from the scope of UCC Article 3. But Section 3-104(c) states that a check that satisfies all other conditions of Section 3-104(a) remains a negotiable instrument, even if it is not "payable to bearer or to order." Therefore, the strike-through fails to achieve its intended purpose, and **Answer (A) and Answer (C) are incorrect answers**.

Neither of the steps taken by Alex will remove the check from the scope of UCC Article 3, so **Answer (D) is the correct answer**.

15. **Answer (D) is the correct answer**.

A check that fails to state a payee is payable to bearer under Section 3-109(a)(2). Because the absence of a named payee does not remove the check from the scope of UCC Article 3, **Answer (A) is an incorrect answer**.

As noted above, a check without a named payee is bearer paper. Therefore, the electrician is a holder under Section 1-201 because he possesses bearer paper. Section 3-301(i) identifies a holder as a person entitled to enforce the instrument (notwithstanding his theft), **making Answer (B) an incorrect answer**.

(Appreciate, however, that the last sentence of Section 3-305(c) provides Greg with a defense to payment, good against the electrician because he is not a holder in due course.)

Because the electrician stole bearer paper, he can negotiate the check to a party that could satisfy all of the requirements of Section 3-302 and become a holder in due course. Therefore, **Answer (C) is incorrect**.

Issuance, under Section 3-105(a), requires delivery. Delivery, under Section 1-201, requires a voluntary movement. The electrician stole the check, so it was not delivered and, therefore, not issued. Even so, Greg (the drawer) is the issuer of the unissued check under Section 3-105(c), which states that the term "issuer" applies "to issued and unissued instruments." Thus, **Answer (D) is the correct answer**.

16.   **Answer (B) is the correct answer.** Lucas made a promise to pay "Stan," so the promise is not payable to bearer under Section 3-109(a). But because the promise is payable to "Stan," rather than "the order of Stan" (or "Stan or his order"), the promise also is not payable to order under Section 3-109(b). This writing fails to include the magical words of negotiability required by Section 3-104(a)(1), so this writing is not a negotiable instrument and falls outside the scope of UCC Article 3. Therefore, **Answer (C) and Answer (D) are incorrect answers**. But just because a promise is not covered by UCC Article 3 does not necessarily mean that the promise is unenforceable under other law (subject to whatever requirements are imposed by the other law). Therefore, **Answer (A) is an incorrect answer** and **Answer (B) is the correct answer**.

17.   Section 3-104(a)(2) mandates that a negotiable instrument be payable on demand or at a definite time. A note "payable on the date of our mother's death" is not payable on demand under Section 3-108(a). And while death is a certainty, the exact date of death is not "readily ascertainable" when Shannon executes the note, so the note, without more, will not be payable at a definite time. A note that is neither payable on demand nor payable at a definite time is not a negotiable instrument under UCC Article 3. One way to capture the intended result, while staying within the scope of UCC Article 3, is to make the note payable on a specific date safely beyond the date on which the person may die, followed by an acceleration clause (permitted by Section 3-108(b)(ii)) triggered by the actual death. For example, the mother, now 83, may be expected to live to an age not more than 100 years. This language, then, might work: "Payment shall be due on the 25th anniversary date of this note; provided, however, that all amounts shall automatically and immediately be due and payable upon the earlier death of our mother, Jennifer."

18.   **Answer (C) is the correct (that is, "false") answer.** Section 4-403 permits a "customer" to place a stop-payment order on a check. Typically, the customer on a checking account is the drawer. In this question, the bank, rather than Carmen, is the drawer (the issuer of the cashier's check). As noted in Official Comment 4 to Section 4-403: "A cashier's check . . . purchased by a customer whose account is debited in payment for the check is not a check drawn on the customer's account . . .; hence, a customer purchasing a cashier's check or teller's check has no right to stop payment of such a check under subsection (a)." Carmen may ask her bank to place a stop-payment order on the cashier's check, but the decision to place the order itself rests with the bank. **Answer (C), then, is false and, accordingly, correct**.

Section 3-103 defines a "remitter" as "a person who purchases an instrument from its issuer if the instrument is payable to an identified person other than the purchaser." Carmen is purchasing the cashier's check from her bank, the issuer. If, as suggested in the answer, the bank makes the check payable to the seller (rather than to Carmen), then Carmen is a remitter. **Answer (A), then, is true and, accordingly, incorrect**.

Carmen has purchased a cashier's check. Section 3-104(g) states that a cashier's check is a draft on which the drawer and the drawee are the same bank (or branches of the same bank). (A teller's check, by contrast, is typically issued by a bank but drawn on an account at a different bank.) **Answer (B), then, is true and, accordingly, incorrect**.

Section 3-201 states that a "negotiation" requires a transfer of possession from a non-issuer to a person who, by taking possession, becomes a holder. The issuer (drawer) of the cashier's check is Carmen's bank; Carmen is not the issuer (regardless of the name of the original payee). If the cashier's check is payable to Carmen, then Carmen can negotiate the check to the seller by indorsing and delivering the check to the seller. If the cashier's check is payable to the seller, then Carmen can negotiate the check to the seller merely by delivering the check to the seller. So regardless of the name of the original payee, Carmen can negotiate the check to the seller. **Answer (D), then, is true and, accordingly, incorrect.**

19. Section 3-104 defines a cashier's check and a teller's check in subsections (g) and (h), respectively. Both are checks drawn by a bank. A cashier's check is drawn on the same bank (or branch of the same bank), whereas a teller's check is drawn on a different bank (or payable at or through a different bank). In general, then, if the drawer and the drawee on a check are the same bank, then the check is a cashier's check. But if the drawer and the drawee on a check are different banks, then the check is a teller's check.

20. **Answer (C) is the correct answer.** If Jane raises no challenges to liability, then Patrick should win the lawsuit merely by producing the note that is in his possession. Jane issued the note either payable to bearer, or to the order of Patrick. In either case, his possession of the note makes him a holder under Section 1-201 and a person entitled to enforce the instrument under Section 3-301(i). Under Section 3-308(b), Patrick's proof of his enforcement status is sufficient to win the lawsuit, **making Answer (C) the correct answer.**

Unless Jane raises in her pleadings an issue with respect to her signature, the authenticity of her signature is admitted. *See* § 3-308(a). Therefore, **Answer (A) is an incorrect answer**.

Issuance, under Section 3-105, requires delivery. Section 1-201 defines "delivery" in terms of a voluntary movement (as contrasted with a theft, for example). The facts indicate that Jane delivered the note to Patrick, so presumably she will not be asserting a defense based on loss or theft. Absent any challenge by Jane, Patrick need not prove how he came into possession of the note. Therefore, **Answer (B) is an incorrect answer**.

The facts do not suggest any delay by Patrick that would trigger a problem with the statute of limitations (found in Section 3-118). Nor does any provision of UCC Article 3 require Patrick to present the note as a condition to payment (or as a predicate to a lawsuit). The facts indicate that the note came due in recent months, suggesting that it was payable on a specific date, rather than on demand. So presentment is not necessary to trigger dishonor under Section 3-502. No provision in UCC Article 3 requires Patrick to prove that he timely presented the note to Jane, so **Answer (D) is an incorrect answer.**

21. Nate is correct (the lawsuit is time-barred), but for a different reason than he asserts. Section 3-104(a) states that a negotiable instrument must be payable in "money," a term defined in Section 1-201 as "a medium of exchange currently authorized or adopted by a domestic or foreign government." Therefore, Nate's promise to pay in Indian Rupees, rather than in U.S. Dollars, does not remove the note from the scope of UCC Article 3. Nevertheless, this note is not a negotiable instrument. Payment is directed "to Romi Purewal." This language fails to make the instrument payable to bearer or to order, as required by Section 3-104(a)(1) (and as further discussed in Section 3-109). It is for this reason that Nate's promise falls outside the scope of UCC Article 3, leaving Romi with a

lawsuit that appears to be time-barred under the facts.

22. **Answer (D) is the correct answer.** The "and/or" language could be interpreted as "Wallace AND Helen" or "Wallace OR Helen." If the former, then both Wallace and Helen must indorse (but in no particular order). *See* § 3-110(d) (second sentence). If the latter, then either parent may indorse. *See* § 3-110(d) (first sentence). Which interpretation is correct? The third sentence of Section 3-110(d) resolves the dilemma in favor of an interpretation that fosters ease of negotiability (i.e., one, rather than two, indorsements): "If an instrument payable to two or more persons is ambiguous as to whether it is payable to the persons alternatively, the instrument is payable to the persons alternatively." *See also* § 3-110, cmt. 4 (last sentence) ("For example, an instrument payable to X and/or Y is treated like an instrument payable to X or Y."). Therefore, either Wallace or Helen may indorse. Both parents need not indorse. Therefore, **Answer (D) is the correct answer**, and **Answer (A) and Answer (B) are incorrect answers**.

Answer (C) is an incorrect answer because Helen need not indorse if Wallace indorses.

23. Section 3-204(d) permits Rosaria to indorse the check by using the misspelled name of "Rosie Giacconi" or the correct name of "Rosaria Giacona." Either form of indorsement should be effective. However, as noted in Official Comment 3, "because an indorsement in a name different from that used in the instrument may raise a question about its validity and an indorsement in a name that is not the correct name of the payee may raise a problem of identifying the indorser, the accepted commercial practice is to indorse in both names." To avoid any problems, Rosaria may wish to raise the issue with the teller at the time of deposit and comply with the teller's suggestion. Section 3-204(d) authorizes the teller to demand a signature in both names.

24. A promise or order to pay is always conditional on the general creditworthiness of the maker or the drawer. That condition exists, even though it is rarely, if ever, stated in the instrument. To expressly state that payment of the promise or order is conditional on the presence of funds in a particular account or source is a difference only in degree. And if the former concern fails to render the payment obligation conditional, so, too, should the latter concern. As noted in Section 3-106, cmt. 1 (last paragraph), limiting payment to a particular account or source may affect marketability, but it need not remove the obligation from the scope of UCC Article 3.

NEGOTIABLE INSTRUMENTS: PERSONS ENTITLED TO ENFORCE; DEFENSES TO PAYMENT; HOLDER IN DUE COURSE DOCTRINE

25.   **Answer (A) is the correct answer.** Section 3-301 addresses which party has the right to enforce a negotiable instrument. The statute provides three options. The first two options extend enforcement rights to a holder (who, by definition under Section 1-201, must have possession) and a nonholder in possession with the rights of a holder. If FinCo does not have possession, it has no enforcement rights under Section 3-301(i) or (ii). Section 3-301(iii) affords enforcement rights to a nonpossessor who can satisfy one of the two cross-referenced statutes. If ZinnCorp has possession, then Section 3-309 is inapplicable because the note is not stolen, lost, or misplaced. Further, no facts in the problem suggest that Section 3-418(d) (a "mistake" statute) is applicable. Therefore, FinCo fails to meet any of the three enforcement options of Section 3-301 if it does not have possession of the note (which remains in the possession of ZinnCorp), **making Answer (A) the correct answer.**

Answer (B) is an incorrect answer. If FinCo takes possession of the note, which is unindorsed by payee ZinnCorp, then FinCo is not a holder under Section 1-201. But FinCo can be a nonholder in possession with the rights of a holder by asserting ZinnCorp's enforcement rights as a holder via the "shelter doctrine" of Section 3-203(b). As a nonholder in possession with the rights of a holder qualifies for enforcement rights under Section 3-301(ii), **Answer (B) is an incorrect answer.**

Answer (C) is an incorrect answer. Failure of consideration (or a defense of nonperformance) may provide ABC Company with a defense to payment, but it does not preclude FinCo from asserting enforcement rights under Section 3-301 (if FinCo otherwise qualifies thereunder).

Answer (D) is an incorrect answer. ABC Company may, absent notice of the sale of the note, have a defense if it continues to make post-sale payments to ZinnCorp (and ZinnCorp fails to pass those payments along to FinCo), but that defense does not preclude FinCo from asserting its enforcement rights under Section 3-301 (if FinCo otherwise qualifies thereunder).

26.   **Answer (D) is the correct answer.** A check that is complete, but for the name of a payee, is treated as a negotiable instrument payable to bearer, under Section 3-109(a)(2). Ginny's possession of bearer paper makes her a holder under Section 1-201. A holder is a person entitled to enforce the check under Section 3-301(i). Therefore, **Answer (D) is the correct answer.**

Answer (A) is incorrect. Ginny's failure to give value for the check prevents her from qualifying as a holder in due course under Section 3-302, but it does not affect her ability to assert enforcement rights as a holder under Section 3-301(i).

Answer (B) is incorrect. As noted above, John unleashed bearer paper when he lost a check that he signed, and which was complete but for the payee's name. And a party who finds bearer paper is no different from a person who finds a $5 bill — both can assert enforcement rights in what they have found.

Answer (C) is incorrect. Ginny may find bearer paper, but that does not make her the legal owner of what she has found. Article 3 severs property rights from enforcement rights, and a party need not have the former to enjoy the latter.

Appreciate that John can use the last sentence of Section 3-305(c) as a defense if Ginny demands payment (Ginny is not a holder in due course under Section 3-302 for obvious reasons, and the check is a lost instrument). But Ginny may not be the party who asserts enforcement rights. Instead, that party may have taken the check directly or indirectly from Ginny, and that party may be a holder in due course, leaving John without the defense. But maybe we should not feel sorry for John, who should have refrained from signing the check until the last possible moment.

27.   **Answer (C) is the correct answer.** Section 3-110(d) states in relevant part: "If an instrument is payable to two or more persons not alternatively, it is payable to all of them and may be negotiated, discharged, or enforced only by all of them." The check is payable to "Elaine *and* Robert Jackson" (emphasis added). Therefore, only acting as a unit may Elaine and Robert enforce the check. For this reason, **Answer (C) is the correct answer** and **Answers (A), (B), and (D) are incorrect answers**.

Answer (D) also is incorrect for the additional reason that it is a nonsense answer. The key word on the payee line is "and." It makes no difference whether a last name appears after any or all of the first names of the human payees.

28.   **Answer (B) is the correct answer.** A thief who possesses bearer paper is a holder under Section 1-201, and a holder is a person entitled to enforce the instrument under Section 3-301(i). The last sentence of Section 3-301 also confirms this result: "A person may be a person entitled to enforce the instrument even though the person is not the owner of the instrument or is in wrongful possession of the instrument."

Answer (A) is incorrect. Section 3-301(iii) confers enforcement rights on certain nonpossessors.

Answer (C) is incorrect. The name of a thief who has stolen bearer paper will not appear on the instrument, yet the thief is a holder and a person entitled to enforce the instrument. Also, the holder of order paper may fail to indorse the instrument prior to delivering the instrument to the recipient, yet the recipient may be a person entitled to enforce the instrument under Section 3-301(ii) even though the recipient's name appears nowhere on the instrument.

Answer (D) is sometimes, but not always, correct; therefore, Answer (D) is an incorrect answer. For example, Smith is the holder of a note payable to the order of Smith. Smith sells all of her rights, title, and interest in the note to Jones, but she fails to deliver the note (which is not stolen, lost, or misplaced) to Jones. Jones may be the owner of the note, but Jones fails to qualify as a person entitled to enforce the note under Sections 3-301(i) (lack of possession prevents Jones from being a holder), 3-301(ii) (no possession), or 3-301(iii) (Section 3-309 is inapplicable because the note is not lost, stolen, or misplaced, and Section 3-418(d) is inapplicable because the note has yet to be paid by mistake).

29.   **Answer (D) is the correct answer.** Gwen is signing the check in her capacity as president

for MegaCorp. Sometimes agents (including corporate officers) are personally liable if they sign instruments and the signature fails to reveal the agency status and the name of the principal. *See generally* § 3-402(b). Even so, Section 3-402(c) states that Gwen is not personally liable for signing the check (which indicated that it was drawn on MegaCorp's account) because she was acting with corporate authority when she signed it. Therefore, **Answer (D) is the correct answer** and **Answers (A), (B), and (C) are incorrect answers**.

If Gwen had signed a note, rather than a check, she could be personally liable to a holder in due course under Section 3-402(b) (so **Answer (B) could be a correct answer under revised facts**).

Answer (C) also is incorrect because Gwen's signature liability as drawer does not turn on timely notice of dishonor. *See* § 3-414(b) (drawer liable on dishonor, but no mention of timely notice thereof).

30.   **Answer (C) is the correct answer.** This indorsement is a blank indorsement under Section 3-205(b) because it does not name an intended indorsee. Therefore, Thief has stolen bearer paper and has become a holder. A holder is a person entitled to enforce the check under Section 3-301(i).

Answer (A) is incorrect. This indorsement is a special indorsement under Section 3-205(a) because it identifies a person to whom the instrument is payable — the account number. *See* § 3-110(c) (indicating that a person may be identified "in any way, including by . . . account number"). The special indorsement makes the check "order paper," and a Thief who steals order paper fails to qualify as a person entitled to enforce the instrument under either Section 3-301(i) (not a holder because the check identifies the bank account as the party to be paid) or Section 3-301(ii) (a thief who steals order paper fails to enjoy the rights of a holder under the shelter doctrine of Section 3-203(b) because the involuntary exchange of possession precludes "delivery" under Section 3-203(a)).

Answer (B) is incorrect for the same reason that Answer (A) is incorrect. This indorsement is a special indorsement because it directs payment to a particular person. A special indorsement creates order paper, and a Thief who steals order paper will not enjoy PETE status under Section 3-301.

Answer (D) is incorrect for at least two reasons. First, its correctness cannot be determined without knowing the nature of Grace's indorsement. Second, the answer incorrectly suggests that enforcement rights turn on a timely demand for payment. Section 3-301, which conveys enforcement rights, makes no such suggestion.

31.   The issuer would prefer that the initial demand for payment come from the possessor. Regardless of who makes the first demand, the issuer who honors that request and makes payment will assert the defense of previous payment against the party who makes the second demand. If the party who makes the second demand has possession of the instrument, it is conceivable that the possessor may enjoy the status of a holder in due course. Such a party would not be subject to the defense of previous payment. But if the party who makes the second demand for payment is the nonpossessor, such a party cannot be a holder in due course and would be subject to the defense of previous payment. Therefore, the issuer prefers that the initial demand for payment come from the possessor, which allows the issuer to raise a good defense of prior payment against the subsequent nonpossessor who demands payment.

32.   **Answer (A) is the correct answer.** To be a holder in due course, FinCorp must give "value." § 3-302(a)(2)(i). FinCorp promised to pay $40,000 for the note: $30,000 to CompuTech, and $10,000 to one of CompuTech's creditors. FinCorp has completed its payment obligations. Therefore, on the assumption that FinCorp meets all other requirements, FinCorp is a holder in due course for the full amount of the note, $50,000, which makes Answer (A) the correct answer and **Answer (B), Answer (C), and Answer (D) incorrect answers**.

Answer (B) suggests that FinCorp's status is somehow limited to the amount of value that it has given. But that suggestion ignores the commercial reality that FinCorp, and similar purchasers, seek to make a profit. So **Answer (B) is an incorrect answer.**

Answer (C) would be correct, under the formula of Section 3-302(d), if FinCorp had paid $30,000 to CompuTech but had not yet paid $10,000 to CompuTech's creditor (or had made the $10,000 payment after learning of the maker's defense to payment). But the facts state that FinCorp fully performed its payment obligations prior to learning of the maker's defense, so the formula of Section 3-302(d) is inapplicable. Therefore, **Answer (C) is an incorrect answer**.

Answer (D) suggests that the $10,000 payment may not constitute "value" and FinCorp's status as a holder in due course is somehow capped at what FinCorp has paid directly to CompuTech (the $30,000). Neither suggestion is correct, **making Answer (D) an incorrect answer.**

33.   Yes. If FinCorp has yet to make the $10,000 payment when it learns of the maker's defense, then FinCorp has given value only to the extent that it has performed on its promise of payment. *See* § 3-303(a)(1). This means that FinCorp "may assert rights as a holder in due course of the instrument only to the fraction of the amount payable under the instrument [$50,000] equal to the value of the partial performance [$30,000] divided by the value of the promised performance [$40,000]." *See* § 3-302(d). The formula yields an answer of $37,500 (which represents the $30,000 payment, plus a *pro rata* percentage (3/4) of the bargained-for profit of $10,000 [$50,000 note, minus FinCorp's purchase price of $40,000]).

34.   **Answer (D) is the correct answer.** Bank, the holder of the $25,000 note (and, accordingly, a person entitled to enforce the note under Section 3-301(i)), has only a security interest in the note. Therefore Section 3-302(e) applies. Under that provision, Bank's rights as a holder in due course are limited to the amount of the unpaid secured loan ($20,000 minus payments of $8,000) if the obligor, First Church, has a defense "that may be asserted against the person who granted the security interest" (Dealer). The facts state that First Church has such a defense. So Bank can enforce the note to the extent of $12,000, **making Answer (D) correct and Answers (A), (B), and (C) incorrect.**

The result seems fair, given the general rule that a secured party (Bank) has no greater rights in the collateral than its debtor (Dealer). So if Dealer is subject to a defense, then Dealer's creditors (e.g., Bank) also should be subject to the defense. Put another way, Bank does not own the note outright. On the contrary, Dealer and Bank both have a property interest in the note. And Bank's enforcement rights are limited to its property interest in the note. Furthermore, the collateral serves the purpose of making Bank merely whole (rather than giving Bank a windfall from any surplus by which the collateral value exceeds the amount of the unpaid secured loan). In this case, Bank made a $20,000 loan to Dealer, and Dealer has repaid $8,000. Bank needs only $12,000 to be made whole, and Section 3-302(e) permits Bank to recover that amount (but no more) from First Church, the maker of the note.

35.   **Answer (A) is the correct answer.** Bank, the holder of the $25,000 note (and, accordingly, a person entitled to enforce the note under Section 3-301(i)), has "only a security interest in the instrument." Therefore, the initial reaction may be to invoke Section 3-302(e) again and limit Bank's rights to $8,000, the amount of the unpaid secured loan, as discussed in the previous answer. But the language in Section 3-302(e)(ii) is not met under these revised facts. As before, First Church has a defense. But under the revised facts, this defense cannot "be asserted against the person who granted the security interest" because that person, Providence Finance, is (as stated in the facts) a holder in due course (and, under Section 3-305(b), therefore takes the instrument free of First Church's mere contract defense). And because Section 3-302(e) does not apply, Bank can assert rights as a holder in due course against First Church for the full amount of the note, $25,000 (**making Answer (A) the correct answer** and **Answers (B), (C), and (D) incorrect answers**).

Awarding $25,000 to Bank seems inconsistent with the policy reasons of Section 3-302(e) discussed in the previous answer. Bank seems to enjoy a windfall of $17,000 (the amount by which the $25,000 payment from First Church exceeds $8,000, the unpaid amount of Bank's $22,000 secured loan to Providence Finance). But under UCC Article 9 (particularly Section 9-608(a)(4)), Bank is required to disgorge the "profit" (also referred to as "surplus") of $17,000 to its debtor, Providence Finance (who, as a holder in due course, also would have been able to recover the full $25,000 from First Church in any lawsuit that it initiated).

36.   Yes. The note continues to identify Frank as the party to be paid, so Jack cannot be a "holder" under Section 1-201 or a person entitled to enforce the note under Section 3-301(i). But Jack is a person entitled to enforce the note under Section 3-301(ii) as "a nonholder in possession of the instrument who has the rights of a holder." Frank, a non-issuer (Gwen is the "issuer" under Section 3-105), voluntarily surrendered possession of the note to Jack for the purpose of giving Jack the right to enforce the note. Therefore, the note was "transferred" by Frank to Jack under Section 3-203(a). As a result, Frank's enforcement rights as a holder vested in Jack under Section 3-203(b), often referred to as "the shelter doctrine." So although Jack is not a holder, he does have possession of the note and is entitled to assert the enforcement rights of his transferor, Frank, a holder, thus cloaking Jack with PETE status under Section 3-301(ii).

37.   Yes. David took the note by gift and did not give value, a requirement to be a holder in due course. See § 3-302(a)(2)(i). Also, David obtained the note on October 5, a few days after the maturity date of October 1. Therefore, the note was overdue, and David will have notice of the overdue nature under Section 1-202(a) (either because he "has actual knowledge of it" or "from all the facts and circumstances known to [him] . . . [he] has reason to know it exists"). But while David cannot assert that he qualifies as a holder in due course on his own, he can assert Claire's rights as a holder in due course under the "shelter doctrine" of Section 3-203(a). That provision states: "Transfer of an instrument . . . vests in the transferee [David] any right of the transferor [Claire] to enforce the instrument, including any right as a holder in due course . . . ." (As noted in Section 3-203, cmt. 2, "[t]he policy is to assure the holder in due course [Claire] a free market for the instrument.") As noted by the facts, Claire is a holder in due course. And the movement of the note from Claire to David is a "transfer of the instrument" under Section 3-203(a) because Claire, a non-issuer (Amy, the maker, was the "issuer" under Section 3-105) voluntarily conveyed the note to David for the purpose of

giving David the right to enforce the note. Therefore, David can assert rights as a holder in due course, albeit derivatively. (And because he is asserting Claire's rights, he has the burden of proving those rights, and how he obtained possession of the instrument. *See* § 3-308, cmt. 2 (first paragraph).)

38.   **Answer (C) is the correct answer.** Section 3-302(b) states that notice of a discharge (excluding discharge in an insolvency proceeding) of a party is not the type of notice that prevents a holder from being a holder in due course. (Even so, appreciate that a holder with notice of the discharge takes the instrument subject to the discharge even if the holder is a holder in due course. *See* § 3-302(b).)

Answer (A) is incorrect. To be a holder in due course, a holder must take the instrument without notice that the instrument has been dishonored. *See* § 3-302(a)(2)(iii).

Answer (B) is incorrect. To be a holder in due course, a holder must take the instrument without notice that the instrument contains an unauthorized alteration. *See* § 3-302(a)(2)(iv).

Answer (D) is incorrect. If the transferor steals a note from the maker, the maker has defenses of nonissuance and theft. *See* §§ 3-105(b); 3-305(c) (last sentence). Notice of these defenses prevents a holder from being a holder in due course. *See* § 3-302(a)(2)(vi).

39.   **Answer (D) is the correct answer.** Illegality of the underlying transaction does not automatically prevent George from being a holder in due course, so **Answer (B) is incorrect.** But even if George is a holder in due course, he is subject to Tony's defense of illegality if, under state law, the illegality "nullifies" Tony's obligation. *See* § 3-305(a), (b). Section 3-305, cmt. 1, explains the meaning of "nullify," indicating that an obligation is nullified when it becomes "null and void," rather than merely "voidable." The facts do not disclose whether the illegality of the underlying wager makes the payment obligation void or voidable. Therefore, **Answer (D) is the correct answer** and **Answer (C) is an incorrect answer.**

To be a holder in due course, George must satisfy the requirements of Section 3-302(a). The statute requires George to give value. Any amount of value will suffice to satisfy that requirement. If, however, the holder has given an amount of value that appears to be too low, then perhaps the allegedly insufficient amount could trigger an attack on the holder's good faith (or lack thereof). There is no bright-line rule on this point in Article 3 (and certainly no "20% rule"); the inquiry will be fact-sensitive. Therefore, absent additional facts, **Answer (A) is an incorrect answer.**

40.   **Answer (B) is the correct answer,** but only because of a change in law resulting from the 2002 amendments to UCC Article 3 (which have not been adopted by very many states). Prior to the amendments, Dealer could discharge Celeste's liability on the note without affecting the liability of Gerard, an "accommodation party" under Section 3-419 with a right of recourse under Section 3-419(e) against the discharged party: Celeste, the "accommodated party." § 3-605(b). But in an effort to harmonize UCC Article 3 with the law of suretyship, Section 3-605 was completely rewritten as part of the 2002 revision process. And as revised, Section 3-605 discharges Gerard's liability. If Dealer releases the obligation of Celeste (a "principal obligor" under Section 3-103(a)(11) as an accommodated party), the following rule applies. "Unless the terms of the release provide that the person entitled to enforce the instrument [Dealer] retains the right to enforce the instrument against the secondary obligor [Gerard, under Section 3-103(a)(17), as an accommodation party], the

secondary obligor [Gerard] is discharged to the same extent as the principal obligor [Celeste] from an unperformed portion of its obligation on the instrument." § 3-605(a)(2). By failing to address Gerard's continued liability in the written release, Dealer discharged Gerard's co-maker liability on the note when Dealer agreed to release Celeste from liability for the remaining $10,000. Therefore, **Answer (B) is the correct answer**.

Answer (A) is incorrect because Section 3-605(a) does not require the release to be in writing (although the release should be in writing, for obvious reasons).

Answer (C) and Answer (D) are incorrect answers because Gerard's liability has been discharged under Section 3-605(a) (as discussed above).

41.   **Answer (C) is the correct answer.** The settlement agreement effectively discharges Celeste from further liability on the note. Under Section 3-302(b), FinCo's notice of the discharge does not prevent it from becoming a holder in due course, but the notice is effective against FinCo. Therefore, **Answer (C) is the correct answer,** and **Answer (A) and Answer (B) are incorrect answers.**

Answer (D) is an incorrect answer (and a nonsense answer). A person who is a holder in due course enjoys that status against the world, not just specific parties.

42.   **Answer (C) is the correct answer.** The issue raised by this fact pattern is addressed in Section 3-602. Subsection (b) states in part: "[A] note is paid to the extent payment is made by or on behalf of a party obliged to pay the note [Jack and Jill] to a person that formerly was entitled to enforce the note [Lender] only if at the time of the payment the party obliged to pay [Jack and Jill] has not received adequate notification that the note has been transferred and that payment is to be made to the transferee [Wabash Finance]." Therefore, Jack and Jill have a valid payment defense for payments they made prior to receiving notice of Lender's sale of the note to Wabash Finance. And under subsection (c), the financial obligations of Jack and Jill are discharged to the extent of those pre-notice payments.

But is that payment defense (or "discharge") good against Wabash Finance? Can Wabash Finance be a holder in due course? Answers to these two questions are found in subsection (d), which states in part: "[A] transferee [Wabash Finance] . . . , including any such party that has rights as a holder in due course, is deemed to have notice of any payment that is made under subsection (b) after the date that the note is transferred to the transferee [Wabash Finance] but before the party obliged to pay the note [Jack and Jill] receives adequate notification of the transfer." Perhaps rephrased, Wabash Finance can be a holder in due course, but it will be deemed to have notice of (and therefore be subject to) the payment defense or discharge asserted by Jack and Jill. Official Comment 4 confirms both points. Therefore, **Answer (C) is the correct answer.**

Answer (A) is incorrect because Wabash Finance may be a holder in due course if it satisfies all of the conditions stated in Section 3-302.

Answer (B) is incorrect because Wabash Finance will take the note subject to the payment defense and discharge asserted by Jack and Jill.

Answer (D) is incorrect because Wabash Finance's status as a holder in due course is not dictated by payments made before, or after, Jack and Jill are informed of Lender's sale of the note to Wabash Finance.

43.   **Answer (C) is the correct answer.** The note was due and payable on or about August 1. ZinnCorp bought the note on August 20. Therefore, ZinnCorp bought the note with notice that the note was overdue. *See* § 1-202(a). This notice prevents ZinnCorp from becoming a holder in due course, at least on its own. *See* § 3-302(a)(2)(iii). Therefore, **Answer (B) is an incorrect answer.**

Even so, ZinnCorp can be sheltered to the status enjoyed by its transferor, Friendly Finance, under Section 3-203. Friendly Finance, a non-issuer (Maker is the issuer under Section 3-105), delivered the note to ZinnCorp for the purpose of conveying enforcement rights in the note. This means that the "instrument was transferred" under Section 3-203(a). And under Section 3-203(b), the transfer of an instrument "vests in the transferee [ZinnCorp] any right of the transferor [Friendly Finance] to enforce the instrument, including any right as a holder in due course." Friendly Finance may indeed be a holder in due course. Unlike ZinnCorp, Friendly Finance did not have notice on its purchase date of June 15 that the note was overdue (which could not happen until thereafter). Therefore, ZinnCorp should assert that it has acquired Friendly Finance's status as a holder in due course (if such status can be proven), **making Answer (C) the correct answer** and **Answer (D) an incorrect answer.**

Answer (A) is an incorrect answer. Failure of consideration is a personal defense, not a real defense among those mentioned in Section 3-305(a). Therefore, under Section 3-305(b), the defense is not good against a holder in due course, making HDC status quite relevant.

44.   The answer is found in Section 3-305(b). If Finance Company is a holder in due course, then it is not subject to either of Dealer's claims in recoupment that may be enforceable against the Supplier. Therefore, Finance Company, as a holder in due course, is entitled to recover the full $5,000.

45.   Once again, the answer is found in Section 3-305(b). If Finance Company is not a holder in due course, then it takes the $5,000 instrument subject to Dealer's claims in recoupment, but only if those claims arise "from the transaction that gave rise to the instrument." § 3-305(a)(3). Dealer's $700 claim arose from the transaction that generated the $5,000 note, so Finance Company can recover only $4,300 if it is not a holder in due course. Finance Company is not subject to the $1,600 claim, however. That claim arose from a transaction separate from the transaction that generated the $5,000 note. The policy for ignoring the unrelated $1,600 claim is because "it is not reasonable to require the transferee [Finance Company] to bear the risk that wholly unrelated claims may also be asserted." § 3-305, cmt. 3.

46.   **Answer (D) is the correct answer.** If Fidelity Savings is a holder in due course, it can enforce the check against Tim (liable under Section 3-414(b) as the drawer of a dishonored check), subject only to the so-called "real defenses" listed in Section 3-305(a)(1). § 3-305(b). One of the "real defenses" is duress, and the facts strongly suggest that Tim wrote the check under duress. But duress is only a real defense if it nullifies, or voids, Tim's obligation (rather than making it merely voidable). § 3-305(a)(1), cmt. 1. Furthermore, duress "is a matter of degree." § 3-305, cmt. 1 (noting that an instrument signed at gunpoint is void, but one signed under threat of prosecution may be merely voidable). If, under applicable local law, the duress that Tim experienced voids his obligation, then Fidelity Savings cannot enforce the check even if it is a holder in due course. But if, under applicable law, the duress that Tim experienced renders his obligation merely voidable, then Fidelity Savings can

enforce the check free and clear of Tim's defense. The bottom line is that Tim's defense may be a real defense or a personal defense. This flexibility is best stated in **Answer (D), making it the correct answer** and **Answer (B) and Answer (C) incorrect answers.**

Answer (A) is an incorrect answer. Fidelity Bank can assert its status as a possible holder in due course as of the time of initial deposit, not when it retakes the check following dishonor (at which time it would have adverse notice). And if banks could not assert HDC status on dishonored checks, many banks might place longer "hold" periods on availability of funds to reduce the risk of loss arising from possible dishonor. You and I, as customers, would not like that result.

47. **Answer (D) is the correct answer.** Ordinarily, no one after First Bank can become a holder in due course unless First Bank indorses the note. Under the federal holder in due course doctrine, however, the FDIC automatically acquires the rights of a holder in due course when it takes over an insolvent bank. The FDIC can transfer those rights to MegaBank. The final paragraph of Official Comment 5 to Section 3-302 explains these principles. **Answers (A), (B), and (C) are incorrect** for this reason.

48. **Answer (A) is the correct answer.** When asked to pay a negotiable instrument by someone other than the payee, the maker may assert offset claims that the maker has against the payee only if the claims "arose from the transaction that gave rise to the instrument." § 3-305(a)(3). Jill's claim on the certificate of deposit did not arise from the loan transaction in 2013 because she purchased the certificate of deposit earlier, in 2011. Because Jill cannot assert the claim at all, it does not matter whether MegaBank has the rights of a holder in due course. Therefore, **Answer (A) is correct** and **Answers (B), (C), and (D) are incorrect.**

49. **Answer (A) is the correct answer.** Holder in due course status is not conferred upon the purchaser of an instrument who buys it "as part of a bulk transaction not in the ordinary course of business of the transferor." § 3-302(c). MegaBank bought Jill's note as part of a bulk transaction. On the probable assumption that this was not a transaction in the ordinary course of First Bank's business, MegaBank will not become a holder in due course, **making Answer (A) a correct answer** and **Answer (D) an incorrect answer.**

Answer (B) is incorrect. Fidelity Bank is the original payee of the note. Rarely does an original payee qualify as a holder in due course. *See generally* § 3-302, cmt. 4.

Answer (C) is incorrect. Section 3-302 requires a party to give value in order to qualify as a holder in due course. But the statute does not mandate a particular amount or percentage. (The fact that the amount of value is considerably or significantly less than the amount payable under the instrument may be used to attack the holder's good faith.)

50. **Answer (B) is the correct answer.** Under Section 3-402, Clark is liable and Zee may be liable. Section 3-401(a) states: "A person is not liable on an instrument unless (i) the person [Clark] signed the instrument, or (ii) the person [Clark] is represented by an agent or representative [Zee] who signed the instrument and the signature [of Zee] is binding on the represented person [Clark] under Section 3-402." Zee's signature does bind Clark under Section 3-402 because Clark cloaked Zee with the authority to act on Clark's behalf, making Clark "liable on the instrument, whether or not [Clark is] identified in the instrument." § 3-402(a). Because the note reveals Zee's agency status for an *undisclosed* principal, Zee is personally liable on the note if FFC is "a holder in due course that took the instrument

without notice that the representative [Zee] was not intended to be liable on the instrument." § 3-402(b)(2). If FFC falls outside the quoted language, Zee is personally liable on the note unless he "proves that the original parties [Zee and the seller] did not intend the representative [Zee] to be liable on the instrument." § 3-402(b)(2). While Clark's liability can be determined with certainty, more facts are needed to establish Zee's personal liability. Answer (B) correctly statutes this conclusion, **making Answer (B) the correct answer.**

Answer (A) is incorrect because Clark is, and Zee may be, liable.

Answer (C) is incorrect because Clark is liable.

Answer (D) is incorrect because more facts are needed to determine with certainty whether Zee is liable.

51.   **Answer (A) is the correct answer.** Section 3-305(a)(1) lists the so-called "real defenses," which, under Section 3-305(b) are good against even a holder in due course. One of these defenses is "lack of legal capacity . . . which, under other law, nullifies the obligation of the obligor." As discussed in Official Comment 1 (third paragraph), an *ultra vires* act (an act outside the scope of the corporation's authority) which voids (rather than merely renders voidable) the maker's obligation falls within the quoted language. A holder in due course will take subject to such a defense, **making Answer (A) the correct answer.**

Answer (B) is incorrect. An illegal transaction creates a real defense to payment only if the illegality nullifies, or voids, the maker's obligation. Facts are inconclusive.

Answer (C) is incorrect. A seller's knowing, and material, misdescription of goods does not trigger a real defense, even if the misdescription rises to the level of fraud. The buyer may have a cause of action for breach of warranty (or some other lawsuit), but the buyer does not have a real defense.

Answer (D) is incorrect. Duress creates a real defense to payment only if the duress nullifies, or voids, the maker's obligation. Facts are inconclusive. (Also note that duress "is a matter of degree." *See* § 3-305, cmt. 1 (fourth paragraph).)

52.   **Answer (A) is the correct answer.** When Tim wrote "for deposit only" on the check, he made a restrictive indorsement. *See* § 3-206(c). The check was payable to the order of Tim, so upon his receipt of the check he became a holder of the check under Section 1-201. As a holder, his indorsement also is either a blank indorsement or a special indorsement under Section 3-205. Because Tim did not indorse in a manner that directed payment to a particular person, party, or account number, his indorsement is a blank indorsement. For confirmation, see Section 3-205, cmt. 2 (last part of second paragraph). In summary, then, Tim's indorsement is both restrictive and blank, **making Answer (A) the correct answer.**

Answer (B) is incorrect because the indorsement is not special. If Tim had placed an account number in the indorsement (e.g., "for deposit only to account 54321"), then the indorsement would be special under Section 3-205(a). *See* § 3-110(c) (stating that a person may be identified "in any way, including by name, identifying number, office, or account number").

Answer (C) is incorrect because Tim was a holder when he indorsed the check. An anomalous indorsement, defined in Section 3-205(d), is inscribed by a non-holder.

Answer (D) is incorrect because the indorsement is blank, as well as restrictive.

53. **Answer (B) is the correct answer.** The check was taken from Tim, a fiduciary, for value (credit to his account) by Metro Bank, which had knowledge (from the face of the check: "in trust for Meredith Smith, a minor"), of Tim's fiduciary status. And Meredith, through her grandmother, is bringing a claim on the check to recover its proceeds on the basis that Tim breached his fiduciary duty. Therefore, Section 3-307(b) applies. Under that section, Metro Bank has notice of Tim's breach because Tim deposited the check, made payable to Tim in his fiduciary capacity (rather than to himself personally), into his personal account (rather than Meredith's personal account or Tim's fiduciary account). § 3-307(b)(2)(iii). Because Metro Bank is deemed to have notice of Tim's breach, Metro Bank is deemed to have notice of Meredith's claim at the time of deposit. § 3-307(b)(1). And since Metro Bank has notice of Meredith's claim at the time of deposit, Metro Bank cannot be a holder in due course. §§ 3-306, 3-302(a)(2)(v), 3-206(e). Section 3-206(d)(1) then makes Metro Bank liable (Metro Bank being the party "who takes the instrument from the indorsee [Tim] for collection").

The facts do not suggest that ZeeBank knew that Tim violated his fiduciary duties. ZeeBank is the payor bank. ZeeBank may process the check by machine, or by electronic means. It is conceivable that no ZeeBank employee will physically review the check, so ZeeBank should not be liable if payment is made contrary to the intent of the drawer. Furthermore, even if a ZeeBank employee reviewed and noticed the "trust" language on the face of the check, it would not have any independent knowledge or notice that the depositary bank complied with, or disregarded, the drawer's wishes. Therefore, ZeeBank is not liable, a result found in Section 3-206(d)(2) (ZeeBank being a "person who pays the instrument").

The bottom line is that Metro Bank is liable, and ZeeBank is not liable. This result is found in Answer (B), **making Answer (B) the correct answer** and **Answers (A), (C), and (D) incorrect answers.**

54. As Jennifer is asserting a personal defense to payment, Jamestown Bank will win its lawsuit against her only if Jamestown Bank is a holder in due course. § 3-305(b). Jamestown Bank appears to have taken the check in good faith and for value, and no facts suggest that Jamestown Bank had notice of Jennifer's defense. But the absence of Helen's indorsement on a check payable to her order appears to make Jamestown Bank a mere nonholder in possession with rights of a holder, rather than a holder in its own right. Jamestown Bank does not want to be a nonholder in possession asserting the enforcement rights of its transferor, Helen, because Helen's enforcement rights are subject to Jennifer's personal defense. Luckily (for Jamestown Bank), Section 4-205(1) makes Jamestown Bank a holder of the unindorsed check because Helen was a holder under Section 1-201 at the time of deposit (Helen possessed a check payable to her order). As a holder that appears to satisfy all of the conditions of Section 3-302, Jamestown Bank is a holder in due course that can enforce the check against Jennifer free and clear of Jennifer's personal defense.

55. As a result of a 2002 amendment to Section 3-309 (an amendment that only a few states have enacted), the court should rule in favor of Weatherford Company and against ZinnCorp. Section 3-301(iii) permits a person without possession of an instrument to assert enforcement rights in the instrument if the person can satisfy the requirements of Section 3-309. Prior to the 2002 amendments to UCC Article 3, Section 3-309(a) read: "A person not in possession of an instrument is entitled to enforce the instrument if (i) the person was in possession of the instrument and entitled to enforce it when loss of possession occurred . . . ." Under this language, the court could rule against Weatherford Company and in favor

of ZinnCorp because Weatherford Company never possessed the note. But Section 3-309(a) was amended in 2002 to read as follows: "A person not in possession of an instrument is entitled to enforce the instrument if (1) the person seeking to enforce the instrument (A) was entitled to enforce the instrument when loss of possession occurred, *or (B) has directly or indirectly acquired ownership of the instrument from a person who was entitled to enforce the instrument when loss of possession occurred . . .*" (emphasis added). As revised, Section 3-309(a) gives Weatherford Company enforcement rights in the note that it never possessed, because Weatherford Company acquired ownership of the instrument from Farmington Credit, a holder (as stated in the facts) and, therefore, a person entitled to enforce the instrument under Section 3-301(i) when loss of possession occurred. Accordingly, the court should rule in favor of Weatherford Company and against ZinnCorp (at least in those few states that have enacted the 2002 amendments to UCC Article 3).

56.   **Answer (B) is the correct answer.** Section 3-118(a) states: ". . . an action to enforce the obligation of a party to pay a note payable at a definite time must be commenced within six years after the due date . . . stated in the note . . ." The note is payable at a definite time (June 30, 2017), so the applicable statute of limitations is six years from that stated date. Therefore, **Answer (B) is correct** and **Answers (A), (C), and (D) are incorrect.**

57.   **Answer (B) is the correct answer.** Section 3-118(b) states: ". . . if demand for payment is made to the maker [Beth] of a note payable on demand, an action to enforce the obligation of a party to pay the note must be commenced within six years after demand." Since the note is payable on demand, Marci must bring her action within six years after making demand on August 15, 2015. So **Answer (B) is the correct answer** and **Answers (A), (C), and (D) are incorrect answers.**

        Appreciate that if Marci never demanded payment, then her action to enforce the note would be barred "if neither principal nor interest on the note has been paid for a continuous period of 10 years." § 3-118(b).

58.   Helen's concern is misplaced, as the applicable statute of limitations has yet to expire. Under Section 3-118(c) (applicable to "unaccepted drafts," such as the rebate check), Helen must commence her action "within three years after dishonor of the draft or 10 years after the date of the draft, whichever period expires first." Incorporating particular dates into the quoted language, Helen must commence her action within three years of dishonor (before approximately March 1, 2017) or 10 years after the date of the check (before approximately October 1, 2018). As the current month is March 2014, Helen has several more months during which she can initiate a timely lawsuit against MCA for drawer liability under Section 3-414(b).

59.   **Answer (B) is the correct answer.** Section 3-401(a) states: "A person is not liable on an instrument unless . . . (ii) the person [Ima] is represented by an agent or representative [Audra] who signed the instrument and the signature is binding on the represented person [Ima] under Section 3-402." Section 3-402(a) states in relevant part: "If a person acting . . . as a representative [Audra] signs an instrument by signing either the name of the represented person [Ima] or the name of the signer [Audra], the represented person [Ima] is bound by the signature to the same extent the represented person [Ima] would be bound if the signature were on a simple contract." These two statutes working in tandem impose maker liability on Ima through Audra's signature in her capacity as Ima's authorized agent. Because Ima is liable, **Answers (C) and (D) are incorrect.** Section 3-402(b) addresses Audra's personal liability. The instrument fails to reveal that Audra is acting as agent for a disclosed principal, so she cannot avoid personal liability under Section 3-402(b)(1). Therefore, subsection (b)(2) applies. Under that provision, Audra is personally liable to TRZ

Partners (the original payee, and therefore not a holder in due course) unless she "proves that the original parties did not intend [Audra] to be liable on the instrument." Audra's liability, then, turns on the proof she can offer. She may or may not be liable. Answer (B) offers more flexibility, **making Answer (B) the correct answer** and **Answer (A) an incorrect answer**.

60.   Ima remains liable as a maker for reasons stated in the previous answer. Audra's possible liability as a maker turns on the status of ABC Equity Group. Because her signature did not reveal the name of the represented person (Ima), Section 3-402(b)(2) applies. It states in relevant part: ". . . the representative [Audra] is liable on the instrument to a holder in due course that took the instrument without notice that the representative [Audra] was not intended to be liable on the instrument." The facts fail to reveal whether ABC Equity Group is a holder in due course and, if so, whether it acquired the note without notice that Audra was intended to be personally liable. If ABC Equity Group is not a holder in due course, Audra is personally liable unless she proves "that the original parties did not intend [her] to be liable on the instrument." § 3-402(b). The facts do not permit any inference on the intent of TRZ Partners. Even so, the statutory presumption is that Audra will be personally liable to ABC Equity Group unless she carries her burden of proof.

61.   **Answer (B) is the correct answer.** Molly's liability as maker is addressed in Section 3-412, which is silent on the matters of presentment and dishonor. Section 3-412 states that Molly is liable on the note according to its terms. If the note is payable on demand, then presumably the person seeking enforcement must actually demand payment (and Molly has no obligation to voluntarily offer to pay the note prior to such demand). That demand will be a presentment. If the note is payable on a stated date, then by its own terms Molly must pay the note on (or before) that date, or otherwise be in dishonor. But no demand or presentment is required, as the terms of the note dictate when Molly must pay. *Cf.* § 3-502(a) (noting under subsection (1) that a note payable on demand is dishonored if the maker does not pay on the day of presentment, whereas noting under subsection (3) that a note not payable on demand is dishonored if the maker fails to pay on the scheduled date of payment). The correct answer, then, turns on whether the note is payable on demand, or payable at a particular time. For this reason, **Answer (B) is the correct answer** and **Answer (C) is an incorrect answer**.

        Answer (A) and Answer (D) are incorrect answers because they fail to draw a distinction between demand notes and time notes.

62.   **Answer (A) is the correct answer.** Section 3-415(a) states that an indorser's liability is conditional on dishonor. Subsection (a) is expressly subject to the other subsections, however. Subsection (c) states that an indorser's liability is discharged if the indorser is not given notice of dishonor as mandated by Section 3-503. Section 3-503(a) states that unless notice of dishonor has been excused, an indorser's liability may not be enforced unless "the indorser is given notice of dishonor of the instrument complying with this section . . . ." Subsection (c) indicates that "notice of dishonor must be given within 30 days following the day on which dishonor occurs." In summary, then, Eric's indorser liability turns on whether he was given timely notice of dishonor, **making Answer (A) the correct answer** and **Answer (D) an incorrect answer**.

        Answer (B) is an incorrect answer. None of the referenced statutes draws a distinction between a special or a blank indorsement.

Answer (C) is an incorrect answer. None of the referenced statutes draws a distinction between time and demand instruments.

63.   **Answer (D) is the correct answer.** Section 3-415(a) imposes liability on Barry as an indorser when Maker dishonors the note. Barry's liability is "owed to a person entitled to enforce the instrument." § 3-415(a). David, a holder of the note under Section 1-201, is such a person. *See* § 3-301(i) (making a holder a "person entitled to enforce the instrument"). The note has been dishonored, and Barry has received notice of dishonor. The notice was timely under § 3-503(c) (which requires notice be given within 30 days of the day of dishonor) because David informed Barry of the dishonor three weeks after Maker refused to pay. Because notice was timely, **Answer (B) is incorrect.** In summary, then, Barry is liable to David on his indorsement under Section 3-415, **making Answer (D) the correct answer.**

   Answer (A) is incorrect. Section 3-503(b) permits an oral notice of dishonor (although this manner of giving notice is not encouraged for obvious evidentiary reasons).

   Answer (C) is incorrect. Barry's liability as an indorser does not stop with the person to whom he negotiated the instrument. It runs to subsequent transferees, such as David.

64.   **Answer (A) is the correct answer.** The note has been dishonored, and Charlie has received timely notice of dishonor under Section 3-503(c) within 30 days after Maker refused to pay. Therefore, Charlie is liable to David as an indorser under Section 3-415.

   Answer (B) is incorrect. Section 3-503(b) states that notice of dishonor "may be given by any person." Therefore, the fact that Charlie received notice of dishonor from Barry, rather than David, is irrelevant.

   Answer (C) is incorrect. Under the last sentence of Section 3-415(a), an indorser's liability is owed to *subsequent*, not previous, indorsers who pay the instrument. Therefore, Charlie can honor his indorsement contract and recover from Barry as a previous indorser. But if Barry honors his indorsement contract, he can recover only from previous indorsers (and, under Section 3-412, the maker).

   Answer (D) is incorrect. An indorsement accompanied by the phrase "without warranty" is effective to disclaim transfer warranty liability. *See* § 3-416(c) and cmt. 5. But it is not effective to disclaim indorser liability. For that, the indorsement should be accompanied by the phrase "without recourse" (or similar language). *See* § 3-415(b).

65.   An indorsement by a holder is either special or blank. Under Section 3-205(a), a special indorsement "identifies a person to whom it makes the instrument payable." Under Section 3-205(b), an indorsement that is not a special indorsement is a blank indorsement. Charlie's blank indorsement might look like this:

Charlie

Charlie's special indorsement might look like this:

Pay to David

Charlie

66.   If Monica has her choice, she should request Gwen's special indorsement. The nature of the indorsement (special v. blank) has no bearing on Gwen's signature liability under Section 3-

415. But the difference can dictate what might happen if Monica loses the note or has it stolen. If Gwen provides a blank indorsement, she converts the instrument into bearer paper. If Monica loses the note or has it stolen, the finder or the thief will possess bearer paper and become a holder and a person entitled to enforce the instrument (and convey that status to a subsequent taker, who just might be a holder in due course). But if Gwen provides a special indorsement, the note remains order paper (presumably payable to Monica or her order). If Monica then loses the note or has it stolen, the finder or the thief will possess order paper. But without Monica's indorsement, possession of the order paper will not make the finder or the thief (or any subsequent taker) a holder, or give that person enforcement rights. So Monica should request Gwen's special indorsement, which offers more protection if the note is lost or stolen.

67. No. Section 3-205(c) states: "The holder may convert a blank indorsement that consists only of a signature into a special indorsement by writing, above the signature of the indorser, words identifying the person to whom the instrument is made payable." When Gwen delivered the note, indorsed in blank, to Monica, Monica became a holder under Section 1-201 as a person in possession of bearer paper. Therefore, Monica could convert Gwen's blank indorsement into a special indorsement by writing "Pay to Monica Johnson" above Gwen's signature. Monica took action permitted by Section 3-205(c). And because Gwen's potential liability as an indorser under Section 3-415 does not turn on whether her indorsement is special or blank, Gwen has no reason to be upset by Monica's conduct.

68. **Answer (A) is the correct answer.** Section 3-305(d) permits Keith to assert against Dealer any defense or claim in recoupment that Hal could assert against Dealer, "except the defenses of discharge in insolvency proceedings, infancy, and lack of legal capacity." Odometer tampering may give Hal a defense to payment, and Section 3-305(d) permits Keith to assert this defense against Dealer.

Answer (B) is incorrect. Section 3-305(d) does not permit Keith to assert Hal's bankruptcy discharge as a defense to payment. Bankruptcy concerns are a primary reason why a creditor seeks multiple obligors.

Answer (C) is incorrect. "[T]he obligation of an accommodation party [such as Keith] may be enforced . . . whether or not the accommodation party receives consideration for the accommodation." § 3-419(b).

Answer (D) is incorrect. Nothing in Article 3 (or Article 9) mandates that a creditor first exhaust any rights in collateral before suing an obligor for personal liability. The parties could contractually agree to such an atypical plan, however (in which case Answer (D) could be a correct answer).

69. **Answer (C) is the correct answer.** Dealer effectively disclaimed any indorser liability by adding "Without Recourse" to the indorsement. *See* § 3-415(b). Therefore, **Answer (A) and Answer (B) are incorrect answers**. But Dealer did breach one of the six transfer warranties when it negotiated the note to Finance Company. Dealer breached its express warranty concerning the odometer reading, giving Meredith a cause of action for the breach. Therefore, Finance Company has a cause of action against Dealer for breaching the transfer warranty found in Section 3-416(a)(4): "the instrument is not subject to a defense . . . of any party [Meredith] which can be asserted against the warrantor [Dealer]." Because Finance Company has breached a transfer warranty (but has effectively disclaimed any indorser

liability), **Answer (C) is the correct answer** and **Answer (D) is an incorrect answer**.

70. **Answer (C) is the correct answer.** AmeriBank dishonored the check, triggering drawer liability for Holly under Section 3-414(b) and indorser liability for Andrew under Section 3-415(a). Nothing in the former suggests that Holly's signature liability is discharged with the passage of a brief time between issuance and dishonor, **making Answer (B) an incorrect answer.** But Section 3-415(a) is expressly subject to subsection (e), which discharges an indorser's liability if the check is not given to the depositary bank "within 30 days after the day the indorsement was made." Andrew indorsed the check no later than July 15. Luke deposited the check on August 30, more than 30 days after Andrew indorsed the check. Therefore, his signature liability is discharged, **making Answer (C) the correct answer** and **Answer (A) an incorrect answer.**

    Answer (D) is incorrect. Nothing in Article 3 requires Luke to exhaust his post-dishonor remedies against a bank before he can seek recovery from the drawer or a previous indorser.

71. **The correct answer is (A).** The instrument was issued for value ($200,000) given for the benefit of Melissa and Hannah (who intend to use the funds to purchase the office building), and Mark, Ruth, John, and Abigail have signed the instrument to incur signature liability without being a direct beneficiary of the value given ($200,000). Therefore, under Section 3-419(a), Melissa and Hannah are "accommodated parties" and Mark, Ruth, John, and Abigail are "accommodation parties."

    Answer (B) is incorrect. Under Section 3-204(a), the presumption is that a signature is an indorsement, but that presumption is rebuttable by relevant and contrary facts (e.g., terms of the instrument, placement of the signatures, etc.). The facts indicate that Melissa and Hannah signed at the conclusion of the text, typically the place for a maker's signature. The facts state that Mark, Ruth, John, and Abigail signed their names on the back of the last page, often the place for an indorsement. Therefore, the placement of the six signatures suggests that the note was signed by two makers (co-makers) and four indorsers, not six makers (co-makers).

    Answer (C) is incorrect. Because Mark, Ruth, John, and Abigail are not holders (Lender, the payee, will be the holder), their signatures under Section 3-205(d) are anomalous indorsements. Therefore, the first part of Answer (C) is correct. But because the four individuals are accommodation parties, they also are sureties. *See* § 3-419, cmt. 3 (second paragraph) ("An accommodation party is always a surety."). Therefore, the second half of Answer (C) is incorrect, **making Answer (C) an incorrect answer.**

    Answer (D) is incorrect. As anomalous indorsers, Mark, Ruth, John, and Abigail may be entitled to timely notice of dishonor as a predicate to signature liability. *See* §§ 3-415(c), 3-503.

72. **Answer (B) is the correct answer.** Melissa and Hannah, the accommodated parties, have a right of contribution against each other, but they have no rights against the four accommodation parties. Mark, Ruth, John, and Abigail, as accommodation parties, have a right of contribution against each other, and a right of reimbursement against Melissa and Hannah. *See* §§ 3-419(f); 3-116(a), (b). These principles are correctly stated in Answer B: Mark, an accommodation party, has a right of reimbursement from Melissa (an accommodated party) and a right of contribution from John (an accommodation party).

Answer (A) is incorrect. Melissa has a right of contribution (not reimbursement) from Hannah, and no rights against Abigail.

Answer (C) is incorrect. Hannah has a right of contribution (not reimbursement) from Melissa, and no rights against Ruth.

Answer (D) is incorrect. Ruth has a right of contribution (not reimbursement) from John, and a right of reimbursement (not contribution) from Hannah.

73. **Answer (C) is the correct answer.** Building on the previous answer, Ruth (an accommodation party) has a right of reimbursement against Melissa and Hannah (accommodated parties) and a right of contribution against Mark, John, and Abigail (her fellow accommodation parties). Because there are four accommodation parties, each (as among themselves) must pay their full fair share of 25% of the total debt ($200,000) before they can seek contribution from another party. Therefore, if Ruth has paid $60,000, she has a reimbursement claim for the full $60,000 against Melissa and Hannah, and she has a contribution claim for $10,000 against Mark, John, and Abigail (her full fair share is 25% of $200,000 [$50,000]; she has paid $60,000; the excess payment of $10,000 can be recovered via her right of contribution). Answer (C) reflects this analysis, **making Answer (C) the correct answer.**

Answer (A) is incorrect. Ruth does have a reimbursement claim against Melissa for $60,000, but she has a contribution claim against Abigail for only $10,000 (not $15,000).

Answer (B) is incorrect. Ruth has a reimbursement claim (not a contribution claim) against Hannah for $60,000 (not $30,000).

Answer (D) is incorrect. Ruth has a contribution claim (not a reimbursement claim) against Abigail for $10,000 (not $60,000), and she has a reimbursement claim (not a contribution claim) against Hannah for $60,000 (not $50,000).

74. **Answer (C) is the correct answer.** The contribution percentage among the four accommodation parties remains at 25%. But because an accommodated party (Melissa) has paid $100,000, then the percentage is multiplied by the total amount not yet paid by an accommodated party to determine the full fair share to be paid by an accommodation party before a right of contribution arises. The original debt was $200,000. Melissa, an accommodated party, has paid $100,000. This leaves $100,000 that could be paid by one or more of the four accommodation parties. That amount, divided among the four accommodation parties, is $25,000. Therefore, any accommodation party who pays more than $25,000 has a claim of contribution (not to exceed $25,000) against each of the other three accommodation parties. John, an accommodation party, has paid $40,000. His full fair share (as adjusted for payments by accommodated parties) is only $25,000. He has a contribution claim for the excess payment of $15,000 against the other accommodation parties, including Ruth. For this reason, **Answer (C) is the correct answer.**

Answer (A) is incorrect. Unless the note included atypical language that capped liability for any particular obligor, each of the six individuals is jointly and severally liable for the full $200,000. Therefore, Lender continues to have a claim against John for the unpaid $60,000 (indorser liability).

Answer (B) is incorrect. Melissa has a contribution claim against Hannah (the other accommodated party), but not until she has paid more than 50% of the total debt. Melissa has paid $100,000. She has yet to pay more than her full fair share, so she does not yet have a contribution claim against Hannah. If Melissa had paid $150,000, she would have a contribution claim against Hannah for the excess $50,000.

Answer (D) is incorrect. John does have a reimbursement claim against Hannah for $40,000, but he has a contribution claim against Ruth for $15,000 (not $10,000).

75. **Answer (C) is the correct answer.** Both the Club and Malone are co-makers and liable to Dealer in that capacity under Section 3-412. Unless Malone received a direct benefit from the piano, he is an "accommodation party" and the Club is an "accommodated party" as those terms are defined in Section 3-419(a). As an accommodation party, Malone has a right of recourse (reimbursement) against the Club. § 3-419(f). Those rights of recourse have been impaired by Dealer's failure to perfect its security interest in the piano, resulting in Creditor's ability to obtain a perfected security interest that enjoys priority over Dealer's unperfected security interest (*see generally* UCC § 9-322(a)). As a result of this impairment, Dealer's interest in the piano has dropped to $16,000 ($20,000 fair market value, minus Creditor's $4,000 priority claim), an amount that is $1,000 less than the $17,000 unpaid debt. This $1,000 represents an impairment of collateral, and is the amount by which Malone's liability, as an accommodation party, is discharged under Section 3-605(d). Malone can subtract this $1,000 impairment from his $17,000 liability and must pay $16,000 to Dealer, **making Answer (C) the correct answer** and **Answers (A), (B), and (D) incorrect answers.**

76. **Answer (C) is the correct answer.** As mentioned in the previous answer, Malone's rights of recourse have been impaired by Dealer's failure to perfect its security interest in the piano, resulting in Creditor's ability to obtain a perfected security interest that enjoys priority over Dealer's unperfected security interest (*see generally* UCC § 9-322(a)). As a result of this impairment, Dealer's interest in the piano has dropped to $11,000 ($15,000 fair market value, minus Creditor's $4,000 priority claim), an amount that is $6,000 less than the $17,000 unpaid debt. But of that $6,000 difference, $2,000 represents a current unsecured risk ($17,000 debt v. collateral worth only $15,000), leaving $4,000 as the impairment triggered by Dealer's misbehavior. The $4,000 impairment is the amount by which Malone's liability, as an accommodation party, is discharged under Section 3-605(d). Malone can subtract this $4,000 impairment from his $17,000 liability and must pay $13,000 to Dealer, **making Answer (C) the correct answer** and **Answers (A), (B), and (D) incorrect answers.**

77. **Answer (A) is the correct answer.** Section 3-605(a) addresses what effect, if any, a discharge of John's liability (as a principal obligor) has on the continued liability (and recourse rights) of Alice (as a secondary obligor). Section 3-605(a)(1) states in relevant part: "Unless the terms of the release preserve [Alice's] recourse, [John] is discharged . . . from any other duties to [Alice]." The one-sentence release is silent on Alice's recourse rights. Therefore, John has been discharged from any possible reimbursement claim initiated by Alice. Perhaps rephrased, Alice no longer has any reimbursement (or other recourse) rights against John, **making Answer (B) an incorrect answer.** But what effect does the release have on Alice's liability to Dealer? Section 3-605(a)(2) states in relevant part: "Unless the terms of the release provide that [Dealer] retains the right to enforce the instrument against [Alice], [Alice] is discharged to the same extent as [John] from any unperformed portion of [her] obligation on the instrument." Again, the release is silent on Dealer's enforcement rights against Alice, so Alice's liability on the note is discharged, **making Answer (A) the**

correct answer and **Answer (B)** and **Answer (C) incorrect answers.**

Answer (D) is incorrect. Section 3-604(a) permits Dealer to discharge John's obligation. Neither Section 3-604(a), nor any other provision of Article 3, conditions the discharge on Alice's knowledge or consent. The note itself might include such conditional language, but that language would be atypical.

78.   You should tell Sharon that the damages provision in the deposit account agreement probably is not enforceable, and she is entitled to an additional credit of $270 covering the dishonor fees. Section 4-403(c) states: "The loss from payment of an item contrary to a stop-payment order may include damages for dishonor of subsequent items . . ." The bank may respond by arguing that Article 4 expressly permits parties to contractually vary the statutory contours of the bank-customer relationship, citing Section 4-103(a). True, but Section 4-103(a) also states: ". . . the parties to the agreement cannot disclaim a bank's responsibility for its lack of good faith or failure to exercise ordinary care or limit the measure of damages for the lack or failure." Sharon should argue that the bank employee's digit transposition constituted a failure to exercise ordinary care, resulting in damages of $270. Because the contract provision attempts to both disclaim the bank's duty to exercise ordinary care and cap its liability for damages resulting from a breach of that duty, the provision should not be enforceable. Therefore, Sharon should be entitled to recover the additional $270 from her bank.

79.   Maybe, maybe not. Section 4-403(a) requires Sharon to describe the check with "reasonable certainty" when she places the stop-payment order. The phrase is not statutorily defined, and the deposit account agreement offers no guidance. No doubt the bank will argue that Sharon failed to describe the check with "reasonable certainty" because she incorrectly stated the amount of the check, the piece of information by which the bank's computer flags the check for nonpayment. But when a bank's technology relies exclusively on one or two fields of information, a number of courts have imposed a duty on the bank to inform its customers of this requirement. *See In re Rovell*, 232 B.R. 381, 387-88 (N.D. Ill. 1998) (citing cases); *aff'd on other grounds*, 194 F.3d 867 (7th Cir. 1999). A court relying on this precedent could conclude that Sharon's bank breached this duty of disclosure because neither the deposit account agreement nor the stop-payment order form mention the bank's need for the customer to accurately state the amount of the check. As a result of this breach, Sharon's stop-payment order should be deemed effective (it was timely under the facts), permitting her to recover damages resulting from payment contrary to her stop-payment order.

80.   **Answer (C) is the correct answer.** Lisa, the drawer, may create an "accord and satisfaction" in accordance with the three requirements of Section 3-311(a). First, Lisa must tender her full-payment check in good faith. Answer (C) assumes Lisa has acted in good faith. Second, the amount of Tim's original claim was unliquidated or subject to a bona fide dispute. This condition appears to be met. Third, Tim obtained payment of the check, when he deposited it into his bank account. Therefore, Tim's claim is discharged under Section 3-311(b) because the check, in a conspicuous manner, indicated payment in full. Lisa need not pay the $300, **making Answer (C) the correct answer.**

Answer (A) is incorrect. Lisa has met the conditions of Section 3-311, which nowhere asks Lisa to prove material fraud.

Answer (B) is incorrect. Section 3-311 applies, whether the underlying transaction was for services rendered or goods sold.

Answer (D) is incorrect. Section 3-311 favors Lisa if she meets certain conditions, none of which are sensitive to the amount in dispute.

81. The statement is false. Subsection (b), which discharges Tim's claim, is subject to subsection (c), which offers Tim some hope in the case of an inadvertent accord and satisfaction. Under subsection (c), Tim's claim is not discharged if Tim "proves that within 90 days after payment of the instrument, [Tim] tendered repayment of [$2,200] to [Lisa]." So, as a general rule, unless Tim's invoice included a statement that triggered Section 3-311(c)(1), he can timely return $2,200 to Lisa and preserve his original claim against her. But this statement (the general rule) is subject to subsection (d), which states: "A claim is discharged if [Lisa] proves that within a reasonable time before collection of the instrument was initiated, [Tim] knew that the instrument was tendered in full satisfaction of the claim." The check bore a conspicuous full-payment legend, and it was accompanied by a letter explaining Lisa's calculation of her amount. Tim had the requisite knowledge of Lisa's intent to propose an accord and satisfaction before he deposited the check. Therefore, he cannot invoke the general rule of subsection (c) and preserve his claim by timely returning $2,200 to Lisa.

82. Section 3-310 addresses what happens to the underlying contract when a party takes a check as full or partial payment of the obligation arising from that contract. Under subsection (a), the underlying obligation is discharged to the extent of the amount of a cashier's check (or teller's check or certified check). The reason for immediate discharge is that the financial institution effectively substitutes its own payment obligation for the contract obligor's obligation. The contract obligor has to pay for the cashier's check (or teller's check) (and the bank will not certify a check without confirming, and then probably freezing, funds in the obligor's account). It should not have to pay for the special check and still remain liable on the underlying contract. A party who takes the special check is expected to forego pursuing the contract obligor and instead look to the financial institution to honor its obligations on the instrument. But under subsection (b), the result is different if the contracting party pays with a personal check. In that case, the underlying contract obligation is not discharged (because the personal check has yet to be presented for payment and honored). Instead, the contract obligation is merely suspended in the amount of the check (with suspension continuing until the check is dishonored, paid, or certified). If the personal check is dishonored, the suspension is lifted (and the contract obligee, as a general rule, can pursue its contract rights and its rights on the instrument). If the check is paid or certified, then the underlying obligation is discharged.

83. **Answer (D) is the correct answer.** Presentment warranties are made by any "person obtaining payment" of a check and any "previous transferor." §§ 3-417(a), 4-208(a). Frank transferred the check to First Bank at the time of deposit. § 3-203(a). Therefore, he warranted, among other things, that he was a person entitled to enforce the check at the time of transfer. This is a false statement, and therefore a breach of the warranty. Frank was not a holder because the check was payable to Robert (who had yet to indorse the check). He cannot claim enforcement rights as a person with the rights of a holder, because he involuntarily obtained possession of the check (frustrating the "delivery" requirement of the shelter doctrine of Section 3-203). And Frank had possession of the check, so he is not claiming enforcement rights under Section 3-309. In summary, then, Frank cannot claim that he is a person entitled to enforce the instrument under Section 3-301. As a result, he has breached the presentment warranty regarding his enforcement status, **making Answer (D) the correct answer.**

    Answer (A) is incorrect. First Bank presented the check to Second Bank. That action does not trigger a "transfer" because First Bank is not delivering the check to Second Bank for purposes of giving enforcement rights to Second Bank. Instead, First Bank is delivering the check to Second Bank for purposes of payment. *See* § 3-203, cmt. 1 (last paragraph). Absent any transfer, First Bank makes no transfer warranties.

    Answer (B) is incorrect. Section 3-420(a) says that an action for conversion "may not be brought" by a "payee . . . who did not receive delivery of the instrument." Robert is the payee, but he did not receive delivery. Therefore, he has no conversion action. The policy behind this rule is that a payee who has not received delivery has not lost anything (the payee retains a claim on the underlying obligation). *See* § 3-420, cmt. 1.

    Answer (C) is incorrect. The preceding paragraph explained why Robert has no cause of action for conversion. The only other party who might appear to have a conversion action is Jim, the drawer of the check. But Section 3-420(a) says that an action for conversion "may not be brought" by the "issuer . . . of the instrument . . . ." The reason for this exclusion is that Jim's cause of action is against his bank, Second Bank, under the "properly payable rule" of Section 4-401(a). He does not need a conversion action. *See* § 3-420, cmt. 1. No other party is entitled to bring a statutory conversion action, so no party (including Second Bank) can be liable under that theory.

84. **Answer (C) is the correct answer.** The payor bank may not debit Lisa's account for the check because it was jointly payable to both Grace and Meredith. The bank could not pay the check to Grace without Meredith's indorsement. §§ 4-401(a); 3-110(d) and cmt. 4. Without Meredith's indorsement, the check was not yet properly payable. Therefore, **Answer (C) is the correct answer,** and **Answer (A) and Answer (B) are incorrect answers.**

Answer (D) is incorrect. The UCC does not provide any statutory presumption that a financial institution will breach its duty of ordinary care by cashing a check that exceeds a particular amount.

85.   **Answer (B) is the correct answer.** The person presenting a check (such as Grace) warrants that she is entitled to enforce the check. §§ 3-417(a)(1), 4-208(a)(1). Grace, by herself, was not a holder of the check under Section 1-201 because the check was payable to both Grace and Meredith. And Grace also was not a non-holder in possession with the rights of a holder because Meredith never transferred her enforcement rights to her sister. § 3-203(a), (b). Accordingly, Grace was not a person entitled to enforce the check under Section 3-301, triggering her breach of the presentment warranty.

     Answer (A) is incorrect. Grace presented, rather than transferred, the check to the payor bank. A presentment of a check is not a transfer because the person presenting the check does not intend to give the payor bank the right to enforce the check. *See* § 3-203(a) and cmt. 1 (last paragraph).

     Answer (C) is incorrect. Under Section 3-415, Grace's liability as an indorser is triggered by dishonor. Here, though, the check was paid, rather than dishonored.

     Answer (D) is incorrect. A payor bank may be sued as a defendant for conversion under Section 3-420, but it has no statutory cause of action to be a plaintiff in such an action. Instead, the law provides the payor bank with alternative theories of recovery (such as breach of a presentment warranty).

86.   **Answer (C) is the correct answer.** Meredith has a claim against the payor bank for conversion under Section 3-420(a) because the bank paid the check to a person not entitled to enforce it. As previously explained, Grace (on her own) was not a person entitled to enforce the check under Section 3-301. The exclusionary language in the last sentence of Section 3-420(a) that denies standing to a payee who did not receive delivery of the check (such as Meredith) is inapplicable because Grace, a co-payee, received delivery.

     Answer (A) is incorrect. Only the drawee/payor bank has standing to initiate an action against a party for breaching a presentment warranty on the check. *See* §§ 3-417(a), (b); 4-208(a), (b).

     Answer (B) is incorrect. Only a "transferee" or a "collecting bank" has standing to initiate an action against a party for breaching a transfer warranty on the check. *See* §§ 3-416(a), 4-207(a). At best, Meredith (through her co-payee, Grace) took the check by issuance (from Lisa, the drawer) under Section 3-105, but not by transfer (and therefore not as a transferee) under Section 3-203 (which excludes a delivery from the issuer, such as Lisa). And Meredith is a human, not a collecting bank.

     Answer (D) is incorrect. Only the payor bank's customer (in this case, Lisa) has standing to invoke the "properly payable rule" of Section 4-401(a).

87.   The suggestion may have merit, is worthy of further consideration, and should trigger some follow-up investigation and research. "Ordinary care" is defined in Section 3-103(a)(9) as "observance of reasonable commercial standards, prevailing in the area in which the person is located, with respect to the business in which the person is engaged." Whether Cardinal Bank breached its duty of ordinary care in handling these checks is debatable. Additional information would be helpful. Questions that might generate helpful information include the

following: Did Ima make these deposits in a face-to-face transaction with a bank employee? Did the bank employee ask why Ima was depositing checks not originally issued to her? Did the bank employee ask why some checks were not indorsed by the payee? What response(s), if any, did Ima offer? Does the bank have an internal policy on deposits of business checks into personal accounts? Do other banks in the area have internal policies on this matter? Were the checks part of larger deposits that included legitimate checks? What amounts, per check (or per deposit), were involved? Did a bank employee ever contact the original payee (MegaChurch) to investigate the merits of the deposits? Is there any applicable case law on point? Etc.

88.   **Answer (C) is the correct answer.** Smith & Jones intended payment to Alex (the former employee), but Alex (the intended payee) did not receive payment. So Commerce Bank (the drawee and payor bank) did not pay the check in accordance with the instructions of Smith & Jones. Therefore, payment of the check violated the "properly payable rule" of Section 4-401(a), and Commerce Bank cannot charge the account of its customer (drawer Smith & Jones), leaving Commerce Bank with the loss unless another statute permits Commerce Bank to deflect the loss back to its customer, Smith & Jones. And Section 3-405 is such a statute. Smith & Jones entrusted employee John (the bookkeeper) with "responsibility" (§ 3-405(a)(3)(iii), (iv), or (v)), so John's forgery of Alex's blank indorsement on each check "is effective as the indorsement of the person to whom the instrument is payable [Alex] if it is made in the name of that person," as long as Commerce Bank paid the check in good faith. § 3-405(b). Because the law treats the forgery as effective, each check becomes properly payable, allowing Commerce Bank to debit the account of Smith & Jones, and shifting the loss to the drawer / customer. Therefore, **Answer (C) is the correct answer** (and, accordingly, **Answer (A) is an incorrect answer**). That answer seems correct as a policy matter because Smith & Jones is in a better position to monitor the activities of its employees (such as bookkeeper John) who are entrusted with some sort of financial responsibility. Therefore, Smith & Jones, rather than Commerce Bank, should bear the loss.

   Answer (B) is incorrect. Section 4-406 does place the loss on the customer, but only if the customer fails to timely discover alterations, or problems with its own signature. The statute does not attempt to address loss allocation arising from forged indorsements. *See* § 4-406(c) and cmt. 5.

   Answer (D) is incorrect. Under the facts of this problem, Section 3-404(b) does not shift the loss from Commerce Bank to its customer, Smith & Jones. Such loss shifting may occur under Section 3-404(b)(i) if the person whose intent determines to whom an instrument is payable under Section 3-110 did not intend the named payee to have any interest in the check. But Smith, who signed the checks, did intend to pay former employee Alex Johnson (what other reason would Smith have for signing the checks?). Commerce Bank also cannot shift the loss under Section 3-404(b)(ii) because Alex is a real person (albeit an ex-employee), not a "fictitious person." So Section 3-404(b) offers no solace to Commerce Bank.

89.   Smith & Jones, the drawer of the checks, has no cause of action for any transfer warranty breach or presentment warranty breach because under the applicable statutes it was not a party to whom any such warranties were made. In general, only a drawee / payor bank has standing to sue for breach of a presentment warranty, and only a transferee (or a collecting bank) has standing to sue for breach of a transfer warranty. Smith & Jones fails to qualify under any of the referenced statutes. But it may have an action against Fidelity Bank under

Section 3-405(b) for comparative negligence. The second sentence of that statute permits Smith & Jones (as "the person bearing the loss" under the assumed facts) to recover some or all of its loss from Fidelity Bank (as a person taking the check "for value or for collection"), if Fidelity Bank "failed to exercise ordinary care . . . and that failure substantially contributed to loss resulting from the fraud . . . ." Given the right facts, Fidelity Bank may be liable for at least part of the loss. *See* § 3-405, cmt. 4.

90.   Fidelity Bank may indeed be able to recover some or all of its loss from John for his breach of a transfer warranty. The movement of the check from John to Fidelity Bank was a "transfer" under Section 3-203(a): "delivery" (a voluntary movement under Section 1-201) by John, the non-issuer (Smith & Jones, the drawer, was the issuer), to Fidelity Bank for the purpose of giving Fidelity Bank the right to enforce the instrument. Presumably John transferred the instrument for "consideration" (e.g., credit posted to his account). Therefore, he made the six warranties in Section 3-416(a) (or Section 4-207(a)) to his transferee, Fidelity Bank. And because he forged Alex's blank indorsement, he breached the second warranty (signatures are authentic and authorized). Therefore, Fidelity Bank, which took the instrument in good faith, can recover some or all of its loss from John for breaching a transfer warranty.

91.   **Answer (B) is the correct answer.** The "imposter rule" of Section 3-404(a) applies in two situations. First, it applies when an imposter impersonates "the payee of the instrument." Barry impersonates the payee, Gary Thompson, in both Answers (A) and (D), so Section 3-404(a) applies, **making Answers (A) and (D) incorrect answers**. Some might conclude that Section 3-404(a) does not apply to Answer (D) because Barry never forged Gary's indorsement. For the "imposter rule" to apply, we must find an indorsement "in the name of the payee." That phrase is the topic of Section 3-404(c), which states that "an indorsement is made in the name of a payee if . . . (ii) the instrument, whether or not indorsed, is deposited in a depositary bank to an account in a name substantially similar to that of the payee." The quoted language is illustrated by the facts in Answer (D). So, despite no indorsement, Section 3-404(a) does apply in Answer (D), **making Answer (D) an incorrect answer**.

The second situation to which Section 3-404(a) applies is when the imposter impersonates "a person authorized to act for the payee." In Answer (B), Barry is misrepresenting his status as Gary's agent, but he is not misrepresenting that he is Barry. In Answer (C), Barry is misrepresenting that he is Bill. The "imposter rule" applies to the misrepresentation in Answer (C) (**making Answer (C) an incorrect answer**), but it does not apply to the misrepresentation of mere status in Answer (B) (**making Answer (B) the correct answer**). This subtle distinction is best noted in former Section 3-405, cmt. 2 (" 'Imposter' refers to impersonation, and does not extend to a false representation that the party is the unauthorized agent of the payee."). Although this helpful guidance was not carried forward into the current statutory language and commentary, no change in law on this point was intended.

92.   **Answer (B) is the correct answer.** Fidelity provides ZC with a monthly bank statement that provides the minimum information required by Section 4-406(a). Therefore, ZC has the examination and reporting duties imposed by Section 4-406(c). But those duties extend only to unauthorized alterations, and unauthorized signature(s) of the customer / drawer. Section 4-406 does not address loss allocation on checks if the sole tangible mischief is a forged indorsement. *See* § 4-406, cmt. 5 ("Section 4-406 imposes no duties on the drawer to look for

unauthorized indorsements."). Checks #2 and #6 raise concerns with ZC's signature, and check #5 has been altered. Therefore, Section 4-406 may address the loss allocation on these checks. But check #3 bears only a forged indorsement, a problem not covered by Section 4-406. Therefore, **Answer (B) is the correct answer**, and **Answer (A), Answer (C), and Answer (D) are incorrect answers**.

93. **Answer (C) is the correct answer.** As noted in the previous explanation, Section 4-406 does not address loss allocation on checks bearing forged indorsements. Therefore, Section 4-406 has no application to the loss allocation for check #7, **making Answer (D) an incorrect answer**. Section 4-406 does address loss allocation for alterations, and problems with the drawer's signature, so it could apply to checks #1, #2, and #6. But the purpose of Section 4-406 is to place the loss on the customer who breaches its duties to examine and report. In this instance, check #1 was paid during the period covered by the first statement covering the period of mischief. The duties cannot commence until the customer receives the statement, on or about June 12. A breach of any duty might arise thereafter, but not before. Therefore, the policy of Section 4-406 is not advanced by imposing the loss on the customer with respect to problem checks reflected in the first statement. Perhaps rephrased, there is no connection between the breach of the duty, and the loss (chronologically, the loss has occurred before the duty, and any resultant breach, arises). Subsection (d)(1) is not quite so clear, but it does place the initial loss on the customer only "if the bank also proves that it suffered a loss by reason of the failure" of the customer to comply with its duties. It is not enough that the customer breached its duties. Its noncompliance must lead to a loss suffered by the bank. That is difficult to prove, absent somewhat unusual circumstances (e.g., during the period of the customer's noncompliance, a potential defendant suffered financial problems, making it a less attractive defendant by the time the customer finally reported the problem to the payor bank). For these reasons, then, **Answer (A) is an incorrect answer**.

The same reasoning can apply to check #2. It was paid on June 13, *after* the first statement was returned on June 12. But the difference is only one day, and Section 4-406(c) refers to "reasonable promptness." It does not mandate that the customer must review and discover the mischief within minutes, hours, or a few days after receiving the statement, or otherwise be held in breach of its duties. At some time, the appropriate period of "reasonable promptness" for review should terminate, but by any measurement the period should extend for at least a day or two after receipt of the statement. *Cf.* § 4-406(d)(2) (referring to "a reasonable period of time, not exceeding 30 days"). Therefore, Section 4-406 should probably place the loss for check #2 on Fidelity, **making Answer (B) an incorrect answer**.

That leaves check #6. It bears mischief covered by Section 4-406 (concerns with the drawer's signature), and it was paid on July 31, more than a month after ZC received the June statement from which it could have discovered the wrongdoing of its chief financial officer. This is the type of loss, by a repeat offender, that Section 4-406 aims to deflect to the customer who breaches its examination duty, **making Answer (C) the correct answer**.

94. **Answer (A) is the correct answer.** As noted in the previous explanation, Section 4-406 (as a general rule) leaves the loss with the payor bank with respect to checks reflected on the first statement covering the period of mischief. Check #1 is such a check, and Fidelity is not likely to deflect the loss to its customer under Section 4-406 (although it may be able to do so under another statute).

The other three checks (#4, #5, and #6) were paid several days after ZC received the first statement (on or about June 12), a timely review of which could have revealed the wrongdoing and halted the mischief on these checks. Therefore, Section 4-406 may impose the loss allocation on these three checks on ZC, **making Answer (B), Answer (C), and Answer (D) incorrect answers**.

95. **Answer (D) is the correct answer.** Check #5 has been altered. Section 3-404 and Section 3-405 do not address loss allocation for altered checks. Section 3-406 does, however, making it the only one of the three statutes applicable. Therefore, **Answer (D) is the correct answer**, and **Answer (A), Answer (B), and Answer (C) are incorrect answers**.

96. **Answer (D) is the correct answer.** The drawer's signature has been forged (in part) on Check #6. Section 3-404 and Section 3-405 do not address loss allocation for checks bearing forged drawer signatures. Section 3-406 does, however, making it the only one of the three statutes applicable. Therefore, **Answer (D) is the correct answer**, and **Answer (A), Answer (B), and Answer (C) are incorrect answers**.

97. **Answer (C) is the correct answer.** Check #7, drawn by ZC, bears an indorsement of the payee forged by ZC's chief financial officer. Section 3-404 does not apply to this check. The imposter rule (subsection (a)) is inapplicable (ZC was not induced by any imposter), the officers who co-signed the check intended the named payee to have an interest in the check (negating subsection (b)(i)), and the payee was a legitimate supplier (not a fictitious payee) (negating subsection (b)(ii)). Therefore, **Answer (A) and Answer (B) are incorrect answers**, because they include Section 3-404. Section 3-405 could apply, as the check bears a forged indorsement by an employee with responsibility. Section 3-406 also could apply, as it addresses loss allocation with respect to a check bearing "a forged signature" (a phrase that includes forged indorsements). Therefore, **Answer (C) is correct** because it includes both Section 3-405 and Section 3-406. **Answer (D) is incorrect** because it fails to include Section 3-405.

98. **Answer (C) is the correct answer.** Section 4-406(c) imposes on Monica the "examine and notify" duties if, and only if, Oxford Savings "sends or makes available a statement of account or items pursuant to subsection (a) . . ." Subsection (a) requires Oxford Savings to provide, at a minimum, "information in the statement of account sufficient to allow the customer reasonably to identify the items paid. The statement of account provides sufficient information if the item is described by item number, amount, and date of payment." The statute does not require Oxford Savings to describe the payee, **making Answers (A), (B), and (D) incorrect** and **Answer (C) correct**.

99. **Answer (D) is the correct answer.** Under Section 4-406(d), Monica must "determine whether any payment was not authorized because of an alteration of an item or because a purported signature by or on behalf of the customer was not authorized." Monica, the customer, is the drawer on this account. Rephrased, then, the statute addresses loss allocation for unauthorized drawer signatures and alterations, **making Answer (D) the correct answer**.

Answers (A), (B), and (C) are incorrect answers because they suggest Monica has a duty to discover forged indorsements on her checks. As noted in cmt. 5, "[s]ection 4-406 imposes no duties on the drawer to look for unauthorized indorsements." That exclusion makes sense because Monica typically cannot examine a check and determine whether an indorsement has been forged or is otherwise unauthorized. She is expected to know her own signature, but not the signature of others.

100.   **Answer (B) is the correct answer.** To be a "holder" under Section 1-201, a party must be in possession of: (i) bearer paper or (ii) an instrument that identifies the possessor as the party to be paid. The cashier's check, if payable to the order of Mark, is not bearer paper. Additionally, until Mark indorses the check, only Mark can be a holder of the check. Nancy, although in possession, cannot be a holder of a check payable to the order of Mark. So **Answer (A) is incorrect**.

Nevertheless, Nancy, a nonholder in possession, is a person with rights of a holder. It was difficult to reach that conclusion prior to the 2002 amendments to Article 3. The "shelter doctrine" of Section 3-203(b) does not appear to vest Nancy with any rights because the shelter doctrine applies only to protect a transferee whose transferor was *not* the issuer. § 3-203(a). But Nancy took the check from Heritage Bank, the "issuer" under Section 3-105. **(Therefore, Answer (C) is incorrect.)** So it appears difficult to cloak Nancy with the status of a person entitled to enforce. But a 2002 revision to the "Official Comment" to Section 3-203 comes to Nancy's rescue. As revised, the Official Comment states, in relevant part: "A nonholder in possession . . . also includes any other person who under applicable law is a successor to the holder or otherwise acquires the holder's rights. *For example, it should include a remitter that has received an instrument from the issuer but has not yet transferred or negotiated the instrument to another person.*" (Emphasis added.) This italicized sentence applies to Nancy because she is a "remitter" under Section 3-103(a). Nancy purchased the cashier's check from the issuer, Heritage Bank. The cashier's check is not payable to Nancy. Instead, it is payable to Mark. Because Nancy is a remitter and has "not yet transferred or negotiated the instrument to another person," she is a nonholder that should have rights of a holder and, as such, be a person entitled to enforce the cashier's check under Section 3-301(ii). This result is stated in Answer (B), **making Answer (B) the correct answer** and **Answer (D) an incorrect answer.**

101.   **Answer (A) is the correct answer.** Absent contrary agreement, when Mark takes the cashier's check, Nancy's obligation to pay for the piano "is discharged to the same extent discharge would result if an amount of money equal to the amount of the instrument were taken in payment of the obligation." § 3-310(a). In this problem, the cashier's check is for the same amount as the purchase price ($20,000), so Nancy's obligation to pay the purchase price is completely discharged when Mark takes the cashier's check. Under the facts, however, Mark has yet to "take" the check because it was stolen from Nancy. Therefore, Nancy's underlying contract obligation to pay the purchase price is unaffected by the parties' agreement to use a cashier's check.

Answer (B) is incorrect. The first part of the statement is true. Thief has not acted in good faith, nor did Thief give value. Therefore, Thief cannot be a holder in due course. *See* § 3-302(a)(2). Thief can negotiate the stolen check to a party that does take the check in good faith, for value, and without notice of any defenses or claims. However, because the check was payable to the order of Mark, no one other than Mark can ever be a holder. And a party who is not a holder cannot be a holder in due course.

Answer (C) is incorrect. Mark fits within the definition of "claimant" in Section 3-312(a)(2): "a person who claims the right to receive the amount of a cashier's check . . . that was lost, destroyed, or stolen." Under Section 3-312(b), Mark may assert a claim to the stolen cashier's check if he is "the remitter or payee of a cashier's check." Nancy is the remitter, but Mark is the payee of the cashier's check. So far, so good. In addition, however, Mark must provide a "declaration of loss." That term is defined in Section 3-312(c) and requires Mark to declare that he "lost possession of a check." He did not. He never had possession. Thief stole the check from Nancy, not Mark. Therefore, Mark has no standing to assert an enforceable claim to the check under Section 3-312.

Answer (D) is incorrect. While the check was in her possession, Nancy was a remitter. As noted previously, a remitter is a person entitled to enforce the check under Section 3-301 (a nonholder in possession with the rights of a holder). After the check is stolen, she continues to enjoy enforcement rights through Section 3-301(iii) (a nonpossessor) and Section 3-309 ("Enforcement of Lost, Destroyed, or Stolen Instrument").

102.   **Answer (C) is the correct answer.** Section 3-312 provides a statutory mechanism for selected parties to bring a claim for lost, stolen, or destroyed cashier's checks (and also teller's checks and certified checks). Nancy, a remitter, is a "claimant" under Section 3-312(a). She meets (or can meet) all four of the requirements of Section 3-312(b). Therefore, under Section 3-312(b)(1), her claim becomes enforceable on the later of: (i) July 5, when she asserts her claim, and (ii) 90 days after July 1, the date of the check. The check is dated July 1, and a date 90 days thereafter will be later than July 5. So her claim becomes enforceable 90 days after July 1, **making Answer (C) the correct answer** and **Answers (A), (B), and (D) incorrect answers**.

103.   **Answer (A) is the correct answer.** The analysis turns on whether Heritage Bank paid a person entitled to enforce the check. If so, Heritage is excused from paying Nancy's claim (and Answer (C) is the correct answer). § 3-312(b)(2). But if not, Heritage must pay Nancy's claim (and Answer (A) is the correct answer). § 3-312(b)(4). Thief's forgery of Mark's indorsement effectively prevents any subsequent party from being a person entitled to enforce. The instrument is treated as if Mark had not indorsed the instrument. Therefore, no one, other than Mark, can be a holder. And while Thief and subsequent parties (e.g., Pemberton Bank) are nonholders in possession, they do not have rights of a holder, either through the "shelter doctrine" of Section 3-203 or otherwise. Pemberton Bank will receive no greater rights than its customer, Thief. But Thief has no enforcement rights to the check because he stole the check, preventing "delivery" (voluntary movement under Section 1-201). And absent "delivery," there is no "transfer" and the "shelter doctrine" does not apply. § 3-203(a), (b). Accordingly, Thief cannot assert Nancy's (or Mark's) enforcement rights. Because Thief is not a person entitled to enforce the check, so, too, is Pemberton Bank. Therefore, Heritage Bank made payment to a party that was not a person entitled to enforce the cashier's check. Accordingly, Heritage Bank must pay Nancy's claim when it becomes enforceable (§ 3-312(b)(4)), **making Answer (A) the correct answer** and **Answer (C) an incorrect answer**.

Answer (B) is incorrect. A quick perusal of the rules in Section 3-312 reveals that payment on presentment does not, by itself, excuse liability for Nancy's claim, even if that claim does not become enforceable until after presentment.

Answer (D) is incorrect. As discussed in a previous answer, Nancy's underlying contract obligation to pay for the piano is not discharged under Section 3-310(a) until Mark has taken the cashier's check. Mark has never taken the check (which was stolen from Nancy, not Mark). Therefore, Nancy's underlying contract obligation to Mark remains enforceable, and has yet to be discharged.

104. If Thief stole the check after Nancy had written her blank indorsement on the check, then Heritage Bank's payment to Pemberton Bank is a payment to a person entitled to enforce the check, and Heritage Bank is not obligated to honor Nancy's claim when it becomes enforceable. *See* § 3-312(b)(2). Nancy's blank indorsement converts the check into bearer paper. Thief's theft of bearer paper makes Thief a "holder" under Section 1-201 and a person entitled to enforce the check under Section 3-301(i). At the time of deposit, Pemberton Bank enjoys the same status. If Thief does not indorse the check, it remains bearer paper and Pemberton Bank is a holder. If Thief does indorse, Thief presumably will indorse in blank (and Pemberton Bank becomes a holder of bearer paper) or will make the check payable to Pemberton Bank through a special indorsement (and Pemberton Bank becomes a holder of order paper that identifies the bank as the party to be paid). Either way, when Heritage Bank pays Pemberton Bank, it is paying a holder and a person entitled to enforce the check. And under Section 3-312(b)(2), Heritage Bank's payment to a person entitled to enforce the cashier's check discharges any further liability on the check, leaving Nancy with a worthless claim.

The moral of the story for Nancy? Do not place a blank indorsement on a check until you are ready to deposit, cash, or negotiate the check. Otherwise, you are unleashing bearer paper, which could affect your ability to recover any loss.

105.   **Answer (A) is the correct answer.** Arizona Bank is a depository bank under Section 4-105(2) because it is "the first bank to take an item [the check] . . ." Because Arizona Bank is a depository bank, it cannot be an intermediary bank. *See* § 4-105(4) (defining "intermediary bank" in a manner that excludes the depository bank). **Therefore, Answer (B) and Answer (C) are incorrect answers.** Arizona Bank is forwarding the check for the purpose of ultimate collection, making it a collecting bank under Section 4-105(5). But Arizona Bank is not a presenting bank. Generally, the presenting bank is the next-to-last bank in the collection chain. In this case, that bank is FRB-Dallas. **Therefore, Answer (A) is correct** because Arizona Bank is both a depository bank and a collecting bank. **Answer (D) is incorrect** because Arizona Bank is not also a presenting bank.

106.   **Answer (D) is the correct answer.** FRB-Dallas is neither a depository bank (Arizona Bank) nor the payor bank (Dallas National Bank), so it qualifies as an intermediary bank under Section 4-105(4). Because FRB-Dallas is not the payor bank (Dallas National Bank), it is a collecting bank under Section 4-105(5). And because FRB-Dallas is the next-to-last bank in the collection chain, it is the presenting bank under Section 4-105(6). All three terms appear in Answer (D), **making Answer (D) the correct answer. Answer (A), Answer (B), and Answer (C) are each underinclusive, making them incorrect answers.**

107.   **Answer (D) is the correct answer.** Dallas National Bank, the payor bank, is "accountable" (liable) for the check if it "does not pay or return the item or send notice of dishonor until after its midnight deadline." § 4-302(a)(1). A bank's "midnight deadline" is "midnight on its next banking day following the banking day on which it receives the relevant item . . . ." § 4-104(a)(10). Dallas National Bank received the check on Tuesday at 4:30 p.m. Tuesday is typically a banking day, so the bank's midnight deadline appears to be midnight on Wednesday. But Section 4-108 allows a bank to establish a cut-off hour of 2:00 p.m. or later, and most (if not all) banks do establish such a cut-off hour. Therefore, it is probably safe to assume that Dallas National Bank has established a cut-off hour of 2:00 p.m. or 3:00 p.m., which means that a check received at 4:30 p.m. on Tuesday is treated as if it is received on Wednesday. As such, the bank's midnight deadline becomes midnight on Thursday. And if Dallas National Bank fails to make its "pay or dishonor" decision by midnight on Thursday, it will become "accountable" (liable) for the check, **making Answer (D) the correct answer.**

Answer (C) is an incorrect answer. Section 4-302(a)(1) does impose on Dallas National Bank a duty to "settle" for the check no later than midnight of the banking day of receipt. (For a definition of "settle," see § 4-104(a)(11).) Under the analysis of the previous paragraph, the bank's implementation of an afternoon cut-off hour means that Dallas National Bank received the check not on Tuesday, but Wednesday. Therefore, it has until midnight on Wednesday to settle the check. Answer (C) suggests that the settlement deadline is Tuesday, not Wednesday, **making Answer (C) an incorrect answer.**

Answer (A) and Answer (B) are incorrect answers because a check that creates an overdraft, in any amount, can be properly payable. *See* § 4-401(a).

108.   **Answer (A) is the correct answer.** Section 4-401(b) states: "A customer [Shirley] is not liable for the amount of an overdraft if the customer [Shirley] neither signed the item nor benefited from the proceeds of the item." This provision appears to make Answer (D) the correct answer. But a bank can contract around the statutory protections afforded its customers as long as it does not "disclaim . . . responsibility for its lack of good faith or failure to exercise ordinary care or limit the measure of damages for the lack or failure." § 4-103(a). Therefore, the contract provision is enforceable and overrides Shirley's statutory protection found in Section 4-401(b), **making Answer (D) incorrect.** As a result, Paradise Savings should be able to recover the $700 overdraft from Shirley, **making Answer (A) the correct answer.**

    Answer (B) is incorrect. A check is properly payable even if payment creates an overdraft. § 4-401(a).

    Answer (C) is incorrect. Paradise Savings may honor a postdated check (otherwise properly payable) prior to its date, absent timely notice from Hal that the check was postdated (and the facts do not suggest that Hal gave any notice). § 4-401(c). This rule is necessary because the check collection process is automated, and the date of the check is not part of the information found on the MICR line. The date on the check is not expected to come to the attention of any bank employee unless the customer timely discloses to a bank employee the postdated nature of the check. Absent such timely disclosure, the bank may process the check prior to any date thereon.

    Overdraft protection should be the topic of conversation when the customer opens the account. Does the customer want overdraft protection? Will the bank offer it? Will the amount of overdraft protection be capped at a particular amount? Will the bank charge for the overdraft protection? Will it charge interest on the overdraft amount? If so, what will the interest rate be? These and other issues should be addressed by the parties. If the parties have agreed that the bank will *not* offer overdraft protection, but it does so anyway, the customer may have a breach of contract action against the bank.

109.   **Answer (C) is the correct answer.** Marvin's indorser liability, contingent on dishonor, is discharged under Section 3-415(e) because the check was not presented for payment until November 12, more than 30 days after he indorsed the check on or about April 29.

    Answer (A) is incorrect. The check became overdue 90 days after its issue date of April 2. § 3-304(a)(2).

    Answer (D) is incorrect. Section 4-402(a) states that "a payor bank wrongfully dishonors an item if it dishonors an item that is properly payable . . . ." A check is "properly payable" under Section 4-401(a) if the check "is authorized by the customer and is in accordance with any agreement between the customer and the bank." Connie authorized the check when she signed and issued it to Marvin, and the facts do not suggest that payment will violate the deposit account agreement. Therefore, the check appears to be properly payable (**making Answer (B) an incorrect answer**), placing Broadway Bank at risk for a wrongful dishonor lawsuit if it dishonors what appears to be a properly payable check. But the wrongful dishonor statute — Section 4-402(a) — opens with this language: "Except as otherwise provided in this Article . . . ." And Broadway Bank can indeed find relief elsewhere in Article 4. Section 4-404 relieves Broadway Bank from any obligation to pay the check because it is being presented on November 12, a date more than six months after the issue date of April 2. (The statute also permits Broadway Bank to pay the check, but it must do so in good faith.) Therefore, Broadway Bank may dishonor the check without the risk of liability for wrongful dishonor, **making Answer (D) an incorrect answer**.

110. **Answer (C) is the correct answer.** Francine has authorized payment of the check, but only in the amount of $200. Only to the extent of $200 is the check properly payable under Section 4-401(a). Fidelity Bank was not authorized to debit Francine's account for this $1,800 excess, and Francine is entitled to a credit to her account for this amount. The fact that Francine owed Mark an additional $1,800 is irrelevant (and Mark received a $200 credit, not a $2,000 credit). Therefore, **Answer (A) is an incorrect answer**.

Against whom may Fidelity Bank seek recovery of the $1,800? Section 4-209(a) states that an encoder (Integrity Bank) "warrants to any subsequent collecting bank (FRB-Local) and to the payor bank (Fidelity Bank) or other payor that the information is correctly encoded." Integrity Bank breached this warranty. Section 4-209(c) states: "A person to whom warranties are made under this section (Fidelity Bank, under subsection (a)) may recover from the warrantor (Integrity Bank) as damages for breach of warranty an amount equal to the loss suffered as a result of the breach ($1,800), plus expenses and loss of interest incurred as a result of the breach." Under this statute, then, Fidelity Bank recovers the $1,800 from Integrity Bank, rather than the intervening (non-warranting) collecting bank, FRB-Local. Therefore, **Answer (C) is the correct answer** and **Answer (B) is an incorrect answer**.

Answer (D) is an incorrect answer because Section 4-209 does not give Francine a cause of action against the encoder (the warrantor's liability runs to specific parties, and the drawer is not mentioned in that list). But the drawer does not need that cause of action. The drawer has the "properly payable" cause of action against its own bank under Section 4-401(a).

111. **Answer (D) is the correct answer.** Section 4-403 addresses a customer's ability to place a stop payment order on one of the customer's checks. Subsection (b) permits oral, and written, stop payment orders. Therefore, **Answer (D) is the correct answer**. Note that oral stop payment orders are good for 14 days, whereas written stop payment orders are good for six months.

Subsection (a) places two duties on a customer who wishes to place a stop payment order. First, when contacting the drawee bank, the customer must describe the check "with reasonable certainty." Second, the customer must contact the drawee "at a time and in a manner that affords the bank a reasonable opportunity to act on it" before it takes certain action with respect to the check (such as honoring it). Nothing in subsection (a) places the limits on the placement of a stop payment order that are suggested by the other possible answers to this question. Therefore, **Answer (A), Answer (B), and Answer (C) are incorrect answers** (at least as statements of law).

112. **Answer (C) is the correct answer.** Section 4-403(a) permits "a customer" to place a stop payment order on the check drawn by that customer on the account. A cashier's check is drawn by the bank on its own account. Therefore, it is the bank, and not Alice, who is the "customer" who can place a stop payment order on the check. This point is stated in the accompanying Official Comment 4: "A cashier's check . . . purchased by a customer . . . is not a check drawn on the customer's account . . . ; hence, a customer purchasing a cashier's

check . . . has no right to stop payment of such a check under subsection (a)."

Answers (A), (B), and (D) are incorrect answers. Section 4-403(a) describes the customer's right to place a stop payment order. The limitations suggested in these three answers are nowhere to be found in Section 4-403(a).

113. The bank teller may insist on Richard's indorsement, Celia's indorsement, or both indorsements before the bank will handle the check for collection. Alternatively, the bank might not request any indorsements, as Richard is depositing the check into an account on which the payee — Celia — is a customer. One benefit (to the bank) is that an indorsement creates potential signature liability, and a possible source of recovery under Section 4-215(a), if the drawee dishonors the check. The amount of the check may play a major role in how the teller responds.

Without any indorsement, the teller might wonder if the bank can be a holder (and a possible holder in due course) of the check. It would be taking possession of a check that is payable to another person: Celia. Section 4-205(1) comes to the rescue. That provision states, in relevant part: "[T]he depositary bank becomes a holder of [the check] at the time it receives [the check] for collection if the customer at the time of delivery was a holder of the item, and, if the bank satisfies the other requirements of Section 3-302, it is a holder in due course." Therefore, the lack of Celia's indorsement does not preclude the bank from becoming a holder under Section 1-201, a person entitled to enforce the check under Section 3-301, or a holder in due course under Section 3-302. The teller may conclude, then, that there is no particular need to insist on an indorsement unless the bank wants to preserve its rights under Section 4-215(a) (indorser liability).

114. **Answer (D) is the correct answer.** Subsection 4-303(b) permits the drawee to honor the checks "in any order." The accompanying Official Comment 7 also addresses the issue. "As between one item and another, no priority rule is stated. This is justified because of the impossibility of stating a rule that would be fair in all cases, having in mind the almost infinite number of combinations of large and small checks in relation to the available balance on hand in the drawer's account; the possible methods of receipt; and other variables. Further, the drawer has drawn all the checks, the drawer should have funds available to meet all of them and has no basis for urging one should be paid before another . . ." Because the drawee may honor the checks in any order, **Answer (D) is the correct answer and Answer (B) and Answer (C) are incorrect answers.**

In such a problem, the drawer is concerned that one or more checks may be dishonored, triggering assessment of fees and penalties by various parties (such as the drawee or the payee). For that reason, the drawer may prefer that the bank pay checks in order from smallest amount to largest amount. The drawee may believe that the importance of the checks is determined by the amount (the largest perhaps being the mortgage payment or the car payment, dishonor of which could trigger adverse consequences for the customer) and conclude that it is doing the drawer a favor by paying checks in order from largest amount to smallest amount. What is the typical practice? A newspaper article from November 2006 indicated that eight of the nation's largest banks pay checks from largest to smallest (perhaps disappointing customers worried about fees and penalties on dishonored checks).

Answer (A) is incorrect. To the extent that funds are available to pay a check, that check is properly payable. The bank will wrongfully dishonor at least one of the checks if it dishonors all of the checks, triggering liability to Meredith under Section 4-402.

115. Both terms are defined in Section 3-104. The difference between the two checks is that the drawer and the drawee of a cashier's check are the same bank, whereas the drawer and the drawee of a teller's check are different banks. (Alternatively, a teller's check may be drawn by a bank on a nonbank but payable at or through another bank.) Two differences between these types of checks are worth noting. First, the obligation of a drawer of a cashier's check is addressed in Section 3-412, whereas the obligation of a drawer of a teller's check is addressed in Section 3-414. Second, a cashier's check is deemed "accepted" under Section 3-409 at issuance, whereas a teller's check is not. The acceptance (or non-acceptance) dictates the application of specific presentment warranties. *See, e.g.*, §§ 3-417(a) (applies to "unaccepted" drafts), 4-208(a) (same).

116. The term is defined in Section 3-103(a)(15) as "a person who purchases an instrument from its issuer if the instrument is payable to an identified person other than the purchaser." Assume that Tim has agreed to purchase a car from Lisa for $10,000. Lisa is a bit nervous about taking Tim's personal check, so she insists that Tim pay with a cashier's check. Tim visits his bank and purchases a cashier's check. His bank debits Tim's account for $10,000 and may or may not charge an additional small fee for the service. The bank asks Tim to designate the payee. Tim asks that the check be payable to Lisa. Tim has purchased a check from its issuer (his bank), and the check is payable to someone other than himself. Tim is a remitter. Alternatively, Tim may ask that the check be payable to himself (and he will indorse it over to Lisa). If Tim is the named payee, he is not the remitter (but while he possesses the check he is the holder).

117. **Answer (A) is the correct answer.** A bank can charge back a customer's account only if it fails to receive a final settlement. § 4-214(a). First Bank received a final settlement because Prosperity Bank had no right to return the check after its midnight deadline. Prosperity Bank received the check on the morning of July 17. Its midnight deadline under Section 4-104(a)(10) was the following night at midnight. Prosperity Bank did not notify Prosperity Bank that it was returning the check until July 21. Therefore, there has been final settlement of the check, and First Bank cannot charge back the check to ZeeCorp's account, **making Answer (A) the correct answer.** Instead, First Bank should attempt to recover any loss from Prosperity Bank under Section 4-302(a) on the theory that Prosperity Bank became "accountable" (liable) for the check when Prosperity Bank missed its midnight deadline.

Answer (B) is incorrect because the ability to charge back the check does not turn on how many days have passed since the check was deposited.

Answer (C) is incorrect because a depositary bank may recover credit even if it has been withdrawn by the customer. § 4-214(a).

Answer (D) is incorrect because First Bank cannot charge back the check on which there has been final settlement. There has been final settlement on this check because Prosperity Bank missed its midnight deadline. §§ 4-302(a)(1), 4-301(a).

118. **Answer (D) is the correct answer.** Section 4-405(a) states that a bank's authority to pay a check is not terminated by its customer's death "until the bank knows of the fact of death . . . and has a reasonable opportunity to act on it." So death alone does not terminate

University Bank's authority to pay the $300 check, **making Answer (A) incorrect**. Answers (B) and (C) appear to be correct because officers of University Bank had knowledge of Dru's death as early as July 6, giving University Bank plenty of time to act on that knowledge before the check was presented on July 11. But even with knowledge of Dru's death, University Bank "may for 10 days after the date of death pay . . . checks drawn on or before that date . . . ." § 4-405(b). The check was paid on July 11, within ten days after Dru's death (July 4), so the officers' knowledge of Dru's death did not prevent University Bank from paying this check. During that ten-day period University Bank retained the authority to pay the check of its deceased customer, regardless of the knowledge of any of its officers or employees. So **Answers (B) and (C) are incorrect** and **Answer (D) is correct**. Policy reasons for this result are discussed in Section 4-405, cmt. 2.

119. Nancy appears to have satisfied her two statutory duties under Section 4-401(c): she accurately described all of the details of the check, and she gave notice on August 2 — which appears to be timely since it was given more than 24 hours before the check was presented on August 4. (If a court concludes that the notice was not timely, then the matter ends, with Nancy bearing her losses and losing the lawsuit.) On the assumption that Nancy can carry her burden of proof, then she will invoke these last two sentences of Subsection (c): "If [Nancy's bank] charges against [Nancy's account] a check [on August 5] before the date [August 8] stated in the notice of postdating, [Nancy's bank] is liable for damages for the loss resulting from its act. The loss may include damages for dishonor of subsequent items under Section 4-402." At this point, Nancy's bank points to the restrictive language in the bank account agreement, citing its cap on liability under Section 4-103(a): "The effect of the provisions of this Article may be varied by agreement . . . ." At most, then, Nancy's bank is liable for $450, the amount of the check. Nancy should respond by directing her bank to the remaining language of the first sentence of Section 4-103(a): ". . . but the parties to the agreement cannot disclaim a bank's responsibility for its lack of good faith or failure to exercise ordinary care or limit the measure of damages for the lack or failure." Nancy will argue that the bank officer's failure to forward her instructions to the appropriate banking department was a breach of its duty of ordinary care, and Nancy's damages flowed from such breach. The terms of the contract cannot be enforced under these facts, and Nancy should be able to recover her damages under the last two sentences of Section 4-401(c).

120. **Answer (C) is the correct answer.** Section 3-414(b) gives Edith a cause of action against Lisa, the drawer of the check, upon dishonor. This cause of action is mentioned in all four answers. But all four answers cannot be correct.

Section 4-402 creates a cause of action for wrongful dishonor. Subsection (b) states that the "payor bank is liable to its customer." Therefore, Lisa (the drawer-customer) may have a cause of action against Omega Bank for wrongful dishonor. But Edith has no such cause of action. Therefore, **Answer (B) and Answer (D) are incorrect answers**.

Section 4-214(a) gives to Alpha Bank the right of chargeback if it takes such action "by its midnight deadline or a longer reasonable time after it learns the facts." The facts indicate that Alpha Bank took immediate action upon receiving timely notice of dishonor from Omega Bank. Therefore, Edith has no cause of action against Alpha Bank for wrongful chargeback. This cause of action appears in Answers (A) and (B), **making Answer (A) and Answer (B) incorrect answers**.

Of the three possible causes of action listed, Edith has only the cause of action against Lisa on the check, **making Answer (C) the correct answer**.

121. **Answer (C) is the correct answer.** Section 4-402 creates the cause of action for wrongful dishonor. Subsection (b) addresses the scope of liability. It states: "A payor bank is liable to its customer for damages proximately caused by the wrongful dishonor of an item. Liability is limited to actual damages proved and may include damages for an arrest or prosecution of the customer or other consequential damages." Answer (C) captures this language, **making Answer (C) the correct answer**.

    Answer (A) is incorrect. It states the general remedy under the UCC, as found in Section 1-305(a). But the general remedy is trumped by the specific remedy for wrongful dishonor found in Section 4-402(b).

    Answer (B) is incorrect. It states the remedy for breach of ordinary care, as stated in Section 4-103(e).

    Answer (D) is incorrect. It is a made-up formula and has no statutory basis.

122. The question asks for three examples. This answer offers six. It is not an exhaustive list.

    A bank may rightfully dishonor a check: (i) if the check is postdated and the customer has complied with its statutory duties under Section 4-401, (ii) if the customer has placed a stop payment order on the check that meets the statutory requirements of Section 4-403, (iii) that bears the forged signature of the drawer or an unauthorized alteration, (iv) if the customer's account lacks sufficient funds (although the bank may breach its contract with the customer if the parties have agreed that the bank will provide overdraft protection), (v) under the conditions of Section 4-405 (death or incompetence of the customer), and (vi) that is more than six months old under Section 4-404.

123. Under Section 4-403(a), Buyer has the right to place a stop-payment order on a check if Buyer describes the check with "reasonable certainty" and places the order in a timely manner. Some courts require Buyer to prove nothing more, other than its loss.

    Other courts, however, examine whether Buyer truly suffered a loss from the bank's failure to comply with the order. If the bank had indeed honored the order and dishonored the check, Buyer remains liable on the check under Section 3-414(b). And might a party in the chain of collection (e.g., the depositary bank) qualify as a holder in due course, with the right of recovery that is immune from Buyer's personal defenses (such as "I found a better deal elsewhere")? These courts ask Buyer to prove the nonexistence of a holder in due course in the collection chain (alternatively, Buyer must prove that he has a claim or defense that negates his signature liability under Section 3-414(b)).

124. **Answer (D) is the correct answer.** Section 4-403(b) states that a stop-payment order "is effective for six months." Therefore, Seller may wish to present it again after holding it for six months. Six months is approximately 180 days, **making Answer (D) the correct answer**. Appreciate, however, that Section 4-404 permits the drawee to rightfully dishonor a check more than six months old.

    Answers (A), (B), and (C) are incorrect answers because they provide a time period inconsistent with the six-month duration of a stop-payment order under Section 4-403(b).

125.   **Answer (C) is the correct answer.** The term is defined at EFTA § 903(7), 15 U.S.C. § 1693a(7). It means "any transfer of funds . . . which is initiated through an electronic terminal, telephonic instrument, or computer or magnetic tape so as to order, instruct, or authorize a financial institution to *debit or credit an account*" (emphasis added). The term covers both debits and credits, so **Answer (A) is an incorrect answer**. There is no dollar threshold, so **Answer (B) is an incorrect answer**. The difference between Answer (C) and Answer (D) is whether the debit or credit must be made to a consumer's account. The language quoted above merely refers to an "account," suggesting that any account (whether personal or business) will suffice. But the EFTA defines "account" as a bank account "established primarily for personal, family, or household purposes." EFTA § 903(2), 15 U.S.C. § 1693a(2). Therefore, **Answer (C) is the correct answer** and **Answer (D) is an incorrect answer**.

126.   **Answer (B) is the correct answer.** The term "electronic fund transfer" expressly excludes "any automatic transfer from a savings account to a demand deposit account [e.g., a checking account] pursuant to an agreement between a consumer and a financial institution for the purpose of covering an overdraft or maintaining an agreed upon minimum balance in the consumer's demand deposit account." EFTA § 903(7)(D), 15 U.S.C. § 1693a(7)(D).

   Answer (A) is an incorrect answer. Rephrased, the transaction will trigger the definition of "electronic fund transfer." The definition covers withdrawals, whether initiated by the customer or the customer's creditor (assuming that the customer has authorized the creditor to initiate the withdrawal process). And the definition does not include a dollar threshold.

   Answer (C) is an incorrect answer. Rephrased, the transaction will trigger the definition of "electronic fund transfer." One might conclude otherwise, as the statutory definition excludes a funds transfer pursuant to "a transaction originated by check, draft, or similar paper instrument." But the Regulation E Commentary (found in some softback statutory supplements) states that the term "electronic fund transfer" does include a payment pursuant to a customer's delivery of a check to a merchant "to enable the merchant . . . to capture the routing, account, and serial numbers to initiate the transfer, whether the check is blank, partially completed, or fully completed and signed; . . . or whether the check is retained by the consumer, the merchant or other payee, or the payee's financial institution." Regulation E Commentary § 205.3(b), Paragraph 3(b)(1)(v).

   Answer (D) is an incorrect answer. Rephrased, the transaction will trigger the definition of "electronic fund transfer." The definition includes credits to Melissa's account. It does not matter that the initiator of the transfer is not a natural person (e.g., Melissa's corporate employer). Nor does it matter that the reciprocal entry is a debit from a business account.

127.   **Answer (A) is the correct answer.** The grant of rulemaking authority is found in EFTA § 904(a)(2), 15 U.S.C. § 1693b(a)(2). The term "Board" is a reference to "the Board of

Governors of the Federal Reserve System." EFTA § 903(3), 15 U.S.C. § 1693a(3). Therefore, **Answer (A) is the correct answer** and **Answer (B), Answer (C), and Answer (D) are incorrect answers**.

128. **Answer (B) is the correct answer.** The grant of rulemaking authority is found in EFTA § 904(a)(1), 15 U.S.C. § 1693b(a)(1). The term "Bureau" is a reference to "The Bureau of Consumer Financial Protection." EFTA § 903(4), 15 U.S.C. § 1693a(4). Therefore, **Answer (B) is the correct answer** and **Answer (A), Answer (C), and Answer (D) are incorrect answers**.

The Bureau was established pursuant to the Dodd-Frank Wall Street Reform and Consumer Protection Act of 2010. Readers interested in learning more about the Bureau may wish to visit its website here: http://www.consumerfinance.gov/.

129. **Answer (C) is the correct answer.** In drafting the EFTA, Congress delegated some rulemaking authority to the Board. *See* EFTA § 904(a)(2), 15 U.S.C. § 1693b(a)(2). Regulation E states in its "authority" provision (12 C.F.R. § 205.1): "The regulation in this part, known as Regulation E, is issued by the Board of Governors of the Federal Reserve System pursuant to the Electronic Fund Transfer Act (15 U.S.C. 1693 *et seq.*)." None of the other federal regulations, all promulgated by the Board, state that the Board's authority is derived from the EFTA, **making Answer (C) the correct answer**.

Answer (A) is incorrect. Regulation CC states in its "authority" provision (12 C.F.R. § 329.1(a)) that the Board's authority is derived from the Expedited Funds Availability Act.

Answer (B) is incorrect. Regulation M states in its "authority" provision (12 C.F.R. § 213.1(a)) that the Board's authority is derived from the consumer leasing provisions of the Truth in Lending Act.

Answer (D) is incorrect. Regulation Z states in its "authority" provision (12 C.F.R. § 226.1(a)) that the Board's authority is derived from the Truth in Lending Act and the Competitive Equality Banking Act of 1987.

130. **Answer (C) is the correct answer.** A consumer's liability for unauthorized electronic fund transfers is addressed in EFTA § 909, 15 U.S.C. § 1693g. The language is rather tough to follow, and readers may find the liability scheme as stated in Regulation E to be more "user friendly." *Cf.* Regulation E § 205.6. In general, a consumer's liability will not exceed $50 if he or she timely notifies the financial institution within two business days following the consumer's discovery of the loss or theft of the access device (e.g., the card). The liability cap escalates to no more than $500 if the consumer fails to give timely notice of the loss or theft of the access device. If the consumer fails to detect the problem within 60 days after the financial institution has transmitted to the consumer a statement on which the unauthorized EFT is reflected, the consumer's liability is not capped (with respect to unauthorized EFTs that occur after that 60-day period).

In this problem, Meredith discovered the theft of her card on Tuesday morning. She gave notice to her bank that afternoon, so her notice was timely. Therefore, her liability is capped at $50, **making Answer (C) the correct answer** and **Answer (A), Answer (B), and Answer (D) incorrect answers**.

131. Common sense, and written admonitions from our financial institution, remind us not to

place our personal identification number on (or near) the card. Yet, perhaps like Meredith, we disregard our common sense (or written admonitions) and act in a manner that might be deemed negligent (or violate what I call "the clearly stupid rule"). The Regulation E Commentary addresses this matter. "Negligence by the consumer cannot be used as the basis for imposing greater liability than is permissible under Regulation E. Thus, consumer behavior that may constitute negligence under state law, such as writing the PIN on a debit card or on a piece of paper kept with the card, does not affect the consumer's liability for unauthorized transfers." Regulation E Commentary § 205.6(b) (paragraph #2). Therefore, Meredith's liability remains capped at $50, even if she taped her PIN to the card, facilitating Thief's unauthorized access to her account.

132. No. "Except as provided in this section, a consumer [such as Meredith] incurs no liability from an unauthorized electronic fund transfer." EFTA § 909(e), 15 U.S.C. § 1693g(e). The federal statute offers a "worst case" scenario. Contrary contract provisions (or state law) cannot increase Meredith's liability beyond the federal statutory scheme.

133. Yes. While contrary state or contract law may not *increase* Meredith's liability, contrary state or contract law may *decrease* Meredith's liability. "Nothing in this section imposes liability upon a consumer for an unauthorized electronic fund transfer in excess of his liability for such a transfer under other applicable law or under any agreement with the consumer's financial institution." EFTA § 909(d), 15 U.S.C. § 1693g(d). Therefore, if Meredith lived in a state with the hypothetical statute, then her liability would be governed by state law because the state statute imposes less liability than does the EFTA. As a result, Meredith seems to have no liability for the unauthorized electronic fund transfers.

134. The loss allocation does not change. Meredith remains liable only for $50. Under the EFTA, notice is sufficient "when such steps have been taken as may be reasonably required in the ordinary course of business to provide the financial institution with the pertinent information, whether or not any particular officer, employee, or agent of the financial institution does in fact receive such information." EFTA § 909(a), 15 U.S.C. § 1693g(a). Meredith's telephone call to her account representative is a reasonable means of communication (and is expressly authorized by Regulation E § 205.6(b)(5)(ii)). Absent any voicemail message indicating that the representative is away from the office for some period of time, or otherwise indicating that these types of messages should be redirected to another bank employee, Meredith took reasonable steps to inform MegaBank that her access device had been lost or stolen. Such notice remains timely, and her liability under the EFTA remains capped at $50.

135. **Answer (C) is the correct answer.** The unauthorized withdrawals started approximately eight months ago. If Tommy and his wife fail to detect the problem within 60 days after AmeriBank transmitted to them a statement on which the initial unauthorized EFT was first reflected, then Tommy and his wife have uncapped liability with respect to all unauthorized EFTs that occur after that 60-day period. EFTA § 909(a), 15 U.S.C. § 1693g(a). That amount will equal $1,500. Liability for the two unauthorized withdrawals during that 60-day period will not exceed $50 because Tommy and his wife promptly notified AmeriBank after they discovered the problem. *Id.* The total liability, then, will be $1,550, **making Answer (C) the correct answer** and **Answer (A), Answer (B), and Answer (D) incorrect answers.**

If loss is calculated under Regulation E § 205.6, the correct answer seems to be $1,500, rather than $1,550. Regulation E seems to ignore the initial $50 loss until the consumer learns "of the loss or theft of the access device." In this problem, Tommy and his wife have discovered the unauthorized withdrawals, but they have not concluded that their ATM card has been lost or stolen.

136.   The response turns on the interplay between the loss allocation rules of EFTA § 909, 15 U.S.C. § 1693g, and the error resolution provisions of EFTA § 908, 15 U.S.C. § 1693f. Perhaps rephrased, must Tommy comply with the error resolution provisions (including the 60-day notice rule) when invoking the loss allocation rules? Tommy should invoke subsection (e) of the loss allocation rules: "Except as provided in this section, a consumer incurs no liability from an unauthorized electric fund transfer." The loss allocation rules have self-contained notice rules, and nothing "in this section" refers (or defers) to the 60-day notice rule or any other part of the error resolution provisions. Tommy's liability should be calculated solely under EFTA § 909, 15 U.S.C. § 1693g.

137.   **Answer (B) is the correct answer.** Under EFTA § 908(a), 15 U.S.C. § 1693f(a), FirstBank must receive an "oral or written notice" from Holly. Those two options (and only those two options) are stated in Answer (B), **making Answer (B) the correct answer**.

Answer (A) is incorrect because it fails to include the option of oral notice.

Answers (C) and (D) are incorrect because they permit notice by means other than orally or in writing.

138.   **Answer (D) is the correct answer.** Holly's notice must include her name and account number, her belief that an error exists, the amount of the error, and the reasons for her belief. EFTA § 908(a), 15 U.S.C. § 1693f(a). The statute does not require Holly to include any receipts. Therefore, because the question asks for what is *not* required (rather than what *is* required), **Answer (D) is the correct answer** and **Answer (A), Answer (B), and Answer (C) are incorrect answers**.

139.   **Answer (B) is the correct answer.** The statute states that FirstBank must receive Holly's letter "within sixty days after having transmitted to" Holly the statement on which appears the alleged error. FirstBank transmitted the statement to Holly on July 1, so it must receive Holly's letter within 60 days after July 1. Answer (B) correctly states the applicable start date and period, **making Answer (B) the correct answer**.

Answers (A), (C), and (D) are incorrect because they mention an incorrect period of time, state an incorrect start date, or both.

140.   **Answer (B) is the correct answer.** FirstBank received Holly's letter on August 16, well within the 60-day period discussed in the previous answer. Therefore, unless FirstBank provisionally credits Holly's account for the amount of the alleged error, FirstBank "shall investigate the alleged error, determine whether an error has occurred, and report or mail the results of such investigation and determination to [Holly] within ten business days." EFTA § 908(a), 15 U.S.C. § 1693f(a). Because the statute references ten business days, **Answer (B) is the correct answer** and **Answers (A), (C), and (D) are incorrect answers**.

Surprisingly, the statute does not mention when the period of ten business days commences. Possible choices include August 10 (when Holly mails her letter) and August 16 (when FirstBank receives Holly's letter). *Cf.* EFTA § 908(c), 15 U.S.C. § 1693f(c) (referencing a 45-

day period, discussed in the next answer, that is measured from "receipt of notice of the error"). The statute's companion regulation, Regulation E, is more specific and resolves the statutory dilemma. *See* Regulation E § 205.11(c) ("A financial institution shall investigate promptly and . . . shall determine whether an error occurred within 10 business days *of receiving a notice of error.*") (emphasis added). Therefore, unless FirstBank provisionally credits Holly's account for the amount of the alleged error, FirstBank must investigate the merits of Holly's claim and report or mail the results to Holly no later than ten business days after August 16 (the date when FirstBank received Holly's letter).

141. **Answer (D) is the correct answer.** In the previous answer we saw that FirstBank must address the merits of Holly's claim within ten business days of its receipt of her notice. The statute permits FirstBank to "buy" a longer investigation period by provisionally crediting Holly's account within ten business days after receiving her letter. How long is that extended period? And from what date does it start running? "Such investigation shall be concluded not later than forty-five days after receipt of notice of the error." EFTA § 908(c), 15 U.S.C. § 1693f(c). Therefore, **Answer (D) is the correct answer** because it correctly states the duration of the period (45 days) and the starting date of that period (August 16, when FirstBank receives Holly's letter).

Answers (A), (B), and (C) are incorrect because they mention an incorrect length of time for the investigation period. Furthermore, **Answers (A) and (C) are incorrect** because they start the investigation period when FirstBank recredits Holly's account (August 19), rather than when FirstBank receives Holly's letter (August 16).

142. **Answer (A) is the best answer.** If FirstBank determines that no error occurred, the EFTA requires FirstBank to "deliver or mail to the consumer an explanation of its findings within 3 business days after the conclusion of its investigation . . . ." EFTA § 908(d), 15 U.S.C. § 1693f(d). The only difference between Answer (A) and Answer (D) is whether FirstBank can give an oral explanation. Resolution of this issue requires the reader to interpret the intended meaning of "deliver," keeping in mind that Congress specifically mentioned "oral or written notice" and "report or mail" earlier in subsection (a). A federal appellate court addressed the issue in *Bisbey v. D.C. National Bank*, 793 F.2d 315 (D.C. Cir. 1986), concluding that the explanation had to be written. The statute's companion regulation, Regulation E, renders the same conclusion. *See* Regulation E § 205.11(d)(1) ("The institution's report of the results of its investigation shall include a *written* explanation of the institution's findings . . . .") (emphasis added). Therefore, based on existing case law and the language in Regulation E, **Answer (A) is a better answer than Answer (D).**

Answers (B) and (C) are incorrect. They use a notice period other than three business days.

143. **Answer (C) is the correct answer.** The error resolution statute does not specifically provide a remedy for breach (other than mentioning that treble damages are available for certain egregious conduct by the financial institution). The answer is found in EFTA § 916(a), 15 U.S.C. § 1693m(a), which permits Holly to recover "any actual damage," plus "an amount not less than $100 nor greater than $1,000," plus "costs of the action, together with a reasonable attorney's fee as determined by the court" if Holly wins her lawsuit. **Answer (A) is incorrect** because Holly always recovers at least $100. **Answer (B) is incorrect** because the statute does not cap her reasonable attorney's fee. The difference between Answer (C) and Answer (D) is which answer reflects the minimum statutory penalty. The minimum statutory

penalty is $100 (whereas $1,000 is the maximum statutory penalty). Therefore, **Answer (C) is the correct answer,** and **Answer (D) is an incorrect answer.**

144.   **Answer (A) is the correct answer.** Section 4A-104(a) defines a "funds transfer" as "the series of transactions, beginning with the originator's payment order . . ." Section 4A-104(c) defines "originator" as "the sender of the first payment order in a funds transfer." Section 4A-103(a)(1) defines "payment order" as "an instruction of a sender to a receiving bank . . ." And Section 4A-103(a)(4) defines "receiving bank" as "the bank to which the sender's instruction is addressed." To summarize, then, a funds transfer includes at least one payment order, and a payment order requires the recipient to be a bank. Therefore, a funds transfer will involve at least one bank, **making Answer (A) the correct answer.**

   Answer (B) is incorrect. While the typical funds transfer involves a large amount of money, the definition of the term does not include a dollar trigger.

   Answer (C) is incorrect. While some money could physically exchange hands, many funds transfers are accomplished, at least in part, merely by making electronic debits or credits to the affected accounts.

   Answer (D) is incorrect. A funds transfer may involve just one payment order. For example, a corporation might order its bank to move money between two of the corporation's accounts, both of which are maintained by that bank.

145.   **Answer (A) is the correct answer.** Section 4A-103(a)(1) defines "payment order" as "an instruction of a sender to a receiving bank . . ." Section 4A-103(a)(4) defines "receiving bank" as "the bank to which the sender's instruction is addressed." Section 4A-105(a)(2) defines "bank" as "a person engaged in the business of banking . . ." ABC Securities is an investment advisor. It is not engaged in the business of banking. Therefore, BigCo's instruction to ABC Securities cannot be a payment order, **making Answer (A) the correct answer** and **Answer (B), Answer (C), and Answer (D) incorrect answers.**

   If ABC was a bank, then the instruction could be a "payment order" if BigCo transmitted the instruction "orally, electronically, or in writing." § 4A-103(a)(1).

146.   **Answer (B) is the correct answer.** To be a payment order, "the instruction [cannot] state a condition to payment to the beneficiary other than time of payment." § 4A-103(a)(1)(i). Requiring MegaFirm to deliver a notarized billing statement is a condition that removes ABC's message from the definition of "payment order." **Therefore, Answer (B) is the correct answer** (because the question asks you to identify a message that will *not* be governed by UCC Article 4A).

   Answer (A) is incorrect because a payment order can be oral (or in writing, or transmitted electronically). § 4A-103(a)(1).

   Answer (C) is incorrect because the definition of payment order permits one condition: time of payment (i.e., "do not pay for seven business days").

Answer (D) is incorrect because the definition of payment order does not prohibit a sender from transmitting its instruction on a Sunday. True, it is possible that the use of certain electronic means (such as a wire service) may not be available on the weekend. But the sender could still take advantage of other means of transmittal on the weekend (such as oral or written transmission).

147. **Answer (C) is the correct answer.** All of the terms in this question are defined in Sections 4A-103 and 4A-104. ABC's instruction to Fidelity Bank is a payment order. ABC is the sender and Fidelity Bank is a receiving bank. This is the first payment order in the transaction, so ABC is the originator. No other person (including any other sender) will be the originator, so **Answer (A) is an incorrect answer.** Because ABC is the originator, Fidelity Bank becomes the originator's bank (the receiving bank of the originator's payment order). The originator's bank cannot be the intermediary bank (see definition), so **Answer (D) is an incorrect answer.** Fidelity Bank's instruction to Integrity Bank is the second payment order in the transaction. Fidelity Bank is the sender of this payment order, and Integrity Bank is the receiving bank. In response to the message it receives from Fidelity Bank, Integrity Bank will take some action (e.g., credit the account of its customer, MegaFirm). But that action will not be a payment order. Therefore, Integrity Bank is never a sender in the transaction, **making Answer (B) an incorrect answer.** The goal of the transaction is to credit MegaFirm's account at Integrity Bank, making MegaFirm the beneficiary and Integrity Bank the beneficiary's bank. As noted earlier, Integrity Bank also is a receiving bank (on Fidelity Bank's payment order), **making Answer (C) the correct answer.**

148. **Answer (B) is the correct answer.** As noted in previous questions and answers, BigCo's instruction to ABC is not a payment order because ABC is not a bank. ABC's instruction to Fidelity Bank is a payment order, as is Fidelity Bank's instruction to Integrity Bank. Integrity Bank will take action (e.g., credit the account of its customer, MegaFirm), but that action is not a payment order. So the transaction involves two payment orders. The series of payment orders creates a single funds transfer. Therefore, **Answer (B) is the correct answer.**

Answer (A) is incorrect because the transaction involves two, not three, payment orders.

Answer (C) is incorrect because the transaction involves two, not three, payment orders. The transaction also involves only one funds transfer (not two).

Answer (D) is incorrect because the transaction involves only one funds transfer (not two).

149. **Answer (C) is the correct answer.** Section 4A-402(c) states: "With respect to a payment order issued to a receiving bank other than the beneficiary's bank, acceptance of the order by the receiving bank obliges the sender to pay the bank the amount of the sender's order." ABC issued its payment order to Fidelity Bank. Because MegaFirm's account is at Integrity Bank, Integrity Bank is the beneficiary's bank. Fidelity Bank is a bank other than the beneficiary's bank. Therefore, the statute applies. And it tells us that ABC becomes obligated to pay the amount of its payment order ($1 million) when Fidelity Bank "accepts" the payment order. Section 4A-209(a) states that Fidelity Bank (a receiving bank other than the beneficiary's bank) accepts ABC's order when it "executes" the order. Section 4A-301(a) states that Fidelity Bank executes the order "when it issues a payment order intended to carry out" ABC's order. Fidelity Bank executed ABC's order when it transmitted its

message to Integrity Bank. At that moment, ABC became obligated to pay $1 million to Fidelity Bank, **making Answer (C) the correct answer.**

Answer (A) is incorrect. ABC incurs no liability merely by transmitting its own message to Fidelity Bank. ABC may yet cancel the message, or it may fail to reach Fidelity Bank, or Fidelity Bank may not act on the message.

Answer (B) is incorrect. Fidelity Bank must not only receive the message; it also must then act on the message before ABC incurs liability.

Answer (D) is incorrect. The statutes trigger ABC's liability before Integrity Bank actually credits MegaFirm's account.

150. Section 4A-402(b) states: "With respect to a payment order issued [by Fidelity Bank] to the beneficiary's bank [Integrity Bank], acceptance of the order by the bank [Integrity Bank] obliges the sender [Fidelity Bank] to pay the bank [Integrity Bank] the amount of the order [$1 million] . . . ." Rephrased, Fidelity Bank becomes liable for $1 million when Integrity Bank "accepts" Fidelity Bank's payment order. Section 4A-209(b) addresses acceptance by the beneficiary's bank (Integrity Bank). In summary, Integrity Bank accepts Fidelity Bank's payment order at the earliest of the following events: (i) Integrity Bank pays MegaFirm, (ii) Integrity Bank notifies MegaFirm that either it has received Fidelity Bank's payment order or that MegaFirm's account has been credited for the amount of the payment order, (iii) Integrity Bank receives payment from Fidelity Bank, or (iv) the opening of the next funds-transfer business day following the payment date of Fidelity Bank's payment order.

151. **Answer (D) is the correct answer.** The statutory authority is found in Section 4A-406. Subsection (a) states: ". . . the originator [ABC] of a funds transfer pays the beneficiary [MegaFirm] . . . at the time a payment order for the benefit of the beneficiary [MegaFirm] is accepted by the beneficiary's bank [Integrity Bank] . . . ." And subsection (b) states: "If payment under subsection (a) is made to satisfy an obligation, the obligation is discharged to the same extent discharge would result from payment to the beneficiary [MegaFirm] of the same amount." Rephrased, BigCo's contractual liability to MegaFirm is discharged when Integrity Bank accepts the payment order that it received from Fidelity Bank, **making Answer (D) the correct answer.** When does that acceptance occur? In summary, Section 4A-209(b) states that Integrity Bank accepts Fidelity Bank's payment order at the earliest of the following events: (i) Integrity Bank pays MegaFirm, (ii) Integrity Bank notifies MegaFirm that either it has received Fidelity Bank's payment order or that MegaFirm's account has been credited for the amount of the payment order, (iii) Integrity Bank receives payment from Fidelity Bank, or (iv) the opening of the next funds-transfer business day following the payment date of Fidelity Bank's payment order.

Appreciate that the above statutory language indicates that *the originator* pays MegaFirm upon Integrity Bank's acceptance. The originator is ABC Securities, not BigCo. Somewhere during this transaction BigCo will have to provide its agent, ABC, with $1 million.

Answers (A), (B), and (C) are incorrect because the events listed in those answers are too premature, all occurring before Integrity Bank (the beneficiary's bank) accepts the payment order that it received from Fidelity Bank.

152. **Answer (D) is the correct answer.** Fidelity Bank must attempt to recover the $9 million overpayment from the beneficiary (MegaFirm), not the beneficiary's bank (Integrity Bank).

The statutory authority that addresses the correctness of Answers (B), (C), and (D) is found in Section 4A-303(a). In relevant part, that statute says: "A receiving bank [Fidelity Bank] that (i) executes the payment order of the sender [ABC] by issuing a payment order in an amount [$10 million] greater than the amount of the sender's order [$1 million] . . . is entitled to payment of the amount of the sender's order [$1 million] . . . The bank [Fidelity Bank] is entitled to recover from the beneficiary of the erroneous order [MegaFirm] the excess payment received [$9 million] to the extent allowed by the law governing mistake and restitution." Rephrased, the statute obligates ABC to pay the amount of its payment order ($1 million), and Fidelity Bank takes the loss for its error ($9 million) unless it can recover that amount from MegaFirm under equitable principles (which may be possible, if BigCo owed only $1 million to MegaFirm). Therefore, **Answer (D) is correct** and **Answers (B) and (C) are incorrect**.

Answer (A) is incorrect. Fidelity Bank has executed ABC's message, notwithstanding Fidelity Bank's mistake. § 4A-301(a) ("A payment order is 'executed' by the receiving bank [Fidelity Bank] when it issues a payment order *intended to carry out the payment order received by the bank*.") (emphasis added); cmt. 1 ("A receiving bank has executed an order even if the order issued by the bank does not carry out the order received by the bank. For example, the bank may have erroneously issued an order . . . in the wrong amount . . . .").

153.   ABC's ability to cancel or amend its payment order is addressed in Section 4A-211. Subsection (a) allows ABC to communicate its intent orally, electronically, or in writing. Under subsection (b), ABC's communication must be received by Fidelity Bank "at a time and in a manner affording [Fidelity Bank] a reasonable opportunity to act on the communication before [Fidelity Bank] accepts [ABC's] payment order." Five hours have passed since ABC transmitted its payment order to Fidelity Bank. It is possible that Fidelity Bank has already accepted ABC's payment order, leaving ABC with no remedy under subsection (b). If Fidelity Bank has already accepted ABC's payment order, then ABC must turn to subsection (c), which states: "After a payment order has been accepted, cancellation or amendment of the order is not effective unless [Fidelity Bank] agrees or a funds-transfer system rule allows cancellation or amendment without agreement of [Fidelity Bank]." Furthermore, under subsection (c)(1), "cancellation or amendment is not effective unless a confirming cancellation or amendment of the payment order issued by [Fidelity Bank] is also made." The bottom line is that we need more facts before we can determine whether ABC can cancel or amend its erroneous payment order.

154.   A payment order can take the form a debit transfer or a credit transfer. If the instruction is initiated by the person who will receive payment, we have a debit transfer. If the instruction is initiated by the person who will make payment, we have a credit transfer. *See* § 4A-104, cmt. 4. The italicized language indicates that payment orders under UCC Article 4A must be credit transfers.

155.   **Answer (C) is the correct answer**. Section 4A-201 defines "security procedure." Nowhere does it mention that the procedure must be "commercially reasonable." Therefore, **Answer (C) is the correct answer**. Appreciate, however, that a security procedure that is *not* commercially reasonable may make the bank liable if it acts on unauthorized payment orders issued in the name of its customer. *See* § 4A-202.

Answer (A) is incorrect. The last sentence of Section 4A-201 states: "Comparison of a signature on a payment order or communication with an authorized specimen signature of the customer *is not by itself* a security procedure" (emphasis added).

Answer (B) is incorrect. A security procedure must be "established *by agreement* of a customer and a receiving bank" (emphasis added). § 4A-201.

Answer (D) is incorrect. "A security procedure may require the use of algorithms or other codes, identifying words or numbers, encryption, callback procedures, or similar security devices." § 4A-201. The operative word is "may."

156. **Answer (B) is the correct answer.** A bank may be able to deflect to its customer any and all liability for an unauthorized payment order if the payment order is "verified pursuant to a security procedure" and "the security procedure is a commercially reasonable method of providing security against unauthorized payment orders." § 4A-202(b). As noted in subsection (c), "[c]ommercial reasonableness of a security procedure is a question of law . . ." And as noted in the accompanying Official Comment 4 (second paragraph), "[w]hether the receiving bank complied with the procedure is a question of fact." Answer (B) accurately states the "law v. fact" distinction, **making Answer (B) the correct answer.**

Answer (A) is incorrect. First Bank has the burden of proving "that it accepted the payment order in good faith and in compliance with the security procedure . . ." § 4A-202(b). BizCorp does not have the burden of proving noncompliance.

Answer (C) is incorrect. The statute does not require the payment order to meet or exceed a minimum dollar amount before imposing a duty on the bank to prove that the security procedure is commercially reasonable.

Answer (D) is incorrect. The statute requires First Bank to prove that it accepted the payment order in good faith, even if the security procedure is commercially reasonable.

157. **Answer (D) is the correct answer.** If both parties carry their respective burdens of proof, and the court concludes that the security procedures are commercially reasonable, then "a payment order received by [First Bank] is effective as the order of [BizCorp], whether or not authorized . . ." § 4A-202(b). This statement is captured in Answer (D), **making Answer (D) the correct answer.** Note, however, that even if the unauthorized payment order is deemed effective as BizCorp's payment order, BizCorp may avoid taking the loss if it can carry its burden of proof under Section 4A-203. Without knowing the details of the unauthorized payment order, loss allocation cannot be determined, so the statements in Answer (B) and Answer (C) are premature, **making Answers (B) and (C) incorrect answers.**

Answer (A) is incorrect because Article 4A does not allocate loss for unauthorized payment orders in an equitable fashion, at least as between the customer (BizCorp) and its bank (First Bank).

158. **Answer (B) is the correct answer.** If evidence reveals that the hacker compromised First Bank's computer system, then BizCorp can use Section 4A-203(a)(2) to its advantage. As a result, First Bank "is not entitled to enforce or retain payment of the payment order." Even so, Section 4A-505 precludes recovery by BizCorp "unless [BizCorp] notifies [First Bank] . . . within one year after the notification [of the unauthorized payment order] was received by [BizCorp]." This statute of repose is best captured by Answer (B), **making Answer (B) the correct answer,** and **making Answer (A), Answer (C), and Answer (D) incorrect**

answers.

Might First Bank (and other financial institutions) attempt to shorten the one-year period by contract? Sure. Would the agreement be enforceable? That issue was addressed in *Regatos v. North Fork Bank*, 804 N.Y.S.2d 713 (N.Y. App. 2005), where the court concluded that the one-year period cannot be varied by agreement.

159.   **Answer (A) is the correct answer.** Using a 360-day year and a 3% interest rate, and ignoring any compounding, the daily accrued interest on $2 million is approximately $167. At the end of a 30-day month, the total interest accrual will be approximately $5,000. Section 4A-204(a) imposes on First Bank the obligation to refund the $2 million, together with "interest on the refundable amount calculated from the date [First Bank] received payment [presumably by debiting BizCorp's account] to the date of the refund." However, BizCorp is not entitled to receive interest unless it notifies First Bank "of the relevant facts within a reasonable time not exceeding 90 days after the date [BizCorp] received notification from [First Bank] that the order was accepted or that [BizCorp's] account was debited with respect to the order." Answer (A) best states this timeliness requirement, **making Answer (A) the correct answer** and **Answer (B), Answer (C), and Answer (D) incorrect answers**.

The period of "reasonable time" can be fixed by agreement, as long as the agreed-upon time is "not manifestly unreasonable." §§ 4A-204(b), 1-302(b).

160.   Neither. The EFTA applies to "electronic fund transfers," defined as "any transfer of funds . . . which is initiated through an electronic terminal, telephonic instrument, or computer or magnetic tape so as to order, instruct, or authorize a financial institution to debit or credit an account." EFTA § 903(7), 15 U.S.C. § 1693a(7). The last word in that definition is "account," defined as "a demand deposit, savings deposit, or other asset account . . . established primarily for personal, family or household purposes . . . ." EFTA § 903(2), 15 U.S.C. § 1693a(2). The agent is withdrawing funds from Megan's business account, rather than her personal account, so the electronic fund transfers are not flowing through an "account" and, therefore, are not "electronic fund transfers," as those scope terms are defined by the EFTA.

UCC Article 4A applies to a "funds transfer" (Section 4A-102), defined in Section 4A-104 in a manner that requires at least one "payment order." But a "payment order," defined in Section 4A-103(a)(1), is limited to credit transfers (where the instruction to pay is given by the person making payment, e.g., Megan) and excludes debit transfers (where the instruction to pay is given by the person receiving payment, e.g., the insurance agent). § 4A-103(a)(1)(ii) and cmt. 4. Absent a "payment order," there is no "funds transfer," and UCC Article 4 will not apply.

So what body of law governs these transactions? Probably traditional contract law and perhaps federal or state bank regulatory law.

161. **Answer (A) is the correct answer.** The answer is found in the federal Truth in Lending Act ("TILA"), part of the Consumer Credit Protection Act. Under TILA § 133(a)(1), 15 U.S.C. § 1643(a)(1), a cardholder's maximum liability for unauthorized use of a credit card is $50. The minimum liability could be $0 (e.g., if the credit card is not an "accepted credit card" or the card issuer has failed to make the required disclosures), but the question asks for Daphne's maximum liability. Therefore, **Answer (A) is correct** and **Answers (B) and (C) are incorrect**.

     Answer (D) is incorrect. Notwithstanding the contract provision that makes Daphne liable for all charges, whether authorized or unauthorized, Daphne's liability for unauthorized charges cannot exceed $50. TILA § 133(d), 15 U.S.C. § 1643(d). Perhaps rephrased, contract law cannot raise the statutory ceiling on a cardholder's liability for unauthorized charges.

162. The answer would change. Federal law provides a "worst case" scenario for cardholders. But federal law defers to contrary state law (or contract provision) when the contrary state law (or contract provision) favors the cardholder. *See* TILA § 133(c), 15 U.S.C. § 1643(c) ("Nothing in this section imposes liability upon a cardholder for the unauthorized use of a credit card in excess of his liability for such use under other applicable law or under any agreement with the card issuer.").

163. **Answer (B) is the correct answer.** The TILA defines "unauthorized use" as "a use of a credit card by a person other than the cardholder who does not have actual, implied, or apparent authority for such use and from which the cardholder receives no benefit." TILA § 103(p), 15 U.S.C. § 1602(p). Linda is the cardholder; her daughter — Penny — is a person other than the cardholder. Penny did not have actual or implied authority to use her mother's credit card. In fact, her mother expressly objected to Penny's use of the card. Nor had Linda acted (or failed to act) in a manner that created the appearance (from the perspective of the merchant) that Penny had apparent authority to use her mother's card. Therefore, Penny's charges are unauthorized. Even so, the federal statute imposes on Linda the liability for the first $50 of unauthorized charges. TILA § 133(a)(1)(B), 15 U.S.C. § 1643(a)(1)(B). For this reason, **Answer (B) is the correct answer and Answer (A) is an incorrect answer.**

     Answer (C) is incorrect. Federal law does not state (or create a rebuttable presumption) that live-at-home kids have apparent authority to use a parent's credit card.

     Answer (D) is incorrect. Once the charges are determined to be authorized or unauthorized, the cardholder agreement places all liability on Linda (the cardholder) for the former, and the statute places all but the first $50 of liability on Francine's Fashions (the card issuer) for the latter. A court has no authority to craft an equitable division of liability.

164. **Answer (C) is the correct answer.** The referenced statute, TILA § 170, 15 U.S.C. § 1666i,

permits Jill to assert her "money back guarantee" dispute against her card issuer since Jill attempted to resolve the dispute with the Club in good faith, the charge exceeded $50, and the transaction occurred in Jill's home state. The difference between Answer (C) and Answer (D) is the ability of Jill to receive a $100 credit for her partial payment of the original $500 charge for the Club membership. She is not entitled to any credit. Subsection (b) of the statute states: "The amount of claims or defenses asserted by the cardholder may not exceed the amount of credit outstanding with respect to such transaction at the time the cardholder first notifies the card issuer or the person honoring the credit card of such claim or defense." She had made a credit card payment, of which $100 was applied against the Club membership charge, before she decided to cancel the membership (and only thereafter did she attempt to notify the Club and actually notify her card issuer). Therefore, the statute permits Jill to avoid paying the $400 balance, but the statute does not permit Jill to receive any credit for payments made on the original $500 charge. So **Answer (C) is the correct answer** and **Answer (D) is an incorrect answer**.

Answer (A) is incorrect. The statute does not exclude charges for a services contract lasting more than six months (but it does exclude tort claims).

Answer (B) is incorrect. Jill does not lose her statutory rights merely because she has partially paid the charge.

165. **Answer (A) is the correct answer.** Under TILA § 161(a), 15 U.S.C. § 1666(a), MegaBank must receive Lauren's "written notice." **Answers (B), (C), and (D) are incorrect answers** because they erroneously suggest that Lauren may provide oral or electronic notice.

166. **Answer (C) is the correct answer.** Under TILA § 161(a), 15 U.S.C. § 1666(a), MegaBank must receive Lauren's written notice "within sixty days after having transmitted to [Lauren] a statement of [Lauren's] account . . . ." MegaBank transmitted the statement on February 20, so it must receive Lauren's written notice within 60 days from the date, **making Answer (C) the correct answer.**

Answer (D) is incorrect. It erroneously suggests that the 60-day period starts running when Lauren receives the statement (February 25), rather than the date of MegaBank's transmittal (February 20).

Answers (A) and (B) are incorrect. They erroneously focus attention on Lauren's act of sending her notice. But the statute focuses attention on MegaBank's timely receipt of Lauren's notice, not Lauren's act of sending the notice (which, for a variety of reasons, might not be received by MegaBank).

167. **Answer (B) is the correct answer.** MegaBank received Lauren's letter on March 22, well within the 60-day period discussed in the previous answer. Therefore, unless MegaBank has already resolved Lauren's billing error, MegaBank is obligated "not later than thirty days after the receipt of the notice" to "send a written acknowledgment thereof" to Lauren. TILA § 161(a), 15 U.S.C. § 1666(a). Applying the law to the facts requires MegaBank to send its written acknowledgment no later than 30 days after March 22, the date on which it received Lauren's letter.

Answer (A) is incorrect. It uses a wrong period (20, rather than 30, days), and a wrong start date (the date Lauren sends her notice, rather than the date MegaBank receives the notice).

Answers (C) and (D) are incorrect. They erroneously focus on Lauren's receipt, rather than MegaBank's transmittal. **Answer (C) also is incorrect** because it uses the wrong period (20, rather than 30, days), and the wrong start date.

168.   **Answer (C) is the correct answer.** MegaBank has a duty to "make appropriate corrections" to Lauren's account or, alternatively, "send a written explanation or clarification" to Lauren, "setting forth . . . why [MegaBank] believes the account of [Lauren] was correctly shown in the statement . . ." TILA § 161(a), 15 U.S.C. § 1666(a). MegaBank must perform this duty "not later than two complete billing cycles of the creditor (in no event later than ninety days) after the receipt of the notice . . . ." *Id.* This rule is stated in **Answer (C), making it the correct answer**.

   Answers (A), (B), and (D) are incorrect answers. They significantly depart from the statutory language.

169.   **Answer (D) is the correct answer.** During the dispute resolution process, MegaBank may not take "any action to collect the amount, or any part thereof," in dispute. TILA § 161(a), 15 U.S.C. § 1666(a). The phrase "action to collect the amount, or any part thereof" excludes from its meaning "the sending of statements of account, which may include finance charges on amounts in dispute . . . if . . . [MegaBank] indicates the payment of such amount is not required pending [MegaBank's] compliance with this section." TILA § 161(c), 15 U.S.C. § 1666(c). In effect, then, MegaBank may continue to reflect the disputed charges (together with related accrued finance charges) on statements mailed to Lauren prior to the completion of its investigation into the matter, as long as MegaBank indicates that Lauren need not pay the disputed amount (or any related accrued finance charges) until MegaBank has completed its investigation. **Answer (D) correctly states the rule, making it the correct answer** and **making Answers (A), (B), and (C) incorrect answers.**

170.   **Answer (D) is the correct answer.** The answer is found in TILA § 161(d), 15 U.S.C. § 1666(d): "Nothing in this subsection shall be deemed to prohibit [MegaBank] from applying against the credit limit on [Lauren's] account the amount indicated to be in error." Therefore, MegaBank may subtract the disputed amount of $183.67 from her available line of credit, even during the investigatory period, **making Answer (D) the correct answer** and **Answers (A), (B), and (C) incorrect answers.**

171.   The answer is found in TILA § 162, 15 U.S.C. § 1666a. After MegaBank receives Lauren's notice, it may not "directly or indirectly threaten to report to any person adversely on [Lauren's] credit rating or credit standing" because of Lauren's failure to pay the disputed amount. MegaBank may not report the disputed amount as "delinquent" to any third party until MegaBank has complied with its investigatory duties and given Lauren a specific period of time in which to pay the disputed amount. If Lauren continues to dispute the charge, MegaBank cannot report the matter as "delinquent" to any third party unless MegaBank discloses that the amount is being disputed; at the same time, MegaBank must inform Lauren of each party to whom it is reporting the delinquency. If MegaBank and Lauren then resolve the matter, MegaBank must disclose the resolution to any party to whom it had previously reported the delinquency.

172.   The cited provision does suggest that, at worst, MegaBank will forfeit $50 for noncompliance with its statutory duties. But another provision offers Lauren additional relief. Under TILA

§ 130(a), 15 U.S.C. § 1640(a), which applies because TILA § 161, 15 U.S.C. § 1666, falls within "part D . . . of this subchapter," Lauren may recover "actual damage" that she sustains from the noncompliance, "twice the amount of any finance charge in connection with the transaction" ($500 minimum, $5,000 maximum), and — if she wins her lawsuit — "costs of the action, together with a reasonable attorney's fee as determined by the court."

173.   **Answer (C) is the correct answer.** This question requires an examination of TILA § 170, 15 U.S.C. § 1666i. Subsection (a) permits Emma to assert her merchant claims or defenses (excluding any tort claims) against her card issuers if she satisfies three requirements. First, she must make "a good faith attempt to obtain satisfactory resolution of a disagreement or problem relative to the transaction" from the merchant. The facts reveal that Emma has done so by writing several letters and making numerous telephone calls seeking redress. Second, the amount of the transaction must exceed $50. (The policy for this requirement is to remove the card issuer from customer-merchant disputes of a *de minimis* nature.) The charge for the purse was only $45 (the dress cost $375), so she must pay the $45 charge for the purse and seek her remedy from the merchant, rather than the card issuer. Therefore, **Answers (B) and (D)**, both of which include the purse, **are incorrect answers**. The third requirement is that "the place where the initial transaction occurred was in the same State as the mailing address previously provided by the cardholder or was within 100 miles from such address." (The policy for this requirement is to protect merchants from the logistical problems associated with litigating against a remote party.) Emma has a Missouri address. She bought the dress in St. Louis (Missouri), so she satisfies this requirement (even though the purchase in cross-state St. Louis occurred more than 100 miles from her billing address). Therefore, she can use the statute to assert her merchant defense, relevant to the dress, against Midtown Bank. As a result, **Answer (C) is the correct answer** and **Answer (A) is an incorrect answer**.

174.   As noted above, Emma can meet the geography test if the out-of-state purchase is within 100 miles of her billing address. She lives in Kansas City, Missouri. Under the revised facts, she purchased the dress and the purse in Kansas City, Kansas, directly across the state line. If we assume that this transaction took place within 100 miles of her billing address (presumably her home address), then she meets the geography test for both the dress and the purse. The purse remains too low to trigger protection, though. The bottom line is the same as above: Emma can use the statute to assert against her card issuer the problem with the dress, but not the purse.

175.   Because Emma used merchant cards to purchase the purse and the dress, she can trigger the statutory protection solely by making a good faith attempt to resolve the problems with the merchants. The statute makes inapplicable the $50 test and the geography test in certain transactions, including transactions in which the merchant "(A) is the same person as the card issuer, (B) is controlled by the card issuer, [or] (C) is under direct or indirect common control with the card issuer . . . ." Because Emma bought the purse at Tilly's and charged the price to her Tilly's credit card, she does not need to meet the $50 test (and while she can meet the geography test, she need not offer any proof on that test). Therefore, she can assert the defective nature of the purse against her card issuer (Tilly's). As before, Emma can assert the defective nature of the dress against her card issuer (Francine's Fashions), but unlike before, she no longer has to satisfy the $50 test and the geography test.

176.   **Answer (D) is the correct answer.** A letter of credit is issued by an "issuer," a term defined in Section 5-102(a)(9). The term includes "a bank or other person." UCC Article 1 defines a "person" as "an individual, corporation, . . . partnership, . . . joint venture, . . . or any other legal or commercial entity." *See* § 1-201(b)(27). As a general rule, then, any human or entity may issue a letter of credit. Issuers are not limited to banks or financial institutions (although they probably issue the overwhelming majority of letters of credit), so **Answer (A) and Answer (B) are incorrect answers. Answer (C) is incorrect** because an individual is a "person," and a "person" can be an "issuer." There is an exclusion found in the definition of "issuer," however. For reasons discussed in Section 5-102, cmt. 5, an "issuer" cannot include "an individual who makes an engagement for personal, family, or household purposes." That exclusionary language is found in Answer (D), **making Answer (D) the correct answer.**

177.   **Answer (C) is the correct answer.** Section 5-104 states that a letter of credit "may be issued in any form that is a record and is authenticated . . . ." Answer (C) contemplates that the issuer will authenticate the letter of credit, satisfying the quoted language and **making Answer (C) the correct answer.**

   Answer (A) and Answer (B) are incorrect answers because Section 5-104 does not contemplate that any party will "acknowledge" the letter of credit.

   Answer (D) is an incorrect answer because the letter of credit need not be in writing. The letter of credit must be a "record." Section 5-102(a)(14) defines a "record" as "information that is inscribed on a tangible medium, or that is stored in an electronic or other medium and is retrievable in perceivable form." Therefore, the letter of credit may, but need not, be in writing if it otherwise meets the definition of "record."

178.   **Answer (A) is the correct answer.** Section 5-105 states: "Consideration is not required to issue . . . a letter of credit . . ." This statement of law is best found in Answer (A), **making Answer (A) the correct answer** and **Answers (B), (C), and (D) incorrect answers.**

179.   **Answer (C) is the correct answer.** Section 5-106(a) states: "A letter of credit is revocable only if it so provides." This statement is best found in Answer (C), **making Answer (C) the correct answer** and **Answers (B) and (D) incorrect answers. Answer (A) is an incorrect answer** because the letter of credit remains enforceable whether or not it is self-described as revocable or irrevocable.

180.   **Answer (D) is the correct answer.** Section 5-106(c) provides a gap-filler of one year if the letter of credit fails to provide an expiration date. Therefore, **Answer (D) is the correct answer** and **Answer (C) is an incorrect answer. Answers (A) and (B) are incorrect answers** because a letter of credit is enforceable, even without a stated expiration date.

181.   A commercial letter of credit is most often used to facilitate payment under a contract for

the sale of goods. The buyer is nervous about paying for goods prior to shipment, and the seller is concerned that it may not receive payment after shipping the goods. The buyer and the seller address these issues through the use of the commercial letter of credit, typically issued by a bank. As a condition to payment, the terms of the letter of credit will require the seller (beneficiary) to offer proof (usually in the form of documents) that it has shipped qualifying goods. A standby letter of credit serves to back up some payment or performance obligation of the applicant. The letter of credit usually requires the beneficiary to present a statement to the effect that the applicant has defaulted. Observe, then, these two material differences. First, the parties expect payment under a commercial letter of credit, but not necessarily under a standby letter of credit. Second, the focus is on the beneficiary's performance under a commercial letter of credit, but the focus is on the applicant's nonperformance under a standby letter of credit.

182. The primary difference between an adviser and a confirmer is the undertaking each assumes. An adviser directly or indirectly notifies "the beneficiary that a letter of credit has been issued, confirmed, or amended." § 5-102(a)(1). But a confirmer agrees "to honor a presentation under a letter of credit issued by another." § 5-102(a)(4). In effect, then, a beneficiary can expect to receive important information from an adviser, but it can demand payment (under the terms of the letter of credit) from a confirmer. This difference is further addressed in Section 5-107. Subsection (a) states that a confirmer "is directly obligated on a letter of credit and has the rights and obligations of an issuer to the extent of its confirmation." Subsection (c) states that an adviser (who is not a confirmer) "is not obligated to honor or give value for a presentation" but merely "undertakes to the issuer and to the beneficiary accurately to advise the terms of the letter of credit, confirmation, amendment, or advice received by that person . . . ."

183. The independence principle is one of the pillars of letter of credit law. It is stated in Section 5-103(d): "Rights and obligations of an issuer to a beneficiary or a nominated person under a letter of credit are independent of the existence, performance, or nonperformance of a contract or arrangement out of which the letter of credit arises or which underlies it, including contracts or arrangements between the issuer and the applicant and between the applicant and the beneficiary." Rephrased, in deciding whether to honor a beneficiary's request for payment, the issuer cannot look beyond the four corners of its letter of credit (and requirements or conditions stated therein). This excludes any review of the underlying contracts between the parties and treats as irrelevant (at least as part of the issuer's decision to honor or dishonor the presentation) the performance or nonperformance of the obligations stated in those underlying contracts.

184. The strict compliance doctrine is codified in Section 5-108(a) (and discussed further in the accompanying cmt. 1). That statute states: "Except as otherwise provided in Section 5-109 [fraud and forgery concerns], an issuer shall honor a presentation that . . . appears on its face strictly to comply with the terms and conditions of the letter of credit." In effect, then, the issuer must pay the beneficiary if, *but only if*, the beneficiary has satisfied each and every condition stated in the letter of credit. Through the years, courts have been asked to resolve the question: "How strict is strict?" The question is of great importance to the issuer, who may find itself between the proverbial rock and a hard place. The issuer may note a discrepancy between the terms of the letter of credit and the materials submitted by the beneficiary. If the issuer uses the discrepancy as a reason to dishonor, it may face a lawsuit

from the beneficiary for wrongful dishonor. If the issuer overlooks the discrepancy and honors the presentation, the applicant may refuse to honor its reimbursement obligation under Section 5-108(i)(1) on the theory that the beneficiary's presentation lacked strict compliance.

185. **Answer (C) is the correct answer.** As a general rule, the basic letter of credit transaction involves three parties: the applicant, the beneficiary, and the issuer. The "applicant" is the person "at whose request or for whose account a letter of credit is issued." § 5-102(a)(2). Morgantown Bank issued the letter of credit at the request of Sunshine Flowers, so Sunshine Flowers is the "applicant." The "beneficiary" is the person "who under the terms of a letter of credit is entitled to have its complying presentation honored." § 5-102(a)(3). Holland Nurseries is the party that will make presentation to Morgantown Bank and request payment. So Holland Nurseries is the "beneficiary." An "issuer" is "a bank or other person that issues a letter of credit . . . ." § 5-102(a)(9). Morgantown Bank is the issuer of the letter of credit.

Answer (C) is the only answer that correctly identifies both Sunshine Flowers as the "applicant" and Holland Nurseries as the "beneficiary," **making Answer (C) the correct answer** and **Answers (A), (B), and (D) incorrect answers.**

186. **Answer (C) is the correct answer.** Under Section 5-108(b), Morgantown Bank must honor or dishonor the documentary presentation by Holland Nurseries within "a reasonable period of time after presentation, but not beyond the end of the seventh business day of the issuer after the day of its receipt of documents . . . ." As noted in cmt. 2, "the seven-day period is not a safe harbor. The time within which the issuer must give notice is the lesser of a reasonable time or seven business days." Because the statute refers to a period not to exceed seven business days, **Answer (C) is the correct answer** and **Answers (A), (B), and (D) are incorrect answers.**

187. **Answer (A) is the correct answer.** The remedies available to Holland Nurseries for wrongful dishonor are found in Section 5-111. Subsection (a) permits Holland Nurseries to recover "the amount that is the subject of the dishonor or repudiation." This amount is $25,000 rather than $15,000 because Holland Nurseries "is not obligated to take action to avoid damages that might be due from the issuer under this subsection." § 5-111(a). Perhaps rephrased, Holland Nurseries has no duty to mitigate. Therefore, **Answers (C) and (D) are incorrect** because they contemplate that Holland Nurseries had a duty to accept the offer from the standby-purchaser to buy the bulbs for $10,000. The only difference between Answer (A) and Answer (B) is the type of additional damages to be awarded. Subsections (d) and (e) mandate recovery of interest and fees and expenses (and subsection (b) permits incidental but not consequential damages), **making Answer (A) the correct answer** and **Answer (B) an incorrect answer.**

188. **Answer (C) is the correct answer.** Article 5 does not provide a statutory basis for a suit seeking restitution. Warren Falls Bank may, however, have a restitution claim under other law. *Cf.* § 1-103.

Answer (A) is an incorrect answer. Section 5-111(a) provides for suits by beneficiaries and their successors against issuers for wrongful dishonor of a proper presentation.

Answer (B) is an incorrect answer. Section 5-108(i)(1) provides a right of reimbursement to an issuer that honors a presentation that strictly complies with the terms of the letter of credit.

Answer (D) is an incorrect answer. Section 5-110(a) establishes warranties that the beneficiary makes when the issuer honors a presentation, the breach of which may result in a cause of action by the issuer against the beneficiary.

189. **Answer (C) is the correct answer.** The Bank must pay under the strict compliance rule of Section 5-108(a) because Bradford Sugar submitted paperwork that strictly complied with the terms of the letter of credit. Because the fraudulent backdating of the shipping date on the bill of lading was not material to either Bradford Sugar or Giacona Chocolates, the fraud/forgery exception found in Section 5-109 is not applicable. As noted in cmt. 1, "[t]he use of the word ['material'] requires that the fraudulent aspect of a document be material to a purchaser of that document or that the fraudulent act be significant to the participants in the underlying transaction."

     Answer (A) is an incorrect answer because the intentional and fraudulent backdating of the shipping date on the bill of lading does not rise to the level of materiality that would permit the Bank to dishonor the presentation.

     Answer (B) is an incorrect answer because the presentation did strictly comply with the terms of the letter of credit, and the fraud/forgery exception in Section 5-109 was not triggered by the facts.

     Answer (D) is an incorrect answer because there is no such "harmless error" exception to the strict compliance rule. Some courts have excused discrepancies between the terms of the letter of credit and the paperwork submitted by the beneficiary, but those discrepancies typically involved technical requests made by the bank in the letter of credit, and not substantive or transaction-sensitive requests made by one of the contracting parties in the letter of credit.

190. **Answer (A) is the correct answer.** Under Section 5-108(a), the Bank must honor a presentation that "appears on its face strictly to comply with the terms and conditions of the letter of credit." The letter of credit requires delivery of a bill of lading that references delivery of "five tons of white refined granulated sugar." But Bradford Sugar delivered a bill of lading for "five metric tons of white granulated sugar." The differences between "five tons" and "five metric tons," and "white refined granulated sugar" and "white granulated sugar" prevent Bradford Sugar's presentation from strictly complying with the terms of the letter of credit. (Note, however, that Bradford Sugar's reference to "WARREN FALLS BANK" and "NUMBER" instead of "WFB" and "NO." probably are acceptable discrepancies from the terms of the letter of credit. Those differences are of a noncommercial, rather than commercial, nature and should be overlooked by the Bank. *See* § 5-108, cmt. 1 (discussing strict compliance).) And the Bank is not charged with responsibility for knowing the degree of importance attached to the differences mentioned. *See* § 5-108(f) ("An issuer is not responsible for . . . (3) observance or knowledge of the usage of a particular trade . . . ."). Therefore, the Bank need not honor the presentation. But if the Bank does honor the presentation, it is not entitled to be reimbursed by Giacona Chocolates. The applicant's reimbursement obligation is triggered when an issuer honors a presentation that strictly complies with the terms of the letter of credit. § 5-108(i)(1). So Giacona Chocolates is not obligated to honor any reimbursement request by the Bank if the Bank honors a presentation that fails to strictly comply with the terms of the letter of credit,

as in this case.

Answer (B) is an incorrect answer for the same reason. Because Bradford Sugar's presentation fails to strictly comply with the terms of the letter of credit, the Bank may rightfully dishonor the presentation and need not worry about a lawsuit for wrongful dishonor.

Answer (C) is an incorrect answer. The independence principle, found in Section 5-103(d), states that the issuer's decision to honor or dishonor the beneficiary's presentation is to be guided by the terms of the letter of credit, not by conversations with its customer or any review of (or suspicion or knowledge of any default under) the underlying contract.

Answer (D) is an incorrect answer. The letter of credit is an example of a documentary, or commercial, letter of credit, rather than a standby letter of credit (most often used as a source of payment when the applicant defaults on its underlying obligations).

191. The last paragraph of the letter of credit incorporates the terms of the current version of the Uniform Customs and Practice for Documentary Credits. As noted in Section 5-101, cmt., "[t]he Uniform Customs and Practice is an international body of trade practice that is commonly adopted by international and domestic letters of credit and as such is the 'law of the transaction' by agreement of the parties." In effect, then, the Bank, Giacona Chocolates, and Bradford Sugar are agreeing to be bound by the rules stated in the UCP. Rather than restate all of these rules, the parties (as is typically done) incorporate them with an appropriate reference.

192. **Answer (C) is the correct answer.** Absent contrary contractual language (not present in this question), a beneficiary enjoys the opportunity to cure the defects of its presentation and resubmit its corrected materials prior to the expiration of the letter of credit. Therefore, **Answer (A) and Answer (B) are incorrect answers** because they suggest otherwise.

The difference between Answer (C) and Answer (D) is whether OmniBank may reject a second presentation if the certificate of default is signed by the same officer again (the chief financial officer), but whose title departs from those mentioned in the letter of credit (chief executive officer or general counsel). OmniBank could, and should, have disclosed this problem to Justin Resources when it dishonored the initial presentation. Because OmniBank failed to do so, it is precluded from raising that discrepancy with respect to the second presentation. *See* § 5-108(c) and cmt. 3. In effect, OmniBank must disclose all known discrepancies at once and cannot hold back, or save, any for later disclosure. Those that are not disclosed are lost. Therefore, OmniBank must honor the second presentation, even if the certificate of default is signed by Justin Resources' chief financial officer, **making Answer (C) the correct answer** and **Answer (D) an incorrect answer.**

193. **Answer (D) is the correct answer.** Because OmniBank honored the request for payment, Justin Resources warranted to OmniBank "that there is no fraud or forgery of the kind described in Section 5-109(a)" and warranted to Dumbarton Industries "that the drawing does not violate any agreement between the applicant and beneficiary or any other agreement intended by them to be augmented by the letter of credit." § 5-110(a). Because Justin Resources had not yet properly accelerated the payments for months five through ten, only $50,000 was due and payable (month number four), rather than $350,000 (months four through ten). Therefore, Justin Resources breached its warranty by saying that $350,000 was due and payable when only $50,000 was due and payable. The facts state that

OmniBank will not assert material fraud, however. Therefore, this breach of warranty can be asserted under Section 5-110(a) only by Dumbarton Industries. OmniBank has no cause of action against Justin Resources for breach of warranty. But because the presentation appeared to strictly comply with the terms of the letter of credit, OmniBank does have a reimbursement claim against Dumbarton Industries under Section 5-108(i)(1). Dumbarton Industries should then sue Justin Resources for breach of warranty under Section 5-110(a)(2). This path of litigation is suggested by Answer (D), **making Answer (D) the correct answer**.

Answer (A) is an incorrect answer. As noted in the introductory language of Section 5-110(a), the issuer must honor the presentation before it can bring an action against the beneficiary for breach of warranty. The problem under these facts is that they do not provide OmniBank with that cause of action.

Answer (B) is an incorrect answer. The independence principle (codified at Section 5-103(d)) prevents OmniBank from reviewing ancillary contracts (like the Sales Agreement) when determining whether to honor the request for payment. But once OmniBank has paid the draft, the independence principle no longer applies, and OmniBank can review and rely on ancillary documents in proving up its claim for a warranty breach. *See, e.g., Mellon Bank, N.A. v. General Electric Credit Corporation*, 724 F. Supp. 360 (W.D. Pa. 1989).

Answer (C) is an incorrect answer. Given the right facts, OmniBank can bring an action against Justin Resources for breach of warranty. But the relevant provision, Section 5-110, is silent on damages. As noted in the accompanying cmt. 3, "[t]he damages for breach of warranty are not specified in Section 5-111 [Remedies]. Courts may find damage analogies in Section 2-714 in Article 2 and in warranty decisions under Articles 3 and 4."

PRACTICE FINAL EXAMINATION: ANSWERS

PRACTICE FINAL EXAMINATION

194. **Answer (C) is the correct answer.** Section 3-104(a) states that a "negotiable instrument" must state "an *unconditional* promise or order" (emphasis added). Section 3-106 offers guidance on the meaning of this phrase. The last sentence of subsection (a) states that a cross-reference "does not of itself make the promise or order conditional." But subsection (a) also warns that a cross-reference that states that the promise or order "is subject to or governed by another record" is prohibited, as well as a statement that "rights or obligations with respect to the promise or order are stated in another record." Answer (C) runs afoul of this latter prohibition, **making Answer (C) the correct answer.**

A cross-reference to prepayment rights stated in another writing is acceptable under Section 3-106(b)(i), so **Answer (A) is incorrect.**

Calculating interest with information found outside the four corners of the writing is permissible under Section 3-112(b), so **Answer (B) is incorrect.**

Sending the reader to a separate writing for rights pertaining to collateral is permitted by Section 3-106(b)(i), so **Answer (D) is incorrect.**

195. **Answer (C) is the correct answer.** Section 3-109(b) states that a promise or order is payable to order if it "is payable . . . (ii) to an identified person or order." Answer (C) — "pay to Jesse Buckman or order" — is such language, **making Answer (C) the correct answer.**

Answer (A) is incorrect because it fails to mention "order" either before (e.g., "pay to the order of Fran Martin") or after (e.g., "pay to Fran Martin or her order") the name of the identified payee.

Answer (B) offers ambiguous language that suggests that the writing is payable to order *and* payable to bearer. Because of the "bearer" reference, the promise is payable to bearer under Section 3-109(a)(3). The opening language of Section 3-109(b) states that an instrument payable to order cannot be payable to bearer, effectively resolving the ambiguity in a manner that makes the writing easier to negotiate (e.g., bearer language trumps order language). *See also* § 3-109, cmt. 2 (first paragraph). Therefore, **Answer (B) is incorrect.**

As noted in Section 3-109(a)(2), the failure to state a payee makes the promise or order payable to bearer. For this reason, **Answer (D) is incorrect.**

196. **Answer (B) is the correct answer.** Section 3-104(a)(2) requires a negotiable instrument to be "payable on demand or at a definite time." The quoted language is addressed in Section 3-108. Subsection (b) indicates that an instrument is payable at a definite time "at a fixed date or dates or at a time or times readily ascertainable at the time the promise or order issued." Payment dates that fall on the first Monday of specific calendar months meet this language, **making Answer (B) the correct answer.**

Answer (A) is incorrect because the date of presentment is not readily ascertainable at the time of issuance. Such language makes the note payable on demand, though, under Section 3-108(a)(i) ("payable . . . at sight").

Answer (B) is incorrect because a promise payable at the holder's discretion is payable on demand under Section 3-108(a)(i).

While most baseball fans would contend that Albert Pujols is a lock for baseball's Hall of Fame following his retirement, the enshrinement date is not "readily ascertainable at the time the promise or order is issued." Tying the payment date to such an event fails to meet the statutory language in Sections 3-104(a)(2) and 3-108, and the promissory note will not be a negotiable instrument governed by UCC Article 3. Therefore, **Answer (D) is an incorrect answer**.

197. **Answer (A) is the correct answer.** A negotiable instrument need not state an execution date or provide for a place of payment. UCC Article 3 fills both drafting gaps. Section 3-113(b) provides: "If an instrument is undated, its date is the date of its issue or, in the case of an unissued instrument, the date it first comes into possession of a holder." And Section 3-111 offers several default rules if the instrument fails to mention a place of payment. Therefore, **Answer (A) is the correct answer.**

Answer (B) correctly observes that the omission of the date is irrelevant, but its suggestion that the absence of a place of payment removes the note from the scope of UCC Article 3 is a misstatement of the law, **making Answer (B) an incorrect answer**.

Answer (C) is incorrect as a nonsense answer. Nowhere does UCC Article 3 suggest a connection between a notarized signature and an unstated execution date.

Answer (D) is incorrect because Section 3-111 dictates the place of payment if the instrument is otherwise silent.

198. **Answer (A) is the correct answer.** Article 3 contains a specific rule to address this common problem. If an instrument contains contradictory terms, words prevail over numbers. § 3-114. The words "four hundred fifty and no cents" therefore prevail over the numbers "$540.00." **Answers (B), (C), and (D) are incorrect** because they do not take this rule into account.

199. No, the trustee is not right; the omitted information does not remove the note from the definition of "negotiable instrument" in Section 3-104(a) and the scope of UCC Article 3. First, Section 3-104(a) does not require the instrument to be dated, and Section 3-113(b) acknowledges that a negotiable instrument can be undated. Second, the absence of any stated payee renders the note "payable to bearer" under Section 3-109(a)(2), satisfying the requirement of Section 3-104(a)(1) that the instrument be "payable to bearer or to order." Third, Section 3-104(a) acknowledges that the promise to pay a fixed amount of money can be "with or without interest," and Section 3-112(a) states: "Unless otherwise provided in the instrument, (i) an instrument is not payable with interest . . . ." Fourth, the omission of a payment date renders the note "payable on demand" under Section 3-108(a)(ii), thereby satisfying the requirement of Section 3-104(a)(2) that the note be "payable on demand or at a definite time." And fifth, Section 3-104(a) does not require the instrument to reference a place of payment, in which case Section 3-111 fills the gap. In summary, then, the note is a "negotiable instrument" governed by UCC Article 3, notwithstanding the trustee's concerns.

200. Any fact pattern in which the thief steals bearer paper will make the thief a PETE. For example, Smith executes and delivers to Jones a check "payable to the order of Jones." Jones places his blank indorsement ("Jones") on the back of the check and places the check in his wallet. Thief steals the wallet. The blank indorsement converts the check into bearer paper. Thief is now in possession of bearer paper, which makes Thief a holder under Section 1-201. As a holder, Thief is a person entitled to enforce the check under Section 3-301(i).

201. Jones buys a negotiable promissory note from Smith. Smith fails to deliver the note for two weeks (but the note is not lost, stolen, or misplaced). Jones is the owner of the note, but during the two-week period in which Jones does not have possession, he will not have enforcement rights. His lack of possession negates PETE status under Section 3-301(i) and Section 3-301(ii), and because the note is not lost, stolen or misplaced, or yet to be paid by mistake, Jones is not a PETE under Section 3-301(iii).

202. Yes. Although Jennifer cannot enforce the dishonored note against Baxter because he indorsed the note "without recourse" (Section 3-415(a), (b)), she can recover damages from Baxter because he breached the "no alterations" transfer warranty in Section 3-416(a)(3). Baxter "transferred" the instrument to Jennifer under Section 3-203(a) because he was not the issuer (Molly is the issuer under Section 3-105), and he voluntarily relinquished possession of the note to Jennifer for the purpose of giving Jennifer the right to enforce the note. Baxter transferred the note to Jennifer for consideration (the facts state that "Baxter sold the note to Jennifer"), so he made all six of the warranties stated in Section 3-416(a), including the warranty that "the instrument has not been altered." The note was altered when Earl wrongfully inserted "2015" as the year of payment. §§ 3-407(a); 3-115 (a), (c), & cmt. 2 (Case #2). Therefore, notwithstanding his status as a holder in due course with no notice of Earl's mischief, Baxter breached the "no alterations" transfer warranty. The warranty breach permits Jennifer to recover from Baxter damages "equal to the loss suffered as a result of the breach, but not more than the amount of the instrument plus expenses and loss of interest incurred as a result of the breach." § 3-416(b).

(If no party filled in the blank with "2015" or "2016" or some other year, the note would be an "incomplete instrument" under Section 3-115(a). The note also would remain a negotiable instrument under Section 3-104, payable at a "definite time" of December 31, 2016, under Section 3-108(b). That section requires the "definite time" to be "readily ascertainable at the time the promise or order is issued," and it need not be determined solely from the text of the note. One could "readily ascertain" the year intended when Molly issued the note by asking Molly what year she and Earl had agreed upon.)

203. No. To be a "negotiable instrument" governed by Article 3, the note must be "payable to bearer or to order *at the time it is issued or first comes into possession of a holder . . . .*" § 3-104(a)(1) (emphasis added). MS Enterprises "issued" the note when it delivered the note to Hammond in March. § 3-105(a). At that time, the note was "payable to bearer" because the note failed to state a payee. § 3-109(a)(2). Also, Hammond became a "holder" under Section 1-201 because he had possession of a note payable to bearer. Therefore, the note was indeed a "negotiable instrument" when MS Enterprises delivered it to Hammond, and the fact that Hammond inserted "Ronald Garcia" rather than, as required by Section 3-109(b), "the order of Ronald Garcia" (or "Ronald Garcia or order") does not remove the note from the scope of Article 3. Article 3 continues to apply, so Ronald can be a holder in due course under Section 3-302 who, under Section 3-305(b), will not be subject to MS Enterprises'

personal defense.

204.   **Answer (C) is the correct answer.** To be a "negotiable instrument" under Article 3, the note must contain Lisa's unconditional promise to pay. § 3-104(a). The provision appears to condition Lisa's promise on the absence of any claims or defenses that she can assert against Dealer. But Section 3-106(d) permits the inclusion of such statutory provisions, and the inclusion does not convert the otherwise unconditional promise into a conditional promise. The promise remains unconditional, and the note can be a "negotiable instrument" under Article 3. Therefore, **Answer (D) is an incorrect answer.** But the legal effect of including such a provision is to prevent subsequent takers, like Dealer, from becoming a holder in due course. §§ 3-106(d); 3-302(g). Therefore, **Answer (A) is incorrect**. And **Answer (C) is correct**, and **Answer (B) is incorrect**, because Dealer's notice of the provision is irrelevant. The provision prevents Dealer from becoming a holder in due course whether or not Dealer has notice of the provision at the time of negotiation.

For additional reading, see Section 3-106, cmt. 3. Also observe that, as a result of the 2002 amendments to Article 3, an instrument that fails to include such a statutory statement "has the same effect as if the instrument included such a statement." § 3-305(e).

205.   **Answer (B) is the correct answer.** Answer (B) appears to be incorrect because Elliott's discharge gives him a defense to payment, and Wanda had notice of that discharge when she took the note. But notice of a discharge (excluding a discharge in an insolvency proceeding) is not notice of a defense. § 3-302(b). Therefore, notwithstanding Wanda's notice of the discharge at the time she took the note, she still can be a holder in due course.

Answer (A) is incorrect. To be a holder in due course, Wanda must give "value." § 3-302(a)(2)(i). "Value" is defined in Section 3-303 and includes taking the instrument "as payment of . . . an antecedent claim against any person . . . ." Therefore, Wanda gave value when she took the note as payment of Elliott's pre-existing debt.

Answer (C) is incorrect. To be a holder in due course, Wanda must take the note without notice that the instrument is overdue. § 3-302(a)(2)(iii). Unless the maturity date of the single principal payment has been accelerated, the note is not overdue merely because Adam fails to make a scheduled interest payment. § 3-304(c).

Answer (D) is incorrect. To be a holder in due course, Wanda must take the instrument without notice that Adam does not have a defense to payment. § 3-302(a)(2)(vi). Wanda's notice, or lack thereof, is examined when she takes the note, not thereafter. Therefore, if Wanda learns of Adam's defense sometime after taking the note, the notice does not prevent Wanda from being a holder in due course.

206.   **Answer (C) is the correct answer.** Section 3-415(a) imposes indorser liability on Matt upon dishonor of the note. But subsection (a) is subject to subsection (c), which discharges Matt's signature liability if he is not given notice of dishonor if required by Section 3-503. Section 3-503 states that unless notice of dishonor is excused by Section 3-504, Matt's signature liability cannot be enforced unless he is given timely notice of dishonor. Under Section 3-503(c), notice of dishonor is timely if it is given within 30 days following the date of dishonor. Therefore, Matt is not liable for his indorsement unless he is given notice of dishonor within 30 days from yesterday (the date of dishonor), **making Answer (C) the correct answer and Answer (A), Answer (B), and Answer (D) incorrect answers.**

207. The answer is found in Section 3-419(a), which states: "If an instrument is issued for value given for the benefit of a party to the instrument ('accommodated party') and another party to the instrument ('accommodation party') signs the instrument for the purpose of incurring liability on the instrument without being a direct beneficiary of the value given for the instrument, the instrument is signed by the accommodation party 'for accommodation.'" Charlene will not be an accommodation party. The statute indicates that such a party must be a "party to the instrument." Charlene did not sign the note; she signed a separate guaranty. So she is not an accommodation party (but she is a surety). The statute also says that an accommodation party cannot be "a direct beneficiary of the value given for the instrument." Alex is a corporate shareholder, and the loan given to Wallace Corporation is enhancing the value of Alex's shares. But this enhanced value merely makes Alex an "indirect" (rather than "direct") beneficiary of the loan. *See* § 3-419, cmt. 1. Unlike Charlene, Alex did sign the note (as an anomalous indorser solely for the purpose of incurring signature liability), making him an accommodation party.

208. **Answer (A) is the correct answer.** Liability of representatives, and represented persons, is addressed in Section 3-402. Subsection (b) addresses liability of Harry, the representative. It opens with a condition to any liability: Harry must sign his own name to the instrument. If he does not, he is not personally liable (assuming he signs within his agency authority). Harry will not be personally liable if he signs the name of the represented person, Danny Davis, **making Answer (A) the correct answer.**

Answer (B) is incorrect. Harry is executing the note within the scope of his agency, so Danny is bound by the terms of the note "whether or not [he is] identified in the instrument." § 3-402(a).

Answer (C) is incorrect. Harry is not personally liable because "the form of the signature [in Answer (C)] shows unambiguously that the signature is made on behalf of the represented person who is identified in the instrument." § 3-402(b)(1).

Answer (D) is incorrect. The signature in Answer (D) does not unambiguously disclose the name of Danny, the represented person. Therefore, it is possible (although not a certainty) that Harry may be personally liable. *See* § 3-402(b)(2) (indicating that Harry is liable "to a holder in due course that took the instrument without notice that [Harry] was not intended to be liable on the instrument" and to other parties unless Harry "proves that the original parties did not intend [Harry] to be liable on the instrument").

209. **Answer (D) is the correct answer.** By increasing the amount from $350 to $3,350, Grant made an "alteration" to the check under Section 3-407(a). Nevertheless, Pasco Savings, the drawee (who presumably paid the check in good faith and without notice of the alteration), can enforce the check under Section 3-407(c) "according to its original terms." Therefore, Pasco Savings may debit Alice's account for $350, **making Answers (A) and (B) incorrect answers.** And Pasco Savings can recover the balance of $3,000 from Everett Bank for breaching the presentment warranty that "the draft has not been altered." §§ 3-417(a)(2), 4-208(a)(2). The warranty breach permits Pasco Savings to recover damages "equal to the amount paid by the drawee [$3,350] less the amount the drawee received or is entitled to receive from the drawer [$350, under Section 3-407(c)] because of the payment." §§ 3-417(b), 4-208(b). Therefore, **Answer (D) is the correct answer** and **Answer (C) is an incorrect answer.**

If evidence revealed that Alice failed to exercise ordinary care in preparing the check, and that failure substantially contributed to the alteration, Alice could incur some, and perhaps all, of the loss. § 3-406(a). If evidence revealed that Pasco Savings did not exercise good faith when it paid the check, it cannot bring an action against Everett Bank for breaching a presentment warranty. § 3-417(a). Also appreciate that the "no alterations" warranty imposes liability regardless of the warrantor's knowledge or notice of the alteration.

210.   **Answer (B) is the correct answer.** Normally, a drawer (Arco Products) will attempt to recover its loss from the drawee (Tuttle Savings) under the "properly payable rule" of Section 4-401. Once the loss is allocated between the drawer and the drawee, the drawee will attempt to shift any of its loss to the presenting bank or a previous transferor for breaching a presentment warranty. If Section 3-404 or Section 3-405 are applicable, then Article 3 also allows a drawer who bears any loss to initiate an action directly against any party (e.g., a depositary bank like Allied Bank) that failed to exercise ordinary care, if that failure substantially contributed to the loss resulting from the fraud. Section 3-404 does apply to these facts because Kate, who forged the drawer's signature, did not intend for the named payees to have an interest in the checks, triggering subsection (b)(i). Arco can then invoke subsection (d) and sue Allied Bank. Because Kate's co-conspirator was an Allied teller, Allied Bank may have failed to exercise ordinary care, a failure that may have contributed to Arco's loss. Therefore, Arco Products can bring an action directly against Allied Bank for this breach, **making Answer (B) the correct answer**. (Similar analysis would arise under Section 3-405, if Kate was an employee with "responsibility.") For a case involving similar facts, and a good discussion of a drawer's ability to sue a non-drawee, see *Gina Chin & Associates, Inc. v. First Union Bank*, 500 S.E.2d 516 (Va. 1998).

    Answer (A) is incorrect. These checks were not issued by a party who was duped by any physical misrepresentation. Therefore, the "imposter rule" of Section 3-404(a) does not apply.

    Answer (C) is incorrect. The "properly payable rule" addresses loss allocation between the drawer (Arco Products) and the drawee (Tuttle Savings). The drawer has no such action against any other party (such as Allied Bank, the depositary bank).

    Answer (D) is incorrect. Transfer warranties are made to subsequent transferees (and collecting banks), not to drawers. Therefore, Arco Products (the drawer) cannot be a plaintiff in such an action.

211.   **Answer (A) is the correct answer.** The "properly payable rule" of Section 4-401(a) allows Tuttle Savings, the drawer, to withdraw funds from Arco's account only if the checks were properly payable. Each of these checks bears multiple forged signatures (drawer's signature and indorsement). Arco should argue that it did not authorize these checks and demand that Tuttle Savings repost the funds to its account.

    Answer (B) and Answer (C) are incorrect answers. Warranties on checks are made to transferees, collecting banks, and payor banks. See §§ 3-416(a), 3-417(a), 4-207(a), and 4-208(a). They are not made to drawers. Therefore, Arco cannot be a plaintiff in an action based on a breach of a transfer or a presentment warranty.

    Answer (D) is incorrect. Section 3-420, the conversion statute, denies standing to a drawer (presumably because it has a cause of action against its bank under Section 4-401 for violating the "properly payable rule"). See § 3-420, cmt. 1.

212. **Answer (B) is the correct answer.** Bayview Bank, which presented the check for payment, made four warranties to Wellford Savings at presentment. (Wellford Savings presumably paid the check in good faith; facts do not suggest otherwise.) *See* §§ 3-417(a), 4-208(a). The second of the four warranties is a "no alterations" warranty. Milton's replacement of "Friendly Finance" with "Milton Garvis" as the payee is an "alteration" under Section 3-407(a) (an unauthorized change that purports to modify the obligation of the drawer and/or the drawee). Bayview Bank's lack of knowledge of the alteration (which was done in an expert manner) is irrelevant. The "no alterations" warranty includes no knowledge or notice qualifier. Bayview Bank breached this presentment warranty, giving Wellford Savings a cause of action for the breach, and **making Answer (B) the correct answer.**

Answer (A) is incorrect. Section 3-418(b) may give Wellford Savings a cause of action against Bayview Bank for recovery of the $1,500 on a mistake theory. Wellford Savings has standing as the person "paying" the instrument, and Bayview Bank is a potential defendant as "the person to whom . . . payment was made." But subsection (b) is subject to subsection (c). And because the alteration was done in an expert manner, not noticeable by the average person, Bayview Bank can successfully avoid liability on a mistake theory by arguing (under subsection (c)) that it "took the instrument in good faith and for value."

Answer (C) is incorrect. Even if Bayview Bank indorsed the check (which the facts do not specifically state), an indorser has no liability under Section 3-415 until the check is dishonored. This check was paid, not dishonored.

Answer (D) is incorrect. The "properly payable rule," codified in Section 4-401, governs the relationship between the drawer (Gwen) and the drawee (Wellford Savings). It is inapplicable to any other relationship, and it gives no cause of action to Wellford Savings against Bayview Bank (the depositary bank).

213. **Answer (B) is the correct answer.** Like Bayview Bank, Milton breached the "no alterations" presentment warranty. Wellford Savings can sue Milton for the breach because Milton is "a previous transferor of the draft." *See* §§ 3-417(a)(ii), 4-208(a)(ii). Milton transferred the draft under Section 3-203 to Bayview Bank at the time of deposit. The movement was voluntary, so it constituted a "delivery" as defined in Section 1-201. Milton, the purported payee, was not the issuer; Gwen, the drawer, was the issuer under Section 3-105. And Milton gave the check to Bayview Bank for the purpose of giving the bank enforcement rights in the check. Therefore, Milton transferred the check to Bayview Bank and can be sued, as a previous transferor, by Wellford Savings for breaching the "no alterations" presentment warranty.

Section 3-418(b) gives Wellford Savings a cause of action against Milton for recovery of the $1,500 on a mistake theory. Wellford Savings has standing as the person "paying" the instrument, and Milton is a potential defendant as "the person . . . for whose benefit payment was made." As noted in the previous answer, subsection (b) is subject to subsection (c). But Milton cannot invoke subsection (c). He is the fraudster who gave no value. As such, he did not "take the instrument in good faith and for value," nor did he "in good faith change[] position in reliance on the payment . . . ." § 3-418(c). Therefore, Wellford Savings may recover its loss from Milton on a mistake theory.

Wellford Savings has no cause of action against Milton for breaching a transfer warranty because it did not take the check by transfer. It took the check by presentment. *See* § 3-203, cmt. 1 (last paragraph). Therefore, Wellford Savings has no standing to sue Milton for breaching any transfer warranty.

In summary, then, Wellford Savings should attempt to recover the $1,500 from Milton on a mistake theory, and for breaching a presentment (but not a transfer) warranty. Therefore, **Answer (B) is the correct answer** and **Answer (A), Answer (C), and Answer (D) are incorrect answers**.

214. The statement is true. Grant made the transfer warranties to Norm because the movement of the note from Grant to Norm constituted a "transfer of the instrument" under Section 3-203(a): Grant, a non-issuer (Marty was the issuer/maker), delivered the note to Norm for the purpose of giving Norm the right to enforce the note. Also, Grant received consideration of $4,100 at the transfer. Therefore, the preface language of Section 3-416(a) is satisfied, and Grant made the transfer warranties to Norm. Len, the party identified in the note as the maker, has a defense under Section 3-401 against liability because his signature was forged. Len can assert this defense against Grant, so Grant has breached the warranty that the note is not subject to any defense that can be asserted against him.

215. The statement is true. Because Marty made the note payable to himself, he was in possession of an instrument that directed payment to himself. Therefore, Marty was a "holder" under Section 1-201 and thus a person entitled to enforce the note under Section 3-301. So Marty did not breach the PETE warranty.

Appreciate, though, that if Norm brings an action against Marty, it probably will not be under Section 3-416. Instead, Norm will sue Marty as the issuer/maker of the instrument under Section 3-412. Although unauthorized, Marty's forgery of Len's signature is effective as Marty's own signature, as maker, in favor of any person "who in good faith pays the instrument or takes it for value." § 3-403. Norm may be such a person.

216. **Answer (D) is the correct answer.** FRB-Buffalo (which is neither the depositary bank, nor the payor bank) is both an "intermediary bank" and a "collecting bank," as those terms are defined in Section 4-105.

Answer (A) is incorrect. Ellen is not a "maker" under Section 3-103(a)(7) because the facts involve a check, not a note.

Answer (B) is incorrect. The parties and terms are mismatched and should be switched. Commerce Bank is a "drawee" under Section 3-103(a)(4) as the person being ordered by Ellen, the "drawer" under Section 3-104(a)(5), to make payment.

Answer (C) is incorrect. Prosperity Bank, the first bank to take the check, is a "depositary bank" under Section 4-105(2). As such, it cannot be an "intermediary bank" under Section 4-105(4).

217. **Answer (D) is the correct answer.** By encoding the check, Prosperity Bank warranted "to any subsequent collecting bank and to the payor bank . . . that the information is correctly encoded." § 4-209(a). No other party made that warranty. Therefore, only Prosperity Bank can be sued for breaching the warranty, **making Answer (D) the correct answer** and **Answers (A), (B), and (C) incorrect answers**. Commerce Bank (the payor bank under Section 4-105(3), and therefore a party to whom the warranty was made) can, as a party that took the check in good faith, bring an action against Prosperity Bank for damages "equal to the loss suffered as a result of the breach, plus expenses and loss of interest incurred as a

result of the breach." § 4-209(c).

After paying $2,700 to Commerce Bank, Prosperity Bank may seek to recover that loss from its customer, Fran, on a variety of possible theories (e.g., mistake, unjust enrichment, etc.).

218. As between the two financial institutions, Graham Bank will take the loss. The check (an "item" under Section 4-104(a)(9)) was presented to Western Savings on the morning of Monday, August 1, so Western Savings had until midnight on Tuesday, August 2 (its "midnight deadline" under Section 4-104(a)(10)), to return the check or send notice of dishonor. Because Western Savings did not return the dishonored check or send notice of dishonor until Thursday, August 4, Western Savings became "accountable" (liable) for the amount of the check. § 4-302(a)(1). Nevertheless, Section 4-302(b) permits Western Savings to shift the loss to Graham Bank if Graham Bank breached any of its presentment warranties. Graham Bank breached the presentment warranty under Section 4-208(a)(1), regarding its status as a person entitled to enforce the check. Meredith forged American Utility Company's indorsement, preventing anyone other than the named payee from being a person entitled to enforce. So notwithstanding Western Savings' failure to give timely notice of dishonor, Graham Bank will take the loss because it breached a presentment warranty.

(The facts stipulate that Sections 3-404, 3-405, and 3-406 do not apply. Absent that stipulation, the forged indorsement might be deemed effective under one or more of those provisions. If the forged indorsement is deemed effective, Graham Bank may not breach the PETE presentment warranty, leaving Western Savings "accountable" for the check under Section 4-302(a).)

219. The "midnight deadline" is defined in Section 4-104(a)(10) as "midnight on [the bank's] next banking day following the banking day on which it receives the relevant item or notice or from which the time for taking action commences to run, whichever is later." The term appears in Article 4, usually in the context of a deadline by which a bank must take certain action. For example, assume Payee deposits a check at Depositary Bank on the morning of Monday, June 1. Section 4-202(a)(1) imposes on Depositary Bank (as a collecting bank) the duty to exercise ordinary care in presenting the check or sending it for presentment. Subsection (b) states that Depositary Bank "exercises ordinary care under subsection (a) by taking proper action before its midnight deadline following receipt of an item, notice, or settlement." Therefore, Depositary Bank should present the check, or send it for presentment, no later than midnight on Tuesday, June 2. Also, assume the check is presented to and received by Payor Bank on the morning of Wednesday, June 3. Under Section 4-302(a)(1), Payor Bank becomes "accountable" (liable) for the check if it "does not pay or return the item or send notice of dishonor until after its midnight deadline" (which, under the facts, is midnight on Thursday, June 4).

220. **Answer (D) is the correct answer.** Section 4-403(a) permits Kerry to place a stop-payment order on a check "by an order to the bank describing the item . . . with reasonable certainty received at a time and in a manner that affords the bank a reasonable opportunity to act on it . . . ." Kerry described the item "with reasonable certainty" by giving the employee all relevant information about the check (e.g., payee, amount, check number, etc.). And Kerry placed the order on August 6, giving the bank a "reasonable opportunity" to act on her request before the check was presented for payment on August 9. Kerry described the check with reasonable certainty and in a timely manner, satisfying the conditions of Section 4-403.

So the stop-payment order should be effective.

Answer (A) is incorrect. Nothing in the statute prohibits stop-payment orders more than three days after the issue date.

Answer (B) is incorrect. The statute does not require the customer to place the order before the payee receives the check.

Answer (C) is incorrect. Section 4-403(b) permits oral stop-payment orders.

221.   **Answer (B) is the correct answer.** A check becomes overdue after 90 days. § 3-304(a)(2). This check was issued in February, then lost and not found until November. More than 90 days have passed, and this check is now overdue. A person taking a check with notice that the check is overdue cannot become a holder in due course. § 3-302(a)(2)(iii). First Fidelity Bank, the depositary bank, will examine the check upon receipt and will discover that more than 90 days have passed since issuance, giving it notice that the check is overdue. This notice prevents First Fidelity Bank from becoming a holder in due course. Therefore, **Answer (C) is an incorrect answer**. Even so, a check can be properly payable even if it is overdue (so **Answer (A) is an incorrect answer**). The standard for determining whether a check is properly payable is whether payment is authorized by the drawer. § 4-401(a). The facts do not suggest that this check was unauthorized. Under Section 4-404, the payor bank has no obligation to its customer to pay a check that is more than six months old. This check is now that old, so the payor bank may rightfully dishonor it upon presentment, **making Answer (B) the correct answer.**

Answer (D) is incorrect. A depositary bank, as well as any other bank involved in the collection and payment of checks, may qualify as a holder in due course if it (or, under Section 3-203(b), its transferor) meets the conditions stated in Section 3-302.

222.   **Answer (B) is the correct answer.** A balance inquiry does not trigger a debit or a credit to the consumer's account. Absent such a debit or credit, there is no "electronic fund transfer" as defined in EFTA § 903(7), 15 U.S.C. § 1693a(7). **Therefore, Answer (B) is the correct answer.**

Answer (A) is an incorrect answer. Rephrased, the transaction does trigger an electronic fund transfer. A cash deposit results in a credit to the customer's account. The amount is immaterial under the definition.

Answer (C) is an incorrect answer. Rephrased, the transaction does trigger an electronic fund transfer. The deposit of a check results in a credit to a customer's account. The amount of the check is immaterial.

Answer (D) is an incorrect answer. Rephrased, the transaction does trigger an electronic fund transfer. A cash withdrawal results in a debit to a customer's account. Again, the amount of the withdrawal is immaterial.

223.   **Answer (D) is the correct answer.** A consumer's liability for unauthorized electronic fund transfers is addressed in EFTA § 909, 15 U.S.C. § 1693g. The language is rather tough to follow, and readers may find the liability scheme as stated in Regulation E to be more "user friendly." *Cf.* Regulation E § 205.6. In general, a consumer's liability will not exceed $50 if he or she timely notifies the financial institution within two business days following the consumer's discovery of the loss or theft of the access device (e.g., the card). The liability cap

escalates to no more than $500 if the consumer fails to give timely notice of the loss or theft of the access device. If the consumer fails to detect the problem within 60 days after the financial institution has transmitted to the consumer a statement on which the unauthorized EFT is reflected, the consumer's liability is not capped (with respect to unauthorized EFTs that occur after that 60-day period).

In this problem, Grace discovered the theft of her card on Tuesday morning. She did not notify her bank until Friday afternoon, more than two business days following her discovery. Therefore, her notice was not timely. As a result, her liability is calculated (under Regulation E § 205.6(b)(2)) as "the lesser of $500 or the sum of: (i) $50 or the amount of unauthorized transfers that occur within the two business days, whichever is less; and (ii) The amount of unauthorized transfers that occur after the close of two business days and before notice to the institution, provided the institution establishes that these transfers would not have occurred had the consumer notified the institution within that two-day period." Using the facts, then, her liability is the lesser of $500 and the sum of (i) $50 and (ii) $250 (Friday withdrawal, the only withdrawal after the two-day period concluded at Thursday midnight). The answer should not exceed $300, **making Answer (D) the correct answer** and **Answers (A), (B), and (C) incorrect answers.**

224. **Answer (C) is the correct answer.** Under EFTA § 908(a), 15 U.S.C. § 1693f(a), FirstBank must receive an "oral or written notice" from Gordon "within sixty days after having transmitted to" Gordon the statement on which appears the alleged error. The transmittal date was July 1. **Answer (C) is correct** because it contemplates oral or written notice, and a 60-day period that starts on July 1.

Answer (A) is incorrect because it refers to a 30-day period, rather than a 60-day period.

Answer (B) is incorrect because it omits oral notice and refers to a 45-day period, rather than a 60-day period.

Answer (D) is incorrect because it omits oral notice and runs the 60-day period from July 5, rather than July 1.

225. **Answer (B) is the correct answer.** All of the terms in this question are defined in Sections 4A-103 and 4A-104. ZinnCo's message to Fidelity Bank is a payment order. ZinnCo is the sender and Fidelity Bank is a receiving bank. This is the first payment order in the transaction, so ZinnCo is the originator. No other person (including any other sender) will be the originator, **making Answer (C) an incorrect answer**. Because ZinnCo is the originator, Fidelity Bank becomes the originator's bank (the receiving bank of the originator's payment order). Fidelity Bank's instruction to Integrity Bank is the second payment order in the transaction. Fidelity Bank is the sender of this payment order, and Integrity Bank is the receiving bank. In response to the message it receives from Fidelity Bank, Integrity Bank will take some action (e.g., credit the account of its customer, MegaCorp). But that action will not be a payment order. There are only two payment orders in this funds transfer, **making Answer (A) an incorrect answer**. The goal of the transaction is to credit MegaCorp's account at Integrity Bank, making MegaCorp the beneficiary and Integrity Bank the beneficiary's bank. As Integrity Bank also is a receiving bank (of the second payment order), **Answer (B) is the correct answer**. And because Integrity Bank is the beneficiary's bank, it cannot be an intermediary bank, **making Answer (D) an incorrect answer.**

226. **Answer (C) is the correct answer.** Section 4A-402(c) states: "With respect to a payment order issued to a receiving bank other than the beneficiary's bank, acceptance of the order by the receiving bank obliges the sender to pay the bank the amount of the sender's order." ZinnCo issued its payment order to Fidelity Bank. Because MegaCorp's account is at Integrity Bank, Integrity Bank is the beneficiary's bank. Fidelity Bank is a bank other than the beneficiary's bank. Therefore, the statute applies. And it tells us that ZinnCo becomes obligated to pay the amount of its payment order ($2.5 million) when Fidelity Bank "accepts" the payment order. Section 4A-209(a) states that Fidelity Bank (a receiving bank other than the beneficiary's bank) accepts ZinnCo's order when it "executes" the order. Section 4A-301(a) states that Fidelity Bank executes the order "when it issues a payment order intended to carry out" ZinnCo's order. Fidelity Bank executed ZinnCo's order when it transmitted its message to Integrity Bank. At that moment, ZinnCo became obligated to pay $2.5 million to Fidelity Bank, **making Answer (C) the correct answer.**

    Answer (A) is incorrect. ZinnCo incurs no liability merely by transmitting its own message to Fidelity Bank. ZinnCo may yet cancel the message, or it may fail to reach Fidelity Bank, or Fidelity Bank may not act on the message.

    Answer (B) is incorrect. Fidelity Bank must not only receive the message; it also must then act on the message before ZinnCo incurs liability.

    Answer (D) is incorrect. The statutes trigger ZinnCo's liability before Integrity Bank actually credits MegaCorp's account.

227. **Answer (C) is the correct answer.** Adam, an innocent victim, remains liable for the first $50 of unauthorized charges. TILA § 133(a)(1)(B), 15 U.S.C. § 1643(a)(1)(B). The cardholder, therefore, never completely escapes liability (at least if we assume that Diamond Bank has complied with all of its statutory duties and disclosures). The TILA does not allocate losses between Diamond Bank (the card issuer) and Barrington Jewelers (the merchant), so Diamond Bank absorbs the liability for $8,325.88 (all but the first $50 placed on Adam). This loss allocation is stated in Answer (C), **making Answer (C) the correct answer** and **Answers (A), (B), and (D) incorrect answers.**

    Note, however, that Diamond Bank (the card issuer) may have contractual rights allowing it to charge some or all of losses back to Barrington Jewelers (the merchant).

228. **Answer (C) is the correct answer.** Under TILA § 161(a), 15 U.S.C. § 1666(a), MegaBank must receive Grace's written notice within 60 days after it transmitted to Grace the statement on which appeared the transaction in question.

    Answer (A) is incorrect. It erroneously suggests that Grace can give oral notice. It also erroneously states a 30-day response period (rather than the correct 60-day period).

    Answer (B) is incorrect. It erroneously states a 30-day response period (rather than the correct 60-day period) that starts on the receipt date of August 2 (rather than the transmittal date of July 28).

    Answer (D) is incorrect. It erroneously suggests that Grace can give oral notice. It also uses the wrong start date (August 2, instead of July 28) for the 60-day response period.

229. This question requires an examination of TILA § 170, 15 U.S.C. § 1666i. Subsection (a) permits Jeff to assert his merchant claims or defenses (excluding any tort claims) against his

bank if he satisfies three requirements. First, he must make "a good faith attempt to obtain satisfactory resolution of a disagreement or problem relative to the transaction" from the merchant. Second, the amount of the transaction must exceed $50. And third, Jeff must prove that the transaction took place "in the same State" as Jeff's mailing address, or "within 100 miles from such address." He must satisfy all three requirements in order to successfully assert against his bank the product defects as a reason not to pay the charges. (Appreciate that the statute waives the $50 test and the geography test if Jeff used a merchant card to purchase the items from that same merchant.)

230. **Answer (B) is the correct answer.** Marine Bank, the issuer of the letter of credit, has the right to reimbursement from ABC under Section 5-108(i)(1) because Marine Bank honored Outboard Industries' presentation, which, under the facts, strictly complied with the terms of the letter of credit.

Answer (A) is an incorrect answer. Marine Bank's payment obligations are dictated by the letter of credit; they are independent from the lease and its contractual terms. § 5-103(d). Therefore, Marine Bank is not excused from paying under the letter of credit merely because ABC is excused from paying Outboard Industries under the terms of the lease.

Answer (C) is an incorrect answer. As already noted, Marine Bank's payment obligations are controlled by the letter of credit. Marine Bank cannot (and has no statutory right to) seek permission from the applicant, ABC, in making its decision to honor or dishonor the beneficiary's request for payment.

Answer (D) is an incorrect answer. As already noted, Marine Bank has a statutory right of reimbursement from ABC because Outboard Industries submitted paperwork that strictly complied with the terms of the letter of credit.

231. **Answer (D) is the correct answer.** The lease remains in force and effect, notwithstanding the use of the letter of credit. Therefore, ABC may have a contract claim against Outboard Industries if Outboard Industries has breached the terms of the lease. Furthermore, because Marine Bank has honored the presentation, Outboard Industries warranted to ABC, the applicant, "that the drawing does not violate any agreement between the applicant and beneficiary or any other agreement intended by them to be augmented by the letter of credit." § 5-110(a)(2). Therefore, ABC may have a warranty claim against Outboard Industries if the drawing violated the terms of the lease. Both the contract claim and the warranty claim are mentioned in Answer (D), **making Answer (D) the correct answer.**

Answer (A) is an incorrect answer because ABC may have both a contract claim and a warranty claim against Outboard Industries.

Answer (B) is an incorrect answer because it is incomplete. It fails to recognize that ABC may also have a contract claim.

Answer (C) is an incorrect answer because it is incomplete. It fails to recognize that ABC may also have a warranty claim.

232. **Answer (A) is the correct answer.** Marine Bank had a statutory obligation to honor Outboard Industries' presentation because the presentation strictly complied with the terms of the letter of credit. § 5-108(a). If Marine Bank dishonors that presentation, then the dishonor will be wrongful. Wrongful dishonor gives Outboard Industries, the beneficiary, a cause of action against Marine Bank (but not against ABC, the applicant). § 5-111(a).

Therefore, **Answer (A) is the correct answer** and **Answer (B) is an incorrect answer.**

Answer (C) is an incorrect answer. Outboard Motors made a presentation that strictly complied with the terms of the letter of credit, so it will have a claim for wrongful dishonor against Marine Bank upon dishonor. Outboard Motors may have violated the terms of the lease (possibly giving ABC a contract claim or a warranty claim against Outboard Motors), but its payment rights (and Marine Bank's reciprocal payment obligations) under the terms of the letter of credit are dictated solely by those very terms (not the lease). *See* § 5-103(d).

Answer (D) is an incorrect answer. Even if the FDIC's insurance program treats a payment obligation under a letter of credit as an insured deposit, the program does not provide any coverage until the obligor (in this case, Marine Bank) has become insolvent. No facts suggest that Marine Bank has become insolvent.

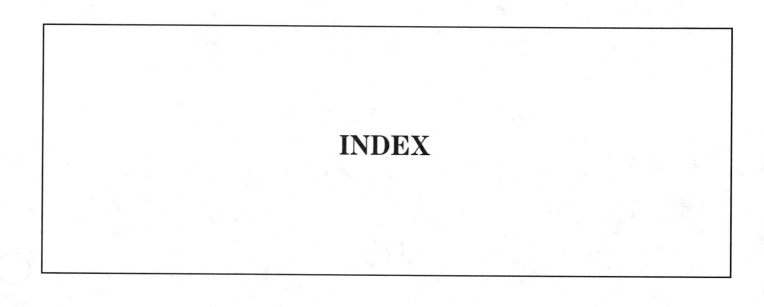

INDEX

INDEX